Strategic Corporate Finance

Applications in Valuation and Capital Structure

JUSTIN PETTIT

BICENTENNIAL

1807

WILEY

2007

BICENTENNIAL

John Wiley & Sons, Inc.

Published by John Wiley & Sons, Inc., Hoboken, New Jersey.
Published simultaneously in Canada.

For general information on our other products and services or for technical support, please
contact our Customer Care Department within the United States at (800) 762-2974, outside
the United States at (317) 572-3993 or fax (317) 572-4002.

Wiley also publishes its books in a variety of electronic formats. Some content that appears in
print may not be available in electronic formats. For more information about Wiley products,
visit our Web site at www.wiley.com.

The author wishes to acknowledge the generous permission of Blackwell Publishing in
allowing him to reuse "Corporate Capital Costs: A Practitioner's Guide" (*Journal of Applied
Corporate Finance*, Vol. 12, No. 1, Spring 1999) and "A Method For Estimating Global
Corporate Capital Costs: The Case of Bestfoods" (*Journal of Applied Corporate Finance*, Vol.
12, No. 3, Fall 1999) in Chapter 1 of this book.

Library of Congress Cataloging-in-Publication Data:

Pettit, Justin, 1965-
Strategic corporate finance : applications in valuation and capital structure/Justin Pettit.
    p. cm.—(Wiley finance series)
Includes bibliographical references and index.
ISBN-13: 978-0-470-05264-8 (cloth)
ISBN-10: 0-470-05264-3 (cloth)
1. Corporations–Finance. 2. Capital. 3. Value. I. Title.
HG4026.P468 2007
658.15—dc22

2006021653

Printed in the United States of America.

10 9 8 7 6 5 4 3 2

√ MW 3-30-08

Additional Praise for
Strategic Corporate Finance

"Strategic Corporate Finance *provides excellent insight into the key financial issues that corporations are dealing with every day.*"

—Rhod Harries, VP and Treasurer, Alcan

"*This book is a MUST for all corporate finance professionals. I have never read a corporate finance book before that provides such a complete and integrated overview of which relevant value drivers and implications should be considered before making strategic corporate finance related decisions—M&A projects, equity and debt financing, Asset and Liability Management, rating, pensions. You financial advisors out there: These are the relevant questions and necessary answers your industrial clients are expecting from you!*"

—Dr. Dietmar Nienstedt, Head of Mergers & Acquisitions, LANXESS AG

"*In* Strategic Corporate Finance: Applications in Valuation and Capital Structure, *Pettit brings a fresh and practical approach to corporate finance, effectively bridging the gap between theory and practice. He addresses timely and pertinent topics that corporations face constantly. I have often relied on Pettit's prior works as useful references, and it will be nice to have them all in one place. I highly recommend his work to anyone looking for a practical and actionable guide to corporate finance.*"

—David A. Bass, Vice President, Treasurer Global Operations, Alcon Laboratories, Inc.

To Krista, Trevor, and Madeleine, for their support, patience, and laughter.

Contents

Preface

S trategic Corporate Finance provides a "real-world" application of the principles of modern corporate finance, with a practical, investment banking advisory perspective. Building on 15 years of corporate finance advisory experience, this book serves to bridge the chronic gap between corporate finance theory and practice. Topics range from weighted average cost of capital, value-based management and M&A, to optimal capital structure, risk management and dividend/buyback policy.

Chief Financial Officers, Treasurers, M&A and Business Development executives, and their staffs will find this book to be a useful reference guide, with an emphasis more on actionable strategic implications, than tactical methodology per se. Board members and senior operating executives may use this book to better understand issues as well as to prompt questions to ask, and frameworks to employ, to get them to the answers they need. Similarly, investors who read this book will benefit from an improved practical understanding of the corporate finance issues, the degrees of freedom in their management, and their impact on company performance and value. Investment bankers and consultants will use this book for training, and as a general reference guide. Finally, students who wish to better understand how their corporate finance knowledge, skills, and tools might be put to use in the real world should read, and re-read, this book.

Each chapter in this book represents a recurring theme or topic in terms of actual client questions. The material is based on real-world advice and includes much of the thought process and some of the analytics that were undertaken to develop the recommendations. In getting to these views, significant input is drawn from the literature—both the theory and the empirical research—as well as our own empirical work. Early work in the public domain is cited.

This book is organized into three parts. Part One addresses the "left-hand side" of the balance sheet and related performance measurement and valuation topics. Part Two deals with the "right-hand side" of the balance sheet and topics in optimal capital structure. Part Three addresses enterprise management in a holistic approach, as corporate finance issues increasingly require. Each chapter begins with an executive summary to make reading this book a realistic possibility for the reader.

Part One outlines the principal topics in managing the left-hand side of the balance sheet, following the prevalent "Fix, Sell, Grow" mantra in use today, with an intrinsic value perspective. Chapter 1 provides a comprehensive user's guide to the weighted average cost of capital and all the practical complications that arise in estimating and applying WACC in practice. In Chapter 2 we put this benchmark for value creation to use. Our solution is a deep dive on how to find the sources of value creation, by overcoming the allocation and cost accounting issues that often plague the economic profit framework, as well as traditional performance measures. Chapter 3 makes the case for divestitures, outlining who, why, how, and when. Chapter 4 tackles growth, a difficult step for many that remains under-served by much of the existing literature today, and a topic that demands thoughtful consideration by value-based management enthusiasts. Chapter 5 rounds out Part One with today's hot topic of excess cash: when it matters and what to do about it.

Part Two moves to the right-hand side of the balance sheet to address optimal capital structure. Chapter 6 provides an executive's guide to credit ratings, with trends and implications of today's new ratings climate, discussion of the quantitative approaches to ratings and their limitations, an understanding of the qualitative analysis, and specific discussion around ratings challenges like pensions, excess cash, notching, and the investment grade versus speculative grade worlds. Chapter 7 outlines a framework for optimal capital structure, with special consideration to the key factors and what is different today, and their implications for financial policy. Chapter 8 is a handbook for setting dividend and share repurchase policy, with special attention given to today's growing problem of too much cash. Chapter 9 addresses stock liquidity, an important problem for many smaller and middle market domestic companies, as well as American Depositary Receipts (ADRs) and the vast majority of stocks listed on overseas exchanges.

Part Three elevates the discussion to an enterprise-wide perspective of capital management. Chapter 10 introduces the strategic risk management concept and frameworks, with examples of the interplay between process control efforts, financial and operational hedging, and capital structure solutions. Chapter 11 outlines best practices in financial hedging. Chapter 12 serves as an enterprise risk management (ERM) case study by showing how corporate pensions can be re-engineered to create considerable shareholder value.

List of Figures

List of Tables

Acknowledgments

I would like to thank Steve O'Byrne for kindly providing the impetus and resources to produce this book. I would also like to thank Don Chew for his help, and David Champion and Krista Pettit, for teaching me not to write like a scientist. Joel Stern and Bennett Stewart deserve special thanks for their original inspiration, as well as Paul Pilorz and the many other Stern Stewart alum who have provided a valuable sounding board and support network over the years.

Thanks also to the many coverage bankers who repeatedly entrusted me with clients and their questions: Bill Brenizer, Kevin Cox, Rob DiGia, Hakan Erixon, David Gately, Chris Hite, Andrew Horrocks, Tom Ito, Eric Kaye, Karl Knapp, Jan Krizan, Michael Martin, David McCreery, Jeff McDermott, Steve Meehan, Evan Newmark, Michael Robinson, Alejandro Przybygoda, Jeff Sine, Steve Trauber, and Brian Webber, just to name a few. I would also like to acknowledge the contribution of the many capital markets bankers who invested time with me on client issues, aiding my own understanding of their respective "crafts," including, Arun Bansal, Mike Collins, John Doherty, Craig Fitt, Tad Flynn, Adam Frieman, Brian Jennings, Michael Katz, Ryan Lee, Kevin Reynolds, Matt Sperling, Tim Steele, Christian Stewart, Selim Toker, and Adriaan VanDerKnapp. From research, I thank Stephen Cooper and his team. Thanks also to Armen Hovakimian and Tom Copeland for methodological assistance, and the many consulting and banking analysts, who have worked with me on these issues and provided invaluable support. All errors and omissions remain purely my own.

Finally, I wish to thank the many clients who have challenged and entrusted me with their corporate finance concerns and encourage them to continue to do so!

About the Author

Investment banker and management consultant Justin Pettit draws on his 15 years of corporate finance advisory experience to bring a uniquely practical perspective to the issues and applications of modern corporate finance theory. He advises Boards and senior executives on financial planning, cash and liquidity, dividends and buybacks, optimal capital structure, funding and financing decisions, capital costs and hurdle rates, risk management, and valuation and business strategy.

A popular guest lecturer in advanced corporate finance at Business Schools, seminars, and public conferences such as the Brookings Institute, the Financial Management Association, and Finance Executives Institute, he leads topics in valuation, value-based strategy, and financial policy. He has reviewed for the *Journal of Applied Corporate Finance*, the *Journal of Pension Economics and Finance*, and *Quantitative Finance*. He has assisted the Canadian Institute of Chartered Accountants and the Certified Management Accountants of Canada with issues of disclosure and valuation and performance measurement, and he has been retained by leading Wall Street Analysts for proprietary research support in these areas.

A highly ranked author on the Social Sciences Research Network (ssrn.com), Justin's publications include articles for the *Harvard Business Review*, *Journal of Applied Corporate Finance*, *Corporate Finance Review*, *Industrial Management*, *Business Quarterly*, *Shareholder Value Magazine*, *Air Finance Journal*, and a chapter for the book, *Real Options and Business Strategy*. Justin holds an MBA from the University of Western Ontario, and a BASc in mechanical engineering from the University of Toronto. His author page is www.ssrn.com/author=102597 and email address is justin_pettit@msn.com.

Managing the Left-Hand Side of the Balance Sheet

CHAPTER 1

The Cost Of Capital

The weighted average cost of capital (WACC) is a critical input for evaluating investment decisions: It is typically the discount rate for net present value (NPV) calculations. And it serves as the benchmark for operating performance, relative to the opportunity cost of capital employed to create value.

Though the Capital Asset Pricing Model (CAPM) has been challenged, it remains the most practical approach to determine a cost of equity. In fact, many perceived limitations arise from challenges in applying the model. We will provide suggestions to deal with the primary difficulties in applying the CAPM: (1) estimating the market risk premium (MRP) for equities; (2) measuring the systematic risk, or beta, of a company; (3) normalizing the riskless rate; (4) estimating an appropriate cost of debt; and (5) estimating global capital costs. Finally, we will also address the related issue of corporate hurdle rates for investment.

The cost of capital is an estimation that should be applied with care to avoid any illusions of false precision. Despite its many degrees of freedom, financial planning time and resources are often better allocated to other areas, such as value creation and risk management. Ultimately, it is the business case, quality of cash flow forecasts, sensitivity analysis, and strategic risk management that will have the greatest impact on value creation.

CALCULATION PITFALLS

WACC is a market-weighted average, at target leverage, of the cost of after-tax debt and equity. We estimate the cost of equity as $Rf + beta \times MRP$, where Rf is the riskless return, market risk premium (MRP) is the expected return premium for bearing equity market risk over the riskless rate, and beta is the systematic risk of the business relative to the market. Estimation of these key inputs (riskless rate, the market risk premium and beta), or degrees of freedom, can lead to a wide range of outcomes.

We normalize the riskless rate with a forward view of the capital markets. We continue to believe that 5 percent is a reliable estimate of the MRP, based on historical data and forward-looking market data.[1] We will provide tools for deriving more reliable estimates of beta in the most problematic areas. This will be especially helpful for business units, unlisted companies, and illiquid stocks with unreliable betas. Direct regression is the most commonly used approach but we also employ alternative methodologies such as constructed betas, portfolio betas, segment regression betas, and multi-variable regression betas.

Beyond these key inputs, the most common pitfalls regard the weightings of debt and equity.

- Financing events per se may not reflect changes in financial policy and may not be permanent changes to the capital structure. Temporary fluctuations in the mix should not affect WACC.
- The WACC for financial institutions is (generally) the cost of equity, as most debt is funding debt (not financing debt) and should be expensed (not capitalized) where the cost of funds is a cost of goods sold (COGS).

Our approach to global corporate capital costs quantifies and captures both sovereign risk and inflation risk. But we recommend that the cash flows be adjusted for the *costs and unsystematic risks* of global investing, coupled with a more rigorous risk analysis. Given the many opportunities for profitable growth abroad, more reliable estimates of global capital costs can help ensure companies will choose to undertake investments that show promise to add value.

The key points of our conceptual rationale and approach are as follows:

- Most companies adjust for sovereign risk. Approaches vary widely between made-up risk premiums and qualitative adjustments to a wide range of quantitative methods, largely based on questionable methods, but most companies do something. Many large-capitalization companies (large caps) approach their five favorite banks each year, with a long list of countries in hand, and compare the responses.
- Most adjustments are too large. Much of the international risk is not systematic risk but is execution risk (poor sourcing and logistics, using too much high-cost expatriate labor, misunderstanding of local market execution) that should be accommodated in the cash flows and not in the discount rate. This parochial view leads to lower growth prospects and lower stock valuations.
- A sovereign risk adjustment for the systematic risk should be made to the cost of debt and the cost of equity. Actual financing choices need

not complicate the picture unless the value of economic subsidies is to be included.

- Sovereign risk premiums may be "triangulated" from country ratings, sovereign yields, stripped Brady yields, and Euros.
- The volatility of a yield is as important as the yield itself. A point estimate of sovereign risk premium may represent false precision. In some cases, a range, derived from the volatility, offers a more practical perspective.
- Avoid quoting a local currency WACC in any market that does not have long-dated local currency borrowings. Though a local currency WACC may be theoretically derived from long-term inflation estimates, the market does not exist for a reason.
- Theoretically, the economic benefit of global diversification can be quantified from country betas and correlations; however, in practice, the numbers are too unstable to be used for financial planning and policy purposes.

MARKET RISK PREMIUM (MRP)

The return premium afforded by stocks over long government bonds (i.e., MRP) is generally believed to be anywhere from 3 to 8 percent. The widely cited Ibbotson and Sinquefeld study (now down from 8 percent, to about 6 to 7 percent) is based on the U.S. arithmetic mean from 1926. It is not that 1926 was an important year in econometric history; this is just when the market tapes started to be archived.

If the study started one year earlier or later, the risk premium would have changed by a full percentage point. Other U.S. studies (employing manual data retrieval) do go back much further (to when the market was largely railroad stocks) and provide estimates closer to the low end of the range.[2] Some studies rely on more recent history and this, again, leads to the lower end of the range.

Provided the data represent a "random walk" and there are no discernible trends up or down, more observations will lead to greater predictive accuracy. However, structural economic changes over the past century make the early data less relevant for estimating expected returns today. Macroeconomic factors have conspired such that, in our opinion, a shorter history is more appropriate.

Based on the arithmetic average of annualized monthly return premiums and on forward looking multiples, stock market investors today are likely to expect about a 5 percent premium for bearing the market risk of equities. The risk of holding equities has generally declined; at the same time, the risk of investing in government bonds has increased, reducing the premium between these two security classes. Though this is based on monthly returns on the S&P 500 index (which included only 90 stocks before 1957) and on U.S. Treasury long bonds, results are similar using a value-weighted index of all NYSE, AMEX, and NASDAQ stocks as a market proxy.

Converging Volatilities and Returns

The volatility of stock returns versus bond returns has decreased. The trailing average standard deviation of annualized monthly stock returns fell from 25 percent in the 1950s to about 16 percent in 2004. During that period, the standard deviation of bond returns increased from 4 percent to almost 12 percent. Similar trends emerge when using 10-year and 20-year averaging periods as 30 years.

Consistent with changes in relative volatility over the past century, the premium that investors received for stocks relative to bonds fell from over 10 percent to about 5 percent. This drop in the risk premium was attributable to a reduction in the level of stock market risk and to an increase in real required returns on bonds.

Why Is The Market Risk Premium Lower?

Several factors contribute to support the notion that earlier history may be less relevant to the *ex post* derivation of expected equity returns. We speak to the possible causes below:

Regulation and Public Policy   Prudent monetary policies of the Federal Reserve and its foreign counterparts, as well as the general liberalization of regulatory policies, appear to have reduced the volatility of business cycles.[3] Liberalization of developing economies, establishment of trading blocks, and the increase of international trade have all contributed to global economic growth and stability, despite tremendous political change and upheaval.

Growth and Globalization   Growth in worldwide market capitalization affords more liquidity, less net volatility, and less *net risk*. The growth of emerging markets helps to buffer the down cycles of developed economies. Emerging markets help drive developed economies to invest further in human and technical capital. Emerging market volatility is often, in turn, buttressed by the developed markets. Although claims of a borderless global economy are overstated, there is a reduced sensitivity to the economics of any single nation, which reduces systematic risk.

Risk Liquidity   Despite claims to the contrary, the proliferation of risk management products (insurance, credit, interest rate, f/x, and commodity) has increased risk *liquidity*, allowing it to be isolated, traded, syndicated, and managed. Most individuals invest in the market through funds and institutions leading to an increased sophistication and change in the nature of our equity markets.

Information and Technology   Despite recent accounting scandals, disclosure is more immediate and comprehensive, reducing uncertainty and required returns. Notwithstanding Regulation FD, segment data, reporting requirements, and analyst coverage are all more extensive and of higher quality today than 50 years ago. And technology has reduced the price and raised the quality of information processing.

Labor Mobility   The nature of employment has changed. Tremendous growth in the service sector allows service and manufacturing cycles to be somewhat offsetting. Service economies have fewer fixed costs and are, thus, less susceptible to pricing pressures in times of overcapacity. The trend toward mobile, marketable knowledge workers helps reduce fixed costs and improve resource allocation.

Agency Costs   Hedge funds and large institutional investors today are much more active in influencing companies to maximize shareholder value, which reduces the risk of common stock. This force is supported by the success of LBOs and the widespread adoption of value-based management. The importance of agency costs and ownership concentration in improving corporate performance are well documented.

How Much History?

Consistent with changes over the past century, the premium investors received for stocks relative to bonds fell from over 10 percent to about 5 percent.[4] With such a clear trend in the data toward lower equity premiums, it would be a mistake to go too far back in time when estimating the MRP.

The estimate of the MRP depends on how much history is used. Indeed, one could almost justify any premium. Starting from as recently as 2004 implies a negative premium, −5 percent, while adding all 78 years of available history increases the premium to about 7 percent.

Structural changes in the economy and markets suggest that more recent data provide a better basis for predicting the future. Provided you choose a period that goes back at least as far as the early 1980s, the MRP has drifted down. The questions that one must answer are these: How far will the MRP go down, and can we expect it to cycle back up? We have chosen to use the second part of the past century (instead of 3/4), a sufficiently long period to achieve statistical reliability, while avoiding the potentially less relevant early market returns. Consequently, we estimate the MRP over the long bond to be about 5 percent.

Market-Implied Risk Premium

A market risk premium may be estimated from the market's total capitalization, level of earnings and re-investment, and future earnings growth. For example, the dividend discount model (Gordon growth model) provides a simple one-stage valuation framework that may be re-written for this purpose. The constant growth rate assumption of a simple one-stage model, though problematic for a single company, may be more useful for a broad market.

Solving for cost of equity, the Gordon growth model can be expressed as $Ke = [(Div0/P0)*(1 + g)] + g$, where $Div0$ is the annual market dividend payments; $P0$ is the total market capitalization; and g is the estimated dividend growth rate (Table 1.1). Using a distributed yield rather than a reinvestment rate allows us to cancel both market earnings and capitalization. It is also important to note that increasingly, distributed yield may come in the form of share repurchases rather than dividends—both tactics have similar balance sheet impact in reducing capital employed (cash and equity).

Long-term sustainable growth rates may be estimated as the *product* (return on equity * retention ratio) of returns on equity and re-investment rates (i.e., one-payout ratio). This is an ex-ante approach to estimating future growth rates.[5] Retention growth assumes historical returns on book equity (i.e., net income/book equity) and earnings retention are a proxy for

TABLE 1.1 Market-Implied Cost of Equity

Market-Implied Cost of Equity		Perpetual Growth Rate				
		4%	5%	6%	7%	8%
	1.0%	5.0%	6.1%	7.1%	8.1%	9.1%
	1.5%	5.6%	6.6%	7.6%	8.6%	9.6%
Div Yield	2.0%	6.1%	7.1%	8.1%	9.1%	10.2%
	2.5%	6.6%	7.6%	8.7%	9.7%	10.7%
	3.0%	7.1%	8.2%	9.2%	10.2%	11.2%
	4.0%	8.2%	9.2%	10.2%	11.3%	12.3%

future growth. For example, a 10 percent return on equity and sixty percent re-investment rate implies a 6 percent growth rate.

Based on today's market capitalization, depending on assumed future growth rates and dividend yields, the dividend discount model implies a market cost of equity of 7 to 9 percent and an MRP of about 4 percent, using a riskless rate of about 5 percent (Table 1.1). Estimates of long-term sustainable nominal growth rates now range from 5 to 7 percent, consistent with expected inflation of 2 to 3 percent and real GDP growth of 3 to 4 percent.

The Global Market Risk Premium

A global MRP is most appropriate, given the forces of globalism and capital market convergence. However, practically, the U.S. data will still dominate any market-weighted mean. Furthermore, as markets integrate, develop, and season, the U.S. market may serve as the best proxy for a future global MRP.[6] The United States has the largest economy and the most liquid capital markets. Consequently, the 5 percent risk premium seems appropriate for other markets, after adjusting for differences in tax rates, and so forth.

Recent international studies have provided similar results, yielding MRP estimates in the vicinity of 5 percent. In one 103-year history of risk premiums in 16 countries, the U.S. risk premium relative to Treasury bills was 5.3 percent, as compared to 4.2 percent for the United Kingdom and 4.5 percent for a world index.[7] Again, the historical record may still overstate expectations of the *future* risk premium partly because market volatility in the future may be lower than in the past and partly because of a general decline in risk resulting from new technological advances and increased diversification opportunities for investors. After adjusting for the expected impact of these factors, these same authors calculate forward-looking equity risk premiums of 4.3 percent for the United States, 3.9 percent for the United Kingdom, and 3.5 percent for the world index. At the same time, however, they caution that the risk premium can fluctuate over time and that managers should make appropriate adjustments when there are compelling economic reasons to think that expected premiums are unusually high or low.

Most market studies from other countries also tend to draw on shorter histories: Their earlier data are often unavailable, unreliable, or irrelevant due to significant changes in exchange controls and monetary policy. Foreign market derivations of MRPs are often undermined by unreliable historical information, local tax complications, irrelevant history, and liquidity issues making the analysis and its conclusions suspect for many major and emerging markets. Yet, current and future differences in taxes, treatment of dividends, and so on, may make a global risk premium somewhat premature.

TOWARD A BETTER BETA

The determination of a robust proxy for systematic risk (beta) is often a problematic part of a WACC calculation, especially for business units, private companies, illiquid stocks and public companies with little meaningful historical data. Beta is typically the regression coefficient that describes the slope of a line of "best fit" through a history of dividend-adjusted stock and market returns. Though betas can be reasonable and statistically meaningful, they can be difficult to determine, so do not throw out the baby with the bathwater. We will provide some alternative methods to apply the CAPM with a reliable measure of systematic risk.

Direct Regression

Most typically calculated using the most recent 60 monthly returns, other sampling periods and frequencies can be more appropriate. For example, for sectors affected by the tech bubble or 9/11 a three-year sampling of weekly data may be more appropriate. How much history is relevant to your company or industry? Beyond a qualitative assessment for fundamental changes in risk, check the data.

Potential questions might probe the interpretation and sensibility of the regression coefficients, summary statistics, and residuals. Sorting the residuals will help you to flag and understand suspect data, as well as to guide your choices regarding the amount of history and length of the return periods to be used. If no discernible trend is evident and the data represent a random walk, longer periods can be employed to provide more data and improve reliability. If a trend is evident or sufficient history is unavailable, more data can be derived from the shorter history with weekly or daily returns to provide enough data for a meaningful regression. Analyze the residuals of a regression by plotting or sorting, that is, what is not explained by the regression. Re-regressing the interquartile or interdecile range of data should provide a similar slope (i.e., beta) but can give a much better "fit" (i.e., a more statistically significant coefficient of determination). However, if the slope changes, it begs which slope is correct?

Industry Betas

Many stocks or markets are less liquid or have too little history, potentially leading to spurious results if the beta is determined overly mechanically. A simple solution in such cases, as well as for private companies and business units, is to determine a proxy for systematic risk by calculating an industry beta. The underlying assumption is that the systematic risk is similar for all businesses in that industry. However, these approaches can be sensitive to the selection of peers.

Simple Mean or Median of Unlevered Beta   A simple mean or median of pure-play comparable unlevered betas (i.e., asset betas) may serve as a representative proxy for the company unlevered beta. The unlevered beta is then relevered based on a target capital structure. Asset beta, or unlevered beta, is adjusted to exclude financial risk from the market beta:

Unlevered beta = D/EV*debt beta(1 − tax rate) + (1 − D/EV)*levered beta

D is debt, EV is enterprise value, and debt beta is estimated from credit spreads or direct regression of market data. The beta for a conglomerate can be a weighted average of division betas, based on each division's contribution to the firm's intrinsic value (capitalized operating cash flow may serve as a proxy).

Portfolio Beta   Where leverage ratios are similar across an entire industry, a portfolio beta may serve as a proxy for a company beta. The portfolio beta is derived from a single regression of cross-sectional returns for all company market return points. Include as much data as possible to minimize bias from any point. Avoid grouping, aggregating, or averaging your data.

Secondary Regression by Segment

In cases of highly vertically integrated industries (financial services and resource industries), where there are often only a few pure-play peer companies, a secondary regression by segment can be employed to determine a pure-play beta. This is especially helpful for estimating segment, or line-of-business, costs of capital within integrated industries. The dependent variable is each company's unlevered beta, and the independent variables are the percentage exposures to different business segment (e.g., by revenue, assets, or operating income).

For example, Table 1.2 illustrates the development of an unlevered timber beta of 0.4, versus a higher 0.7 for pulp and paper, within the integrated forest products industry. Though the t-statistics are generally all highly significant, the "other" beta will clearly not be meaningful due to the wide mix of other segments within which it will represent.

Constructed Beta

A constructed beta is especially helpful for illiquid stocks where the beta is artificially depressed by a low correlation to the market due to extremely

TABLE 1.2 Segment Beta Regression Illustration

Company	Market Beta	Debt/ EV (%)	Asset Beta	Products (%)	Pulp and Paper (%)	Timber (%)	Other (%)
Company A	1.00	40%	0.68	15%	40%	40%	5%
Company B	1.90	60%	0.88	40%	50%	0%	10%
Company C	1.30	55%	0.69	40%	35%	20%	5%
:							
Company Z	1.20	30%	0.90	60%	10%	10%	20%
Industry			0.95	0.70	0.40	nmf	

low stock liquidity. Betas can be constructed as the product of an industry portfolio correlation coefficient and a company-specific relative volatility coefficient:

$$\text{Beta} = \text{industry correlation coefficient} \\ \times (\text{company volatility}/\text{market volatility})$$

Volatility of market returns may be measured directly from market data, as can a correlation coefficient for the industry. If the business is not traded, relative volatility may be estimated from the standard deviation of changes in capitalized net operating profit after tax (NOPAT), or earnings before interest and taxes (EBIT), as a proxy for return volatility. If operating results, which are generally available on monthly basis, exhibit seasonality, we suggest regressing the percentage change in capitalized NOPAT or EBIT over the same period last year against respective annual market returns.

Multi-Variable Regression Beta

We have employed a novel approach for hybrid businesses that share the characteristics of multiple sectors. For example, a privately owned industrial biotechnology company shared specialty chemicals, pharmaceuticals and biotechnology characteristics. Our multivariable regression incorporated these characteristics (Table 1.3).

Our illustration predicts an asset beta based on these key characteristics, or value drivers (size, growth, R&D intensity, margins, and capex intensity) relative to those of publicly traded pharmaceutical, biotechnology, and specialty chemicals companies. We found significant and intuitively appealing coefficients with this model.

TABLE 1.3 Multivariate Regression Beta Illustration

Company	Market Beta	Debt/ EV (%)	Asset Beta	Size (ln)	Growth (%)	R&D Intensity	Margins (%)	Capex (%)
Company A	1.50	20%	1.24	8.00	20%	18%	30%	8%
Company B	1.00	0%	1.00	14.00	0%	2%	15%	10%
Company C	1.30	10%	1.19	11.00	5%	6%	12%	12%
:								
Company Z	1.20	15%	1.05	12.00	3%	4%	15%	5%
Hybrid Co.				8.00	15%	12%	18%	3%

THE "RISKLESS RATE"

With the 10-year Treasury at abnormally low levels, we typically normalize the riskless rate. Ten-year Treasuries are near historic lows below 5 percent (and 30-year Treasuries near 5 percent); the 10-year historical average is closer about 5.5 percent. Though many companies use a trailing average to normalize the riskless rate for policy purposes, this will have the perverse effect of continuing lower even as spot rates climb and the forward curve steepens.

The forward curve for 10-year Treasuries is a market-derived estimate for the riskless rate. It tends to asymptote in the 5 percent range. The forward curve is less sensitive to the choice of historical averaging period and provides a stable and objective benchmark for a normalized riskless rate.

In practice, investors use any number of government bond rates as a proxy for the risk-free rate, each with its own strengths and weaknesses.[8] Those who use T-bill rates argue that the shorter duration and lower correlation of the T-bill with the stock market make it truly riskless. However, because T-bill rates are more susceptible to supply/demand swings, central bank intervention, and yield curve inversions, T-bills provide a less reliable estimate of long-term inflation expectations and do not reflect the return required for holding a long-term asset.

For valuation, long-term forecasts, and capital budgeting decisions, the most appropriate risk-free rate is derived from longer-term government bonds. They capture long-term inflation expectations, are less volatile and subject to market movements, and are priced in a liquid market. However, the long end is more susceptible to systematic risk, leading some practitioners to propose adjustments to unlever the risk-free rate with a Treasury beta, leading to a truly riskless rate.

THE COST OF DEBT

WACC is calculated using the marginal cost of corporate debt, that is, the yield the company would incur for borrowing an additional dollar. Interest expense is an inaccurate reflection of a corporation's true cost of debt. Nor is it a marginal cost. The average coupon currently paid by a corporation is the result of yields and credit rating at the times of issuance and may not reflect the market environment or corporate credit quality.

Credit quality and corporate bond ratings are the primary determinants of the cost of debt, and they are influenced by factors such as size, industry, leverage, cash flow and coverage, profitability, and numerous qualitative factors.

WACC is based on an after-tax cost of debt. Higher degrees of financial leverage and cash flow volatility will lead to lower expected values for each dollar of tax shield. There will be fewer profits to shield, a loss in time value from loss carry forwards, and an increased risk of financial distress. Company-specific stochastic solutions are perhaps the best approach to estimating this effect. However, as a short-cut method, this effect can be approximated by analyzing risk-laden corporate debt as risk-free debt less a put option on the assets of the firm, with a strike price equal to the face value of the debt.

Based on option valuation framework, the probability of being able to utilize the interest tax shield decays under increased leverage, volatility, and duration. At the debt's maturity equity-holders can "put" the firm assets to debt-holders in exchange for the face value of debt (in bankruptcy, the debt is effectively forgiven when debt-holders take possession of the assets). If the company's assets' value declines below the face value of its debt, the bondholders suffer a loss. Key inputs in the option valuation are time to maturity and volatility of returns of the underlying asset, in this case the enterprise value.

Specifically, from put-call parity, the probability that a firm will be unable to make a payment on its debt obligations and, thus, will not realize a tax shield is (G). S-call (S) = PV (strike price @ Rf)−Put (S). S is the firm's assets, Call (S) is the value of equity, PV (strike price @ Rf) is the value of riskless debt (Df), and PV (strike price @ Rf)−Put (S) is the value of risky debt (Dr). Hence, assets−equity = risky debt. Dr/Df = (PV (strike price @ Rf)−put (S))/PV (strike price. @ Rf) = 1−put (S)/PV (strike price @ Rf) = G.

Hybrid Instruments

Convertibles can offer issuers significant tax advantages while minimizing cash servicing costs via amortization of the warrant value. WACC estimations are complicated by the introduction of hybrids into the capital

TABLE 1.4 Anatomy of a Convertible

	Stock Price	$28.00
	Conversion Price	$40.00
	Effective Term	5
Equity Portion	Stock Volatility	35%
	Risk-Free Rate	5%
	Value of Warrant	7.45
	Warrants per Bond	18
	Total Warrant Value	134.12
	Par Value	1,000
Debt Portion	Coupon	2.5%
	Discount Rate	5.5%
	Straight Debt Value	871.89
CVT	Intrinsic Value	1,006.01

structure. This is most easily resolved through an effective bifurcation of the instrument's value into debt and equity to reflect the true target debt-equity mix (Table 1.4).

However, the equity content for ratings treatment may not represent the true economic content, and therefore its true economic cost. For example, for ratings agency purposes, cash-pay converts are typically treated as debt until conversion. This is true regardless of how in-the-money they become. Some hybrids, such as the newer long-dated junior unsecured notes receive considerable equity credit from the agencies despite representing no economic dilution to the common shareholders. Mandatory convertibles and trust preferred, receive some equity credit for ratings purposes.[9]

Table 1.5 illustrates the effective WACC of this convertible security as a weighted average of cost of the debt and equity portions. The cost of the debt is the grossed up yield (coupon + accretion); grossed up yield = convertible yield/debt portion of total value; straight debt portion of total value = 1 − warrant value/value of the convertible bond; discount rate (%) based on comparable 10-year corporate bond yields.

The cost of the equity is the cost of warrant equity.[10] The warrant value is estimated using the Black-Scholes or other option pricing formula: exercise price premium = (strike price/share price)−1; risk-free rate = Treasury rate with a tenor matching the option term in years; warrant beta = equity beta*warrant delta*share price/warrant premium.

In the case of the more recent hybrid securities with equity-like features that enable them to be accorded a degree of equity content (typically, C or D bucket treatment by Moody's) for ratings purposes, there is no underlying dilution (or conversion) to the fundamental equity interest either at issue, or

TABLE 1.5   Weighted Average Cost of a Convertible

Cost of Equity	Warrant Beta	3.00
	Market Risk Premium	5%
	Cost of Warrant	15%
	Equity Content	13%
Cost of Debt	Effective Yield	2.5%
	Debt Content	87%
	Grossed Up Yield	2.9%
	Adjusted Tax Rate	20%
	A/T Cost of Debt	2.3%
CVT	WACCvt	4.0%

any point in the future. For WACC purposes in such cases, these instruments (long-dated, junior, subordinated notes) are treated as debt.

GLOBAL CAPITAL COSTS

Under the pressure of a prolonged weakness and uncertainty in the equity market, many companies face unprecedented demand for profitable, long-term sustainable growth. Corporate expansion through foreign direct investment continues to offer investors the prospect of valuable growth opportunities.

Global growth remains an essential part of the strategy of most large companies today. Companies pursuing global growth accomplish something their investors appear unwilling or unable to do themselves.[11] Global diversification is a strategy to cope with economic exposures that market integration and risk management were supposed to eliminate but did not. Despite the development and integration of world financial markets, investors continue to behave as if there are substantial costs to foreign portfolio investment.

But today's corporate financial management practices are decidedly at odds with the strategic benefits of foreign direct investment. There may be no other area where corporate practice diverges so far from finance theory. Many still cling to standard practices and ad hoc rules of thumb where excessive hurdle rates for overseas operations and investments often impede value-enhancing growth.

Though the investment returns in emerging economies are often more volatile than the returns on domestic operations, emerging market investments do *not* contribute as significantly as one might expect to the *net risk* of a multinational corporation's (MNC) portfolio.[12] One of the key issues behind the wide range of approaches, in practice, is the extent to which capital markets are now integrated.

A Segmented Markets Perspective

A local country perspective assumes that country managers operate and invest within the isolation of their own respective local markets. This perspective treats each country operation as a stand-alone investment and uses a "local" version of the CAPM with local equity risk indices, local market risk premiums, debt costs, and country risk premiums. Though this approach reflects managers' intuition that international markets exhibit higher risk, it ignores the more global view of shareholders and the beneficial effects of a diverse MNC portfolio and often leads to numerous practical challenges in obtaining reliable and intuitive results. From a corporate financial policy perspective, this approach introduces considerable complexity, communications challenges, and administrative burden.

An Integrated Markets Perspective

An integrated markets perspective views investments as components of a global portfolio. This approach calls for uniformly allocating the corporate portfolio's net sovereign risk, inflation risk, and diversification effects to each and every country-business unit or investment: one source of capital and one cost of capital for all.

Each element of the corporate portfolio fully bears the risks and benefits of the portfolio, irrespective of its contribution to the systematic risk of the corporate portfolio. Though this works well for the consolidated cost of capital, for country operations and investments, we employ a hybrid perspective that captures each investment's *marginal impact* to the systematic risk of the corporate portfolio.

The Hybrid Perspective

Although world financial markets have become more integrated than they were 25 years ago, several factors continue to contribute to a significant degree of market segmentation. Perhaps most important, investors in all nations are still most comfortable investing in companies in their home markets, leading to the well-documented "home bias" in investor portfolios. But legal, tax, accounting, and regulatory barriers are also at work.

As a result of these impediments to well-functioning markets, many of the world's capital markets, particularly emerging markets, have continued to exhibit signs of illiquidity—or, depending on your interpretation, market inefficiencies—associated with market segmentation. But, far from discouraging foreign direct investment by corporations, these barriers make the *benefits* of foreign direct investment *even greater* than if markets were completely integrated.

In a world that remains at least partly segmented, foreign direct investment is still capable of providing the firm's shareholders with investment opportunities and diversification benefits they cannot obtain on their own. Moreover, as global economies and financial markets continue the process of integration, this diversification benefit of foreign direct investment will gradually disappear; other benefits, notably the reduction in risks (sovereign and inflation) that come with global integration, will take its place.

Our hybrid perspective assumes that a company maintains a dynamic portfolio of foreign and domestic investments that is continuously evaluated for possible expansion, curtailment, or even sale; as a result, the proportionate weightings of each real portfolio element are constantly changing.

To extend the CAPM to the evaluation of operations and investments overseas, we adjust the framework for systematic and unsystematic risk as follows:

- Adjust operating cash flows for project-specific risks and costs. Though simple rules of thumb are easier to use, they obscure fundamental issues, undermine strategic risk discussion, and become inapplicable as conditions change.
- Perform comprehensive risk analysis, such as sensitivity analysis and Monte Carlo simulations, of risk drivers to enhance active risk management for value.
- Adjust the cost of capital for sovereign risk and expected inflation—our proposed methodology follows.

As a practical matter, the risk profiles and volatilities of each market, as well as their correlations between each other, are changing. Therefore, we *do not* employ a country beta relative to the home country as our proxy for the incremental systematic risk to the portfolio for each operation or prospective investment; rather, we assume sovereign spreads best capture the incremental systematic risk. Similarly, we *do not* attempt to quantify the diversification benefit that accrues to the portfolio with each marginal investment. This is constantly changing. Variation within the estimation of any one correlation coefficient is often greater than the difference between any two correlation coefficients.

The instability of sovereign ratings and sovereign risk makes any *point estimate* of WACC an oversimplification in many markets. Historical distribution and standard deviation data can support the development of a range estimate to help quantify the risk of a value-dilutive investment via simulation. For example, the probability that an investment produces a negative NPV due to the true WACC turning out to be higher than the hurdle rate.

The Risks and Returns of Foreign Direct Investment

Beyond profitable growth, there are strategic benefits to global investing. Today's global companies are often more attractive than their domestic peers who missed their chances to go global in part because of inflated international hurdle rates. For many years, Bestfoods was an attractive acquisition target to packaged food companies, ultimately trading at a large premium, in part, due to its highly diversified global portfolio with exposure to faster growing consumer markets.

Consider the case of Japanese foreign direct investment in the United States in the 1980s. These "transplants" enjoyed relief with low-cost manufacturing resulting from an unexpected strengthening of the yen against the dollar. Had production remained in Japan, supply to the large U.S. market would have been uncompetitive. European transplants similarly benefited in this more recent era of Euro strength.

But the returns of global investment cannot be realized without significant risk since global investing entails risks and costs incremental to those domestic investing. We distinguish between unsystematic and systematic risks and propose approaches to the treatment of each. Systematic risk, or market risk, stems from economy-wide perils that affect all businesses; by definition, this would include the currency and sovereign risks of the economy itself. What matters to the well-diversified corporation, and ultimately the well-diversified investor, is any incremental contribution to risk.[13]

Unsystematic Risks and Costs

Foreign direct investment brings new and significant incremental costs (foreign legal and tax, currency repatriation and hedging, and insurance and other transaction costs) that reduce the intrinsic value of the investment or operation. Numerous risks (heightened project uncertainty such as market success, labor strife or other operational challenges) are specific to the investment or operation. Typically, these costs and risks are noncompounding and are best evaluated in cash flow scenario, sensitivity, and simulation analyses. But despite the heroic coaching of finance professors around the world, our experience has shown that these costs and risks are still frequently omitted from the cash flow projections of international investment decisions. Furthermore, they are often "below the line" in the evaluation of any international operations. This creates a need for higher hurdle rates.

Project uncertainty, and the recognition that many international risks and costs are neglected, is the often unspoken rationale to inflate the hurdle rates for these investments. But managers typically have the best information about the potential impact of these risks on the expected stream of operating cash flows. Managers do not have any way to quantify the effect (if there is any) on shareholders' required rate of return, and these risks are diversifiable by investors or companies with global portfolios.

Systematic Risks

We identify the systematic risks to discrete foreign direct investments that can be quantified and treated within the cost of capital framework to manage the MNC portfolio better. However, these risks do not need to be incorporated with arbitrary and excessive risk premiums; rather, they can be addressed more rigorously in a fairly straightforward manner.

Business and Financial Risks   The inherent business and financial risk need not change for foreign direct investments because a company's core business and target capital structure does not typically depend on any particular international operations; we would typically expect these to be applicable worldwide. For example, in industries where operating profit tends to be more volatile and correlated to the market (e.g., semiconductor industry), business risk is high. These risks, measured by the company beta, have been captured in the corporate cost of capital.

Expected Inflation   The rate at which prices are expected to increase, inflation risk, measures the relative strength of a currency in relation to domestic expected inflation and is typically reflected in forward foreign exchange rates. In effect, it represents the risk arising from expected currency devaluation (longer term) due to differentials in long-run inflation expectations (assumes interest rate parity holds over the longer run). These risks implied by the relative risk-free rates between countries, or from inflation-linked government bonds, are incorporated into the cost of debt and cost of capital calculations. This risk should be distinguished from the short-run cases where parity breaks down, and unexpected currency devaluation is a possibility subsumed by sovereign risk.

Sovereign Risk   Sovereign risk is most commonly associated with the risk that a foreign government will default on its loans or fail to honor other business commitments due to change in government or policy. However, sovereign risk is a broad category of risks unique to a country's political and economic environments that include the impact of currency controls, changes in tax or local content laws, quotas and tariffs, and the sudden imposition of labor or environmental regulation:

- **Unexpected devaluation/inflation:** Sharp movements in the relative valuations of currencies, as in Mexico in 1994 and in Russia and much of Asia in 1998, go beyond the weakness implied by expected inflation differentials and are frequently the result of unrealistic currency pegs. Sudden runaway inflation has been "employed" to help satisfy debt obligations (e.g., Bolivia in the 1980s).
- **Policy risk:** A host government, due to leadership or policy changes, may renege on contracts, agreements, or approvals, may prevent currency conversion, or may impede repatriation. Other examples include sudden large changes in tax laws, local content laws, quotas and tariffs, and environmental restrictions. For example, witness the unexpected difficulties faced by MNC loggers and miners in the Pacific Northwest in the 1990s as a result of environmental lobbying.
- **Expropriation:** Host government policy may reduce or eliminate ownership of, control over, or rights to an investment by an overseas firm. This has happened in Russia, Cuba, South America, Israel, and many other countries.
- **War/civil disturbance:** This includes acts of sabotage or terrorism, damage to tangible assets, or interference with the ability of the enterprise to operate. This has been particularly acute in sub-Saharan Africa and the Middle East.

Sovereign risks add a premium to the required rate of return for foreign direct investment. One way of estimating the possible size of this premium is to look at the "insurance premiums" charged by organizations such as the Overseas Private Investment Corporation (OPIC) and the Multilateral Investment Guarantee Agency (MIGA), which guarantee foreign investments against some of the risks cited above. Other market-based methods may be more reliable.

We generally employ multiple sources of information to "triangulate" sovereign risk premiums, such as USD-denominated (Global Euro and stripped Brady) sovereign debt yields. Where bond yields are unavailable or appear unreliable, we use the premiums implied by a basket of similarly rated (S&P country ratings) countries. For the countries that make long-term borrowings predominantly in U.S. dollars (USD) and not in the local currency, we may use Eurobond yields or the stripped yield of their International/Brady bonds as a basis for USD-based risk-free rates. The stripped yield is the yield on the noncollateralized portion of the bond. We do not employ a local currency WACC for currencies that have no long-dated market. Where capital markets are unwilling or unable to quote and make long-dated bets on a currency, neither should corporates. In these cases, we keep WACC in a "hard" currency and recommend that great care be taken in projecting and discounting cash flows to mitigate against uncertain future inflation estimates. The local cost of capital in local currency provides local managers with a reference frame when forecasts are based on local currency with local inflation expectations embedded. But, for purposes of evaluating a contemplated investment in Turkey (or, say, a major expansion of its current operations), a Turkish cost of capital in USD (with no significant revenue inflation) provides a better basis.

For developed countries (and those others who are able and tend to borrow long-term in the local currency), we may estimate USD-based sovereign yields based on S&P sovereign credit rating of such countries and corporate credit spread matrix. We begin by estimating a domestic cost of capital and then add sovereign and expected inflation risk premiums.

This process is a somewhat iterative process, as the *domestic* cost of capital should not reflect the net incremental risk of the *global assets* already reflected in the company beta. We skip this step where the impact is deemed to be immaterial at the corporate level.

Our sovereign risk premiums reflect the country risk; larger markets such as the G7 and other AAA and AA countries have low risk premiums, often less than 50 basis points (bps). Emerging market sovereign risk premiums range from 50 to 100 bps for investment grade credits such as Chile and Poland, to hundreds or even thousands of bps for noninvestment grade credits like Argentina, Indonesia, Peru, and the Ukraine.

For example, Chile USD sovereign debt yields 4.9 percent, and incorporates an incremental required rate of return to compensate U.S. (or globally diversified) investors for bearing Chilean sovereign risk. To determine what portion of that 4.9 percent represents Chilean sovereign risk, we effectively subtract the U.S. sovereign yield from the local country sovereign yield (excluding the effect of compounding) to estimate a 70 bps sovereign risk premium, which is consistent with their country USD rating.

Global Corporate Capital Costs

A helpful way of looking at the cost of capital for foreign countries is in terms of the marginal impact of the two systematic risk components: sovereign and currency risk. Calculating foreign WACC in USD involves adding a sovereign risk premium to the domestic WACC. To calculate foreign WACC in local currency, we also add the expected inflation premium.

TABLE 1.6   Global Capital Cost Illustration

	USD Rating	Sovereign Risk	Standard Deviation	USD WACC	Inflation Risk	LC WACC
Country A	AAA	20	5	8.0%	(20)	7.8%
Country B	AA	35	10	8.4%	—	8.4%
Country C	A	70	15	8.7%	10	8.8%
Country D	BBB	115	30	9.2%	150	10.7%
Country E	BB	240	60	10.4%	nmf	nmf
Country F	B	350	150	11.5%	nmf	nmf

We estimated currency risk from inflation-linked sovereign bonds or from the difference between using expected changes in Consumer Price Index (CPI), LC sovereign bond yields and the implied LC issuer yields based on S&P Country sovereign yields. Local WACC in USD = global USD WACC + sovereign risk premium. Local WACC in LC = local WACC in USD + inflation risk premium.

For example (Table 1.6), in the case of Chile (Country C), where we estimate a sovereign risk premium of 70 bps and an inflation risk premium of 10 bps, a company with a domestic WACC of 8 percent will have a foreign WACC in USD of roughly 8.7 percent and a WACC in local currency of about 8.8 percent.

But any point estimate of sovereign risk may represent false precision. Sovereign risk premiums vary widely even within country ratings, and are subject to sudden change. For noninvestment grade countries, we estimate and illustrate the range for a sovereign risk premium with a Monte Carlo simulation based on historical sovereign yield data.

WACC AND HURDLE RATES

Many companies use a higher required return for investments than their actual cost of capital, often with artificial decrees to compensate for poor sensitivity or risk analysis, free capital and with an excessive reliance on single-point estimates of an internal rate of return (IRR) or NPV. In many companies, capital is "free" because once investment approval is negotiated, it is a sunk cost to managers. Thus, in most cases, capital must be rationed precisely because it is free. Alternatively, when capital bears its own true cost, it becomes plentiful but expensive.

But hurdle rates destroy value:

- Starve growth by systematically obstructing value-adding investment opportunities

- Lead to inflated projections by the proponents of investment opportunities
- Steer the company away from beneficial activities of more comprehensive risk analysis and creative risk management
- Reduce the company's weighted average return on capital by forfeiting positive NPV investment opportunities

To offset the problems of poor risk analysis and free capital, hurdle rates that exceed the cost of capital are frequently imposed on managers. This attempt to subsume a proper risk analysis and compensate for overly optimistic forecasts typically leads to more optimistic forecasts. The practical corollary to the deceptively simple allure of inflated hurdle rates is a reduced emphasis on even simple risk analysis and more optimistic forecasts.

Increasing a project's rate of return does not allow for adequate consideration of the time pattern and magnitude of risk being evaluated. Using a higher discount rate to reflect additional risk indiscriminately penalizes future cash flows relative to less distant ones and geometrically compounds the cost of any risk. It is simplest to use a single cost of capital (per currency) for discounting and hurdle rates. Risk, on the other hand, is best identified and analyzed discretely through scenario or simulation analysis; capital consumption, is best managed through performance measurement and rewards.

Though some negative NPV projects invariably must be undertaken for environmental, health and safety reasons (defensive capital), inflated hurdle rates do not help, and actually exacerbate, this problem because they limit the amount of capital that earns an offsetting return. However, all investments that earn returns above those of the existing business increase the overall return on capital. An inflated hurdle rate results in foregone opportunity, less growth, a lower return on capital employed (ROCE), and a lower value (Table 1.7). We illustrate mathematically that reducing the hurdle rate down from 20 percent (versus an 8 percent WACC and 10 percent ROCE) leads to increasingly higher weighted average returns, more NPV, and larger enterprise values.

Instead of raising the cost of capital, project and business operating cash flows should be adjusted downward to reflect the incremental risks, costs, and uncertainties. Where capital must be rationed, we recommend a ranking to produce the largest incremental NPV available. However, the limitation to any ranking of investments is that this must be done in a static environment with all investment opportunities available for evaluation at the same time, yet this is rarely realistic.

Capital is rarely in short supply as investors are clamoring for opportunity. The greatest constraint, and one of the greatest strategic challenges

TABLE 1.7 Lower Hurdle Rates Lead To Higher Returns and Values

	Profit	Capital	ROCE	EVA	NPV	EV
Company	120	1200	10.0%	24	300	1,500
Projects						
20%	20	100	10.8%	36	450	1,750
18%	18	100	11.3%	46	575	1,975
15%	15	100	11.5%	53	663	2,163
12%	12	100	11.6%	57	713	2,313
10%	10	100	11.5%	59	738	2,438

facing publicly traded corporations, is the opportunity for growth. Stock prices routinely reflect expectations of tremendous growth. In most years, about one half of the aggregate S&P enterprise value can be justified by the present value of current cash flows capitalized as perpetuity. The other half of the market capitalization is predicated on profitable growth over and above today's level of cash flows.

Today's corporate financial policies and practices are at odds with this growth imperative—excessive hurdle rates impede growth—especially organic growth and smaller investments (the least amount of risk) and, ultimately, necessitate large acquisitions (where risk is greatest) to supplement modest growth.

One of the most basic and fundamental tenets of modern corporate finance, and indeed capitalism, is the obligation to maximize shareholder wealth. A tacit promise to maximize NPV is made with passive investments, such as retaining rather than distributing capital, and with active investments, involving the raising of capital. To meet this obligation to maximize shareholder wealth, all positive NPV are to be undertaken and negative NPV investments rejected, or deferred, where possible. Every positive NPV project adds value. Value is maximized when all positive NPV projects are undertaken.

CHAPTER 2

Fix: Finding Your Sources of Value

T raditional earnings approaches to valuation, performance measurement, and strategic thinking have come up short. Managing for value has again become the mantra of today's executive. But the academic literature, mainstream journalists, and even analyst community members, have long interpreted managing for value initiatives as mere advances in metrics and measurement.

Such a narrow interpretation implies little fundamental change to the behavior of the people and processes responsible for the decisions and actions that create value. To create value, value-based management must include a powerful change to both people and processes, including planning, portfolio management, strategic and tactical decision-making, and compensation.

Many strategies fail in the decisions, not the vision. All too often, strategies and their execution are premised on flawed measures and metrics, driving uneconomic decisions and value destruction or suboptimization. The deployment and execution of strategies require countless economic, value-based decisions to be made at all levels within the company: integrations, dispositions, closures, outsourcing, run-length, customer and stock keeping unit (SKU) rationalization, changes to pricing, promotions and value propositions.

Many companies feel pressed to discern where they are creating value and where they are destroying value within their business portfolios. In our experience, roughly 80 percent of companies cannot measure returns on capital or true contribution to value creation below the business unit level. In practice, meaningful measures of customer, product and SKU economic profitability remain a distant dream.

Value-based portfolio management puts the tools for strategic decisions and tactical execution into the hands of value-oriented managers. Yet the application and interpretation of these tools demand care. Despite the seemingly simple call to maximize value, choices are complex as performance measurement and valuation become harder to discern at the more granular levels of the business portfolio.

It takes sound economic analysis and progressive accounting practices to unearth the sources of value creation and value destruction within a corporate portfolio. One must define the key elements of a granular value-based profitability measure and what levers can be used to increase contributions to value, measure, and categorize business and activities along a spectrum of contribution to value, and optimize (analyze, improve, and control) the value of a portfolio of SKUs, customers, and products.

WHY SHAREOWNER VALUE?

Shareowner value is all the buzz in business and valuespeak once again permeates annual reports, mission statements and research reports. Why all the fuss? What about stakeholders?

Capital is a scarce resource that all businesses must compete for and efficiently manage. The limited supply of, and liquid markets for, capital require that its users maximize its value, that is, maximize shareowner value or face the flight of capital to more attractive opportunities.

One of the most basic and fundamental tenets of capitalism is the obligation to maximize shareowner value. An expectation of a return is created with every dollar raised and invested. A tacit promise to maximize value is made to shareowners with each dollar of profit retained rather than distributed. Thus, the litmus test behind any decision to raise, invest, or retain a dollar must be to create more value than the investor might have achieved with an otherwise alternative investment opportunity of similar risk.

If managing for value is embracing the interests of owners, what then of the interests of other stakeholders? Let's start with a look at who these owners are, for they are not rich, young professionals on Wall Street; institutional investors represent the savings of everyday citizens. Our mutual funds, pension plans, life insurance policies, and many small investor holdings represent the vast majority of stock ownership. We invest our savings and bear risk, in the hopes of the best return possible.

But this need not imply a conflict between the interests of customers, employees, owners and the managers, executives, and directors who act as stewards of our savings. Fashionable shareowner stakeholder discussions show a confusion of means and ends. Value maximization, the heart of economic growth, is a long-term proposition that delivers higher economic output and prosperity through productivity gains, employment growth, and higher wages. The interests of stakeholders and of society are best served when our scarce resources are put to their most productive uses.

Management's most important mission is to maximize shareowner wealth; managing for value directs our scarce resources to their most promising uses and most productive users. The societal benefits of managing for value are clear. The more effectively our scarce resources can be deployed and managed, the more robust will be our economic growth and the rate of improvement in our collective standard of living.

Globalism presents investors with an opportunity and a challenge. As historically insular product, labor, and capital markets become increasingly global, companies will continue to face increasing competitive pressures. Under pressure to perform, institutional investors are warming to the notions of shareowner activism and heightened corporate governance. Market liquidity and the emergence of more sophisticated and demanding institutional investors have made the consequences of destroying shareowner value more material to today's employees, executives, and directors.

PERFORMANCE MEASUREMENT PITFALLS

Given that what gets measured gets managed, managers and executives should exercise caution. Though business schools have been teaching valuation concepts for decades, earnings per share and other traditional accounting-based metrics continue to dominate corporate decision making. However, these metrics have many risks and can mask rampant value destruction if the costs of capital and capacity are inadequately addressed. Chronic problems result from using the popular potpourri of performance metrics—top line growth, market share, gross margin, operating income and standard cost—as an implicit proxy for value creation.

Overproduction

Standard cost typically ignores or understates the cost of capital, such as the opportunity cost of capital employed in capacity, inventory, and receivables. Standard cost converts period costs into unit costs: the fixed production costs and the costs of capacity. Excess (unsold) throughput is often capitalized into inventory, reducing perceived unit cost. Because inventory has no income statement cost and a false "absorption" benefit, profit increases with production even if no demand exists for the goods produced.

Plant managers are often directed to minimize unit costs, irrespective of actual demand and will, thus, produce to and expand capacity. Producing as many units as possible, irrespective of demand, maximizes profit per unit. Gross margins and profits will increase with production and capital investment, but inventory levels, utilization, and ultimately returns on capital and economic profit suffer.

In some cases, excess inventory reaches a point where product quality, material flow, and order fulfillment suffer. Other operating burdens include uneven and inflexible production and vast quantities of unnecessary inventory. Excess product is often heavily discounted, wholesaled, or scrapped. Foregone revenue is endemic to this vicious circle because heavy discounting and trade promotion are needed to unload aging surplus product, often at the end of each year or quarter.

Overinvestment

Profit and profit margin measures often drive over-investment and vertical integration because they overlook capital and its cost. Rampant overcapacity plagues many sectors, undermining margins. Increasingly, different businesses and business models consume varying levels of capital at varying costs. Managers are often drawn to higher margin businesses that, on the surface, may seem more attractive. For example, profits and margins are often improved with newer production technology, but they must be to compensate for the higher levels of investment. Because traditional financial measures ignore the returns that shareholders expect, any corporate project with just a positive—but not necessarily an adequate—return above zero can improve a manager's margins, unit cost, and profit and productivity measures. However, such a project can destroy value.

Feed the "Dogs" and Starve the "Stars"

Many managers have a strong affinity for percentages because of their intuitive appeal. But batting averages and shooting percentages do not win games. A focus on percentage margins and rates of return starves the "stars" and feeds the "dogs."

A low-return dog business might be motivated to pursue return expanding growth that, if below the cost of capital, would destroy value to achieve higher margins and returns on capital. A high-return star business might overlook or reject return-diluting growth that, although above its cost of capital and therefore additive to value, will decrease returns on capital and dilute margins (Table 2.1).

Traditional financial measures, being based on traditional business models, have not kept up with the pace of change. New business models are often based on services, outsourcing, partnerships and other innovative ways of doing business. Traditional financial measures are inherently biased against the new service economy. Their blunt nature is too simplistic,

TABLE 2.1   Starving the Stars and Feeding the Dogs

	Starve the Stars			Feed the Dogs		
	A	B	A + B	A	B	A + B
Sales	1,000	1,000	2,000	1,000	1,000	2,000
Margin	20%	15%	18%	5%	8%	7%
Profit	200	150	350	50	80	130
Capital	1,000	1,000	2,000	1,000	1,000	2,000
ROCE	20%	15%	18%	5%	8%	7%
WACC	10%	10%	10%	10%	10%	10%
EVA	100	50	150	(50)	(20)	(70)
NPV	1,000	500	1,500	(500)	(200)	(700)

creating impediments to profitable growth in a world where more service-oriented businesses are being designed around razor-thin margins, but with low capital investment. A bias against viable, long-term investments and economic growth can result from a simplistic, near-term income focus.

MEASURING ECONOMIC PROFIT AND VALUE

Annual reports reveal much about the collective view of managers. But rather than finding a sense of shared purpose, we often find overarching goals that vary widely, interpreted and expressed in terms of market share, revenue dollars, gross margins, expense ratios, earnings growth, price/earnings ratios, returns on capital, and share price performance.

Income statement measures still dominate our language in business, yet profit and profit margin measures often drive overproduction, overinvestment, and uneconomic vertical integration because they overlook capital and its cost. And we increasingly see different businesses and business models consuming varying levels of capital at varying costs.

While the goal ultimately must be expressed in terms of shareowner returns, an operating measure provides a more actionable proxy. The contribution to intrinsic value in any given period is best captured with a measure known as *economic profit* (EP), which is the annual contribution to intrinsic value, or net present value (NPV).[1]

Economic profit = net operating profit after tax-capital employed
× cost of capital

Economic profit measures profit after the cost of all capital employed. It simultaneously captures revenue, cost, and the cost of capital in one measure and properly accounts for the trade-offs between the income statement and balance sheet in creating value. It charges the full cost of your balance sheet to your profit statement.

Economic profit is also the spread between a company's return on and cost of capital, times invested capital. For example, the economic profit for a $1,000 investment in a hot dog stand with a 5 percent return, versus investments of similar risk earning 15 percent, would be negative $100 [$(5\% - 15\%) \times \$1,000$].

Simplistically, one can express intrinsic value as the NPV of all future cash flow. This can also be expressed as the mathematically equivalent sum of capital and the present value of all future economic profits. And while present value concepts are more easily, and therefore more commonly, applied to fixed income valuation, the same concept holds for businesses, albeit with much less certainty in the forward numbers.

A business generating $100 per year, every year forever, can be valued into perpetuity as $1,000, assuming a 10 percent cost of capital, or time value of money ($100/10% = $1,000). This zero-growth base case implies a capitalization factor, or multiplier, of 10 times operating cash flow and is the current operations value (COV). The COV can also be expressed as the sum of capital invested, plus the present value of current EP capitalized into perpetuity, with no growth. The nominal zero-growth assumption implies decay in real terms.

Now, let's try a growth case where operating cash flow grows at a rate of 5 percent per year forever. Though many of us might think that forever is a long time, it may not be long enough to justify some stock prices. Our simple case can be valued on a present value basis at $100/(10% − 5%), or $2,000. The growth case implies a multiplier of 20 times and happens to illustrate a price level common to today's marketplace.

In this example, one half of the value is from the present value of current operating cash flows (forever) and the other half from profitable growth above this level, that is, 50 percent of the value is COV, while the remainder is future growth value. The growth value subsumes expected growth and the value of any real options. For example, 5 percent growth might be a proxy for a 90 percent likelihood of no growth, and a 10 percent chance of 50 percent annual growth.

Book Values Do Not Count!

Confusion between accounting and economics often stops managers from making value accretive portfolio decisions. Bookkeeping entries often create a needless friction that reduces market liquidity for transactions.

For example, idle assets and loss-making businesses that could otherwise be disposed of in return for cash are often needlessly kept to avoid booking a loss on sale, that is a non-cash accounting entry of no economic consequence beyond the possible signaling value of an overdue correction.

Negative EVA Does Not Matter!

Just as the distraction of book values should not prohibit value-creating sales, they need not unduly drive judgment against a business. Though earning a return below your cost of capital is by no means desirable, these returns are typically calculated on a book value, not a market value. And since we know book values do not count, negative EVA calculated on book values are equally misleading. However, using market value capital is not the answer. Since going concern market values have capitalized expectations of future growth in EP, they too are inappropriate indications of the opportunity cost of current period capital.

Regardless of whether a company has positive or negative EP, its intrinsic value is equal to the present value of its future cash flow generation (or capital plus the present value of all future EP). Thus, it is the present value of future EP for each alternative (grow, divest, close) is what matters, not the *level* of EP. EP *growth*, or *improvement* (especially any amount beyond what is already expected, or capitalized into the intrinsic value) that is needed to drive value creation.

For example, the liquidation value of a smelter may be less than the value of continuing operations, despite negative EP. The breakup value may be less for many reasons, including high closure costs, resale values well below book values, and operating synergies. Continuing operations may well have a higher intrinsic value than the shutdown or liquidation of this business. A negative economic profit company can even be a strong buy if this performance and outlook is capitalized by the market (if the stock price is sufficiently low to allow you to earn an adequate return on your own investment). Ultimately, if opportunity for improvement is made possible and this gets capitalized by the market, excess returns will be created.

Negative economic profit is often a flag that indicates the strategy of a business should be reviewed to ensure it is the alternative with the best net present value.

Putting Value into the Profit Equation

Several measurement issues must be addressed to measure value creation and destruction at low, granular levels within the corporate portfolio (customer, SKU, product, brand). Fixed asset values do not represent the true opportunity cost of capital employed.

Book values overstate plant and property value in sectors with chronic overcapacity or high closure costs and are understated for equipment that can remain in service long beyond stated lives. Furthermore, acquired capital is "marked to market" via goodwill, while organic growth is accounted for at book value. The sunk cost of goodwill has more relevance to past portfolio decisions than to future ones.

Net Realizable Value   For granular economic profitability measurement, net realizable value (NRV) is a more accurate measure for the opportunity cost of fixed assets. NRV should be an approximate expected salvage or liquidation value, net of all exit or closure costs (e.g., severance and tax). NRV is a forward-looking measure for the opportunity cost of capital and should be used especially when liquidation can be considered a viable long-term or short-term alternative.

Closing facilities with little or no NRV saves their annual operating cost, but their sale or liquidation provides no economic benefit beyond the potential secondary benefit of reduced supply. In economic terms, this capacity is essentially free.

Business Value   Though many companies are publicly traded, businesses within the corporate portfolio (business units, products, brands, and so forth.) generally are not. Thus, strategic questions must be addressed through their likely impact on intrinsic value, estimated through fundamental valuation. Projecting and then discounting future economic profit or cash flow links performance to intrinsic value.

Because intrinsic value is dependent on expectations, it is sensitive to capitalized current performance as well as changes in performance outlook. For example, most stocks trade with a significant amount of value dependent on expectations of growth. In the case of the Dow Jones Industrial Average (DJIA), future growth values accounted for about 55 percent of the average stock prices at 2003 year-end, with the other 45 percent contributed by the present value of the current operations.

This analysis can help support forecast and terminal value assumptions, as well as an empirical strategic review of COV and growth value (GV) drivers. We can disaggregate future growth value into a performance forecast better to gauge market prices.

Implications for Terminal Values

Terminal values frequently contribute 50 percent or more of the NPV in an economic profit analysis and even higher in the case of a discounted cash flow (DCF) analysis. This is in part because capital is expensed in a DCF, rather than capitalized as it is with EP; thus, EP based NPV analysis is less dependent on terminal value assumptions. Yet, terminal values are one of the most under-researched and overlooked issues in modern corporate finance. They are the weak link in valuation, not the discount rate, as many would believe. We present several terminal value approaches and their underlying rationale below.

Perpetuities   The simplest approach assumes an infinite "steady state" at the end of a forecast period, say, three to five years. Final year cash flow remains constant into perpetuity with new investment equal to the annual depreciation expense and capital constant.

Unfortunately, this finite-growth model typically does not reconcile empirically with how the market values securities because it assumes growth value decays to zero; warranted or not, in practice, one can rarely find a business with zero growth value. Though a single product may have a finite life, a company, business, or product need not resign itself to such a sad fate, thanks to renewable brand, technology, or franchise values. Most businesses and products have an opportunity to reinvent themselves and rebuild growth values.

Few, if any companies, ever trade like a bond with no growth value. This is especially true in cases able to earn more than their cost of capital where growth is expected until excess returns become unavailable, and low return businesses are expected to be "turned around" or sold. Empirically, businesses cannot be expected to trade like a bond with no growth value.

Analysts often address this with simple perpetual growth assumptions for nominal annual economic growth of 3 to 5 percent. Others prefer a market solution. For example, we have found correlation between return on capital, margins, R&D intensity, and the perpetuity growth rate implied in market values, allowing us to build industry-specific tables of appropriate perpetuity growth rates.

Any renewal of growth value does require investment in R&D, brand building, technology, capacity, and so forth. A fade or decay in economic returns, toward the cost of capital, might be assumed where no investment or renewal is planned.

Market Multiples   Market multiples are a common empirical shortcut to the terminal value factor, particularly where valuations that reconcile with the marketplace require large amounts of growth value in the terminal value. Although expecting certainty in long-term forecasting is unreasonable, terminal values suffer from the same problem; all multiples and terminal value assumptions themselves subsume implicit assumptions about expectations for the future.

Typically, market multiples are income statement focused (e.g., 1 × sales, 6 × EBITDA, 20 × earnings), and they may be economic profit-based to incorporate the utilization of capital more systematically.

Multiples should conceptually be based on a sound theoretical construct of value and then established empirically from market value data. Through industry regression analysis of market values, we can develop an industry specific valuation model (market multiple).

Cyclicality will limit the relevant range of history for market multiples, with multiples being lowest in good times and highest in poor times. Economic profit multiples may explain more of the variance in market values and may demonstrate less standard error.

For example, regression analysis of branded food stocks yielded a y-intercept, representing the capital multiple (1.30) and slope (3.5), representing the capitalized economic profit multiple. The theoretical construct in this case is that both coefficients equal one for the current operations value. The coefficient premiums represent GV, incorporated primarily in the economic profit portion. Though negative economic profit is typically capitalized at a lower multiple, this industry has insufficient data to support its statistical determination.

ANALYZING THE CORPORATE PORTFOLIO

A calculation of economic profit involves three components of data: revenue, expense, and capital. The cost of capital is more an economic determination than an input. At the consolidated level, an EP calculation is typically simple with few issues of data availability and clarity. Similarly, intrinsic value can also be determined and benchmarked wherever a financial outlook can be estimated. But at more granular levels (product, brand, SKU, customer), important measurement issues arise. Can the economic benefit (attributable revenue) be appropriately captured? How are indirect cost and capital allocations best handled? How are unit costs best measured?

And does managing for value—be it a portfolio of businesses, products, brands or customers—mean that each manager should grow businesses earning returns above their cost of capital and sell or close all businesses earning returns below their cost of capital (book value issues aside)? Despite the appealing simplicity, we argue against this approach due to four common pitfalls.

Inadequate Time Horizon

Economic profit is a period measure, yet value is determined by the present value of performance in this period plus all periods going forward. A company, business unit, product, or customer may offer negative economic profit now, but each represents considerable value if it is likely to be sufficiently positive in the future to offset the cost of holding the negative. The early years of negative economic profit might be considered the price of a call option on better future, a real option.

Unrecognized Cross-Subsidies and Inappropriate Transfer Pricing

Unrecognized cross-subsidies and inappropriate transfer pricing often mask the sources of true economic performance and value, particularly at more granular levels within a company's portfolio. Cross-subsidies, inadequately addressed via transfer prices, will invariably create incorrect signals of performance and value within the portfolio. Suboptimization can occur where we see only part of the picture; decisions can maximize the value of some parts, functions, or processes, but total value is not maximized because of our incomplete view of the picture.

We have heard how Polaroid cameras were used to feed the sale of film and that razor blades subsidize the razors. Similarly, casinos regularly lose money on food and lodging to capture larger gaming profits. Drug companies try to leverage high research costs across more therapeutic areas. A large printing company might lose money on a high-profile magazine to showcase production quality capabilities. Car retailers nearly give away new cars to generate used car, service, insurance, and financing business.

But these strategies need to be closely managed. For example, many do not realize how unprofitable car financing can be once accounting for the costs of capital employed and risk undertaken. But after appropriately factoring matched maturity funds transfer pricing and associated risk capital, the highly competitive business of consumer lending seems best left to the majors.

Business activities are frequently bundled by default, rather than on purpose. For example, the three activities of consumer financing (origination, servicing, and investment) need not necessarily be bundled. When they are bundled, it is impossible to discern the true nature of the value proposition and sources of value unless economic transfer pricing is employed.

Businesses need to understand the true economics of each activity to make the appropriate decisions around resource allocation and outsourcing.

Misallocations

Top line growth and standard cost reduction can mask rampant value destruction. The misallocation of indirect costs and assets can create misleading signals of performance and value. The variablization of fixed period and sunk costs creates problems (more on this later), but especially when allocations are made without any reference to their underlying cost drivers.

Allocations encompass a variety of line items including external purchases, overhead allocations, and sharing of joint and common costs. These allocations are often of overhead costs, that is, period costs that will be incurred in any event or may notionally represent an allocation of sunk fixed costs like capacity.

Recall that economic costs are not limited to charges from the profit and loss statement but can include the carrying cost (opportunity cost) of capital employed. A true economic profit measure must include a charge for the capital invested in the business. Thus, even shared receivables, payables, goodwill, and fixed assets can give rise to allocation issues. Though activity-based allocations are best, the 80/20 rule is critical to be effective.

Although a capital charge is a necessary component for creating a value based profitability measure, there are issues with how to measure the actual level of capital employed at these low levels. Capital has two main components: net working capital and the fixed assets in place. On the surface, measuring the components of capital would seem to be a simple procedure: Measure the point-in-time levels of working capital plus fixed assets and attribute these to products and customers. But there are difficulties.

Actual versus Optimal Inventory   Actual inventory levels are not likely to be optimal. As discussed earlier, traditional performance measurement and incentive systems, which neglect the cost of capital, focus on plant efficiency. Thus, the observed level of inventory does not reflect the level needed to run the business smoothly, distorting any forward-looking analysis of economic profitability.

When measuring performance *ex post* on a firm level, actual levels of inventory, accounts receivable, and accounts payable must be considered because these are real costs. However, it can be inappropriate to assign the costs of the excess inventory sitting in trailers *ex ante*. These inflated levels of inventory do not represent the true capital investment needed to sell the product; rather they're a sunk cost and a refection of past errors. To assess economic profitability on a forward-looking basis, it can be more appropriate to normalize inventory levels.

Customer versus Product Working Capital   Net working capital is especially susceptible to distortion by inaccurately assigning capital costs to products or customers. While it may be easy to attribute accounts receivable to a customer, it is more difficult to justify that charge when looking at product profitability because the charge is the result of the customer being served. When a product is sold to a large customer, the profitability of that product is influenced by the profitability of that customer.

For example, retail suppliers experience this problem. Many of their products appear unprofitable because they serve few large and numerous small customers. Large customers have the power to force a supplier into longer terms, higher inventory requirements and lower margins. When the product is sold to the small shops, it appears profitable; when it is sold to large customers, it looks unprofitable. It is not the *product*, but the *customer*, that is unprofitable.

Improper Costing

Improper costing, such as the unitization of fixed (period) costs and capital, such as the cost of capacity, often creates misleading signals of performance and value in a business portfolio.

As discussed, costing systems ignore or understate the cost of capital. Indirect overhead costs and excess capacity are often incorrectly treated as a unit cost and capitalized to inventory, rather than expensed as period costs. Capitalization of costs, where there is no cost for capital, makes these costs "free" and creates a *short-term* incentive to overproduce rather than build to order.

Longer term, the unitization of fixed period costs such as capacity leads to a classic death spiral, with rising pricing and declining production. For example, a struggling manufacturing facility with $300 annual depreciation and capacity for 100 units, expects utilization of only 30 percent (30 units) versus prior year utilization of 50 percent (50 units).

Though the "true" fixed depreciation cost (at capacity) is $3 ($300/100) per unit, the prior year fixed cost per unit was $6 ($300/50). But the budgeted per unit fixed cost is now $10 ($300/30). Perceived rising unit costs will lead to higher pricing and further reduce volume, even to internal customers, pushing the plant out of business.

We propose full cost accounting, including the cost of all capital, but with *an assumed 100 percent capacity utilization*. Instead of unitizing fixed costs (including the cost of capital) over actual or budgeted volumes, throughput accounting unitizes them by capacity.

When utilization is less than 100 percent, a portion of overhead remains an unallocated, period cost. Volume variance does not impose any burden on either customer or product profitability.

Using throughput accounting, profitability is independent of utilization and portfolio mix and capacity decisions can be made more correctly and independently. Additionally, comparisons of customer and product profitability can be made across businesses where utilization varies.

Economic Costing for Joint Products

Joint products are products that are produced in tandem, sharing overhead costs or capacity. For example, poultry farmers' primary product is chicken breasts, but a chicken also has wings and drumsticks, which may be sold for some additional revenue. In textiles and apparel, production often leads to some amount of off-quality product. These irregular goods are an involuntary outcome of producing "first quality" products. Over time, variation reduction (aka Six Sigma) efforts can reduce the volume of these irregular byproducts.

Joint production costs are frequently ignored, or allocated, leading to a skewed profitability analysis that misstates profitability and misleads decision making. For example, with the same production cost applied to first quality and irregular products, irregulars are sold at a loss and the cost of quality is not reflected in the first quality products.

For example, first quality products incur a $15 cost after the split-off point and bring in revenue of 135 dollars. The sale of irregulars brings revenue of $7.50 on incremental direct costs of 5 dollars. To understand the economics, we must make an allocation of the joint and common costs according to the product's ability to cover these production costs.[2] First quality products receive a weight of 98 percent because the $120 corresponds to 98 percent of the total contribution made to cover production costs. Therefore, 98 percent of joint production costs are attributed to first quality products. The overall profit is then the difference between revenue, costs after split-off, and allocated costs of the joint production process. However, this approach is difficult if irregular data cannot be matched to first quality data.

A practical alternative is to use scrap rates. Though less accurate than the joint cost allocation method, it uses readily available information that remains superior to standard costing. This method recognizes the cost of quality in the production of first quality products. The production costs for the first quality units are inflated by the scrap rate, and production costs for irregulars are set to zero.

INCORPORATING THE COST OF CAPACITY

A cost of capacity framework is necessary for insight into the short term versus long term. This framework breaks economic profitability of customers and products into two groups. The first group includes only the direct operating costs. It includes the direct variable costs of manufacturing and selling products as well as a charge for the net working capital tied up in running the business. The second group consists of longer-term capacity costs, often step costs that are quite independent of volume.

Short Term versus Long Term

The EP contribution margin shows if the business is value accretive in the short term, covering the variable costs and including variable capital costs. Full cost EP shows if the business is value accretive in the long term, covering all related costs (including all fixed cost and capital, such as the cost of capacity). For example, we evaluated the profitability of global food company portfolio.

Lighter bars show the EP contribution for each of the eight products in the portfolio. Each contributes positively toward indirect costs and capacity except for a low margin product unable to cover even direct economic costs, such as material, labor, and the carrying cost of directly attributable working capital.

Though short-term portfolio decisions are likely to include the potential discontinuation of this product, the more pressing strategic issue may be the longer-term one regarding total capacity. Direct economic profit was determined with full economic costs allocated. Volume variance was expensed as a period cost, not unitized into product cost; most barely cover their full cost. Thus, products and customers fall into one of three categories (Figure 2.1):

1. **Category 1**: Economic profit contribution and EP are negative.
2. **Category 2**: Economic profit contribution is positive, and EP is negative (i.e., the customer/product earns its directly attributable costs).
3. **Category 3**: Economic profit contribution and EP are positive (i.e., all costs are covered).

In the short run, where the costs of capacity and overhead are "sunk" period costs, it is advantageous to serve all customers that have a positive EP contribution. All category 2 and category 3 customers should be served. But for the longer term, all costs must be covered or capital will need to be reallocated and capacity and related overhead costs should be shed. Capacity will be resized longer term for category 3 customers and products, including those that can be migrated to category 3 via a better value proposition.

We worked with one textile company in a competitive sector facing margin pressures and excess capacity. Often, the short-term decision to serve category 2 customers becomes the company's long-term production strategy. It can be difficult to stop serving this business without customer retaliation.

	Category 1	Category 2	Category 3
Revenue – Variable operating costs – Net working capital charge	–	+	+
= Net economic contribution per unit at full capacity – Fixed operating costs – Fixed capital charge = Economic Profit	–	–	+

FIGURE 2.1 Cost of Capacity Framework

This company had excess capacity, at some point, which its sales force filled with aggressive deals for large customers. At that time, the large customer contributed to covering fixed costs. However, longer-term planning often overlooks the excess capacity issue, and these marginal accounts may have a negative spillover effect on pricing levels in the marketplace.

In this case, capacity continued to expand through operational improvements, new equipment, and acquisitions. Too much debt was employed to finance this expansion, leading the company into financial distress. In the airline industry, this behavior often pushes the company into bankruptcy. For example, airlines have the ongoing challenge of filling planes, first with full-fare customers, such as business travelers, and then with restricted fare passengers. Low-fare seats cover variable costs and contribute to fixed cost coverage. Having set a timetable and a predetermined number of planes, the only relevant costs, in the short run, are operating costs. However, when it comes time to redefine fleet size, this decision should depend primarily on the projected number of category 3 customers.

Technological constraints and the "lumpy" nature of capacity costs can often dictate a minimum capacity (e.g., there are few small aluminum smelters). In these cases, capacity should be filled first with category 3 customers and then with the most profitable category 2 customers because they, at least, contribute to fixed cost coverage. This scenario assumes the fixed cost contribution of category 3 customers is equal to or greater than the fixed cost shortfall of category 2 customers, so that overall plant economic profit is still positive. If this is not the case, then neither category 2 nor category 3 customers should be served.

Overall, the long-term outlook for these customers defines the profitable capacity level. The cost of capacity model can support a constant monitoring of cost and capacity, especially when demand is soft. The model is also a useful tool for determining profitable capacity.

Textiles Case Study: How to Evaluate Excess Capacity

We found nearly 80 percent of all sales were in category 2, but this number is made up of a handful of large accounts. The profitability of these customers was sensitive to value drivers such as terms and inventory requirements. After preliminary negotiations with the key accounts, management believed it would be able to turn half of these category 2 sales into category 3 sales, but it would still need to reduce capacity by approximately 50 percent. They produced goods in two plants (A and B) of similar size, equipment, and cost structures. So which one should be closed?

Table 2.2 presents disguised numbers for these two plants. Plant A is running at capacity whereas Plant B has a utilization rate of 50 percent. Plant A produces more premium goods, but plant B produces more "value" merchandise. Differences in direct costs (material) reflect the higher quality inputs used to manufacture premium products. Utilities and other fixed costs are higher in Plant B in the standard cost approach since the overhead is unitized over a smaller quantity. Based on standard profit, Plant A is more profitable and the correct decision would seem to be to keep A and shut down plant B.

TABLE 2.2 Economic Versus Standard Costing

	Plant A	Plant B
Utilization	100%	50%
Unit Price	$ 5.00	$ 4.00
Material	$ 1.10	$ 1.05
Labor	$ 0.95	$ 0.90
Utilities	$ 0.20	$ 0.60
Other Fixed	$ 0.35	$ 0.50
Standard Unit Cost	$ 2.60	$ 3.05
Standard Profit	$ 2.40	$ 0.95
Material	$ 1.10	$ 1.05
Labor	$ 0.95	$ 0.90
Utilities	$ 0.20	$ 0.30
Other Fixed	$ 0.35	$ 0.25
Throughput unit cost	$ 2.60	$ 2.50
Throughput profit	$ 2.40	$ 1.50
Capital charge on NRV	$ 0.50	$ 0.10
Economic cost	$ 3.10	$ 2.60
Economic profit	$ 1.90	$ 1.40

However, this line of reasoning is flawed because of two distortions. First, plant A is more profitable partly because it runs at full capacity, which reduces standard unit cost. Second, premium products are produced in plant A. The capacity problem can be addressed by using throughput accounting. To compare plant cost structures, both should be measured based on the same utilization rates. Throughput accounting corrects for the utilization problem.

To correct for the distortion caused by different product prices, we removed the unit price and looked at only unit cash and economic costs. After making this adjustment, plant A was almost comparable to plant B. The question remained, which plant should we close?

The final factor is the amount of capital tied up in each plant. Though we could look at the accounting books to the historic value of plant, property and equipment, a better measure would consider only the opportunity (not historic) cost of capital. To do this, we recognize that if a plant is shut down, the company realizes a liquidation value based on the net of salvage costs and values associated with the property, plant, equipment, and severance, after taxes (NRV). If the company decides to keep a specific plant, then this is the true amount of capital employed and subject to an opportunity cost.

In this case, plant A had a much higher NRV and, therefore, a higher opportunity cost of not being closed. Including this opportunity cost in the analysis showed that plant B was the "cheaper" of the two. The manufacturer decided to close plant A, shift production to B, and realize the significant liquidation value and reduce outstanding debt.

VALUE-BASED STRATEGIES AND TACTICS

Although countless individual operating actions can create value in any given business, they must all lead to one of four categories measured by an increase in economic profit. Specifically, EP can be increased through strategies that employ the following four means.

Fix

Improve the returns on existing capital through higher prices or margins, more volume, or lower costs. Economic profit margins subsume profit margin and asset utilization:

- Initiate industry efforts to pool and optimize industry-specific assets or activities. These may be established as independent, or jointly owned and operated networks to improve utilization

- Employ "virtual" vertical or horizontal integration to enhance value chain transparency. Improved supply and demand visibility can improve efficiency and utilization through broader network optimization.
- Optimize material flow with dynamic Economic Profit optimization of fulfillment economics. Production economics for companies that move/make things remain largely misunderstood, undermanaged, and suboptimized

Sell

Rationalize, liquidate, or curtail investments in operations that cannot generate returns greater than the cost of capital:

- Outsource unprofitable activities (in-source capacity that cannot be viably outsourced, sold or closed), restructuring a smaller manufacturing footprint, sale or divestiture, withdrawal from unprofitable markets
- Creative business sale strategies, such as employee, customer or management purchases, demergers, spin-offs, and other forms of financial restructuring

Grow

Profitable growth through investing capital, where increased profits will cover the cost of additional capital. Investments in working capital and production capacity may be required to facilitate increased sales, new products, or new markets:

- Make investments that are recorded as expenses, for example, intangibles (brands and capabilities) that drive growth value such as institutional processes and technologies.
- Invest in real options (options to grow, switch, defer, abandon) and scalability.
- With "vanilla" acquisitions increasingly prohibitive, explore creative acquisition strategies such as joint ventures, licensing-in (and out), economic profit earn-outs and creeping acquisitions, asset swaps, and shared service structures.

Optimize Cost of Capital

Reduce the cost of capital but maintain sufficient financial flexibility to support the business strategy through the prudent use of debt, risk management, hybrid capital, real-time capital, and other financial products.

MANAGING FOR VALUE

Measuring and analyzing the sources of value creation and value destruction within a corporate portfolio is only the beginning. Ultimately, improvements must be made to mitigate sources of value destruction while leveraging sources of value creation. Changes might include pricing, terms, promotions, selection, availability, process control and quality, packaging, or other aspects of the value proposition.

Much ado is often made of loss leader strategies, that is, intentionally losing money somewhere to make up for it elsewhere. For example, retailers drop their prices on select visible items (e.g., milk, diapers) to establish an image of value pricing in the minds of shoppers. We have heard how Polaroid sold cameras at a loss to make it up in film. However, these strategies, their performance, and their value need to be quantified and monitored. Once a star, Polaroid fell into bankruptcy as its markets evolved more quickly than the company.

A loss leader strategy creates its own challenges. Though it might appear that dropping a loss leader would improve profitability, this action can reduce sales of profitable products and overall profitability. For example, after lobbying for a price increase and working capital improvements, one supplier was still losing $2 million per year on a product to a large retailer but retained the customer because of $4 million of related, and profitable, sales.

Pricing and Terms

Pricing is a primary lever in the value proposition. Generally, price and volume vary inversely. Price elasticity of demand is a measure that indicates the percentage change in the quantity of a good demanded resulting from a 1 percent change in price. This determines what happens to total revenue when prices are changed and quantities demanded react to these price changes. The analysis may be performed at the company level to include the effects of competitive response or, at the industry level, to examine macro consumer response.

In one case, we drew on a window of historical price/quantity data to estimate the price elasticity of demand to project revenue over some price range. Combined with a total cost curve, this allows an evaluation of pricing strategies to maximize value. We found EP could increase by $10 million with a 4 to 6 percent price increase on many products, but that a 3 to 5 percent price decrease was optimal for high margin goods. Therefore, before dropping any marginal business, the company first proposed price increases to make the business value-accretive. In other cases, it was possible to propose more economic terms, selection and availability that customers still found acceptable.

In addition to fixed assets, an important issue in low-level economic profitability analysis is the net working capital requirements of customers and/or products. Different customers require different levels of working capital.

Identify customers with upside opportunity with an analysis of capital turns and profit margins by customer. In cases where an unprofitable customer is unwilling to accept a price increase, shorter payment terms or reduced inventory requirements may suffice.

Cost Structure

Higher product quality can support a better mix and price. Reduced scrap and rework leads to increased throughput and, therefore, more net operating profit after tax (NOPAT) and a higher return on capital. Higher yields and less downtime lead to capital avoidance, reduced capital charge, and less capital invested below the cost of capital. Reduced variability, risk, and uncertainty leads to less work in process (WIP) and a reduced capital charge. Simplified processes and less material and labor lowers direct costs, supporting higher margins and more volumes and, therefore, more NOPAT and a higher return on capital.

The drive for lower unit costs and higher margins often leads to investments in capacity, equipment, and new technology. However, these investments often destroy value because profits do not rise by enough to cover the cost of additional capital employed.

For example, the domestic textile industry has seen large investments in new capacity and technology, increasing efficiency and capacity. With excess capacity wreaking havoc on pricing and return on capital, the long-term solution calls for more offshore sourcing and domestic capacity closures. But the lowest cost value proposition is hard to find. We have found cases where it is the new, low-cost capacity that should be closed for reasons such as lower cost of closure, higher salvage value, higher cash operating costs, taxes, or more realizable overhead reductions.

Run Length and Material Flow

Single-piece flow is a central element in the lean production system. Pulling smaller lots shrinks the supply chain, speeds cycle time, and reduces complexity, waste, and invested capital (invested capital is reduced both in the form of WIP and finished goods inventory). But the implementation of single-piece flow need not fly in the face of economic run lengths.

CREATING VALUE FROM
PROFITABILITY INITIATIVES

In concert with corporate-wide profitability initiatives, production facilities frequently undertake operating initiatives to harmonize with financial initiatives. Some months or quarters focus on increasing labor productivity and machine uptime and on reducing overtime premiums; at other times, a concerted effort is made to reduce all forms of inventory. Other periods might call for increasing market share and booking sales.

A new production manager was hired with a mandate to improve processes. Productivity metrics plummeted in his first three months as a lean initiative shortened run lengths; inventory was reduced but weekend production was needed to make delivery dates. Overtime increased and profits fell. Inventory fell, but so did earnings before interest and taxes (EBIT). Did intrinsic value rise or fall?

Each initiative leads to financial benefit that is manifested in income statement profitability or balance sheet productivity, and it gets captured in economic profit and intrinsic value per share. The problem arises because no initiative affects only one line item in the EP calculation; most initiatives have EBIT and capital.

Assuming a 10 percent WACC and 40 percent tax rate, profitability initiatives will create intrinsic value when the economic profit impact is positive; EBIT growth contributes 60 cents on the dollar, and reductions in capital employed contribute 10 cents on the dollar.

Table 2.3 speaks to the specific route and impact of company performance. Improved processes should reduce supply lead times (SLTs), allowing sales and marketing to, in turn, leverage lower demand lead times (DLTs) leading to more profit. Improved process control should reduce process variance, and greatly narrow the breadth of the lead-time distributions leading to less supply chain buffer and less capital employed.

Figure 2.2 illustrates the well-known and ignored economic run length concept. Initially, longer run lengths increase EP because less time and cost is spent on setups. But as batch size exceeds demand, production builds to stock rather than to order. The carrying cost (capital charge) of WIP or finished goods increasingly offsets the NOPAT advantage of reduced set-up time and cost. Economic profit is maximized at the economic run length.

TABLE 2.3   How Operating Initiatives Create Intrinsic Value

Root Cause	Impact	Economics
Quality	Throughput, price and mix	More NOPAT, higher ROCE
Downtime	Throughput	More NOPAT, higher ROCE
Lead time variability	Inventory	Less capital, higher ROCE
Process complexity	Material and labor	More NOPAT, higher ROCE

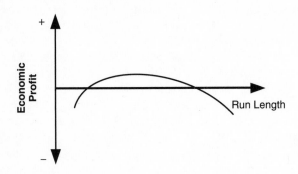

FIGURE 2.2   Economic Run Length

The curve is often much steeper to the left of optimal and declines more gradually when above optimal, thus, the tendency to plan for buffer stock.

The shape of the curve is critical to the implementation of lean production concepts. High-cost products (e.g., catalytic converters containing precious metals) will have a much higher than average cost of carry and, thus, a much steeper decline to the right end of the run length curve—a high cost penalty to over-production. Low-cost products (elastomer engine cradle isolation mounts) will exhibit a much flatter curve, with a low carrying cost penalty to overproduction.

The shape to the left end of the curve is dominated by set-up time and cost; processes with slow, expensive setups will generally exhibit a much steeper curve, indicating a high cost penalty to underproduction. Processes characterized by fast, inexpensive changeovers will generally exhibit a flatter curve indicating a low cost penalty to underproduction.

The goal is to improve processes continuously to minimize the time and cost of changeovers—constantly shifting the economic run length curve to the left—facilitating a migration to single-piece flow. But where to start? Which are the best candidates for shorter runs or better process control? Figure 2.3 illustrates a general road map that prioritizes these initiatives according to the shape of their economic run length function.

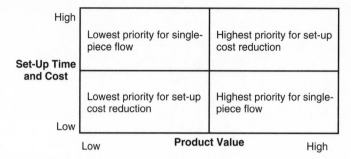

FIGURE 2.3 Product Value versus Set-Up Time/Cost

High-value products with low set-up times and cost offer the most potential benefit, with the smallest risk, from short runs. High-value products with high set-up time and cost profiles should be the highest priority for process improvement initiatives.

Success on this front could then be followed by small lot sizes without as high a cost penalty to underproduction. Low-value products with high set-up times and cost offer the lowest potential benefit and highest potential penalty for reduced run lengths but may offer some payoff to a set-up time and cost reduction initiative. Low-value products with low set-up times offer the lowest payoff for any initiative targeting set-up process reengineering. The minimal cost of underproduction may offer some potential to a single-piece flow initiative.

Inventory

Inventory is often a sign of unoptimized processes and poor process control, realities that take time to improve. Demand uncertainty and variability, SLT, process variation, poor flow control and physical tracking, equipment condition, and limitations contribute to the need for buffer stock in the value chain for raw, WIP, and finished goods.

Reducing inventory without isolating and removing these root causes creates overtime premiums, unplanned downtime, and unfilled orders.

Figure 2.4 illustrates building to order with consideration to lead times, given typical DLT and SLT curves. Lead time is charted horizontally and frequency is charted vertically. Lead-time variability gives the curves their shape, or width; in too many cases, lead times are uncertain and variable. Lead times tend to extend further to the right and are constrained to the left tail by zero, giving the curves their rightward skew.

Demand lead times are often shorter than SLTs (hence, the frequent need for some amount of inventory). Again, the root causes are demand

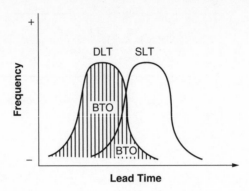

FIGURE 2.4 Modified Build to Order (BTO) Concept

uncertainty and variability, production lead time, process variation, inadequate or completely absent statistical process controls, poor physical tracking, and inadequate preventative maintenance.

The shaded portion of the figure illustrates all potential cases in which the DLT exceeds the SLT. These cases would easily accommodate a pull system of building to hard orders (BTOs). The larger the proportion of overlap, the easier it is to accommodate a lean BTO schedule and win new business on delivery. But a pure lean production system can get into trouble in an environment of little overlap, where SLT may often exceed DLT. These cases lead to expedite orders that wreak havoc on scheduling, cause tremendous amounts of overtime premium, and bottleneck conditions on the floor.

Now, the notion of an economic run length, if it exceeds demand, clearly shows that there are times when it is more economic to build to stock (BTS) than to build to order. From Figure 2.4, we can see these will generally be the cases of low product value and high set-up time/cost (top left quadrant). There are times when SLTs exceed DLTs or are likely to exceed DLTs, and it may be more economical to BTS than BTO.

How do we reconcile the need to go lean and BTO with the practical realities of SLTs that often exceed DLTs and the uncertainty and variability of lead times?

Though economic run length is a constraint to optimize production scheduling, it need not be a constant. Six Sigma initiatives should target the highest value cases (top right quadrant of Figure 2.3) to reduce set-up time/cost to support a reduction in optimal economic run lengths.

Rather than BTOs, we propose a modified, build to "soft" orders (BTO'). BTO' is a synthetic construct of hard orders, plus "unseen" orders, plus a provision for the variability in unseen orders. Each hard order should trigger an unseen order, which is the volume with SLTs greater than DLTs. Thus, though the order has not been received, when it finally is received, it will be too late, giving rise to an expedite order. The third portion of the synthetic order is a provision for variability in unseen orders due to the net variability of DLTs and SLTs. Optimization algorithms can be developed and applied from historical data with economic run length constraints for economic profit maximization.

Though unseen orders and unseen order variability are real life constraints, they should not be constant. Six Sigma initiatives should target the highest value cases to reduce SLTs and reduce net DLT-SLT variability.

Develop a new BTO′ approach to lean production to accommodate real-life constraints of economic run length, unseen orders, and order variability. Improvement initiatives should target the highest value cases to reduce SLTs and net DLT-SLT variability (working with customers, working with vendors, process mapping, set-up time/cost reduction, real-time monitoring of key process parameters with feedback loops and visual queues, basic statistical process controls, physical tracking and flow control, preventative maintenance, and retrofitting newer process controls on old equipment).

EVA and Lean

Jonah, a production scheduler, evaluates producing to demand versus producing to capacity. By going lean with shorter runs, he saves $2 million in inventory, but the changeover costs increase $200,000 annually.

"Unit and total cost, scrap and budget variance all go up," he says, "and profit, earnings per share, machine utilization, absorption, efficiency, and productivity all go down... I don't know." Assuming a 10 percent cost of capital and a 30 percent tax rate, what is the EP impact?

EP = 10% × $2,000,000 capital benefit, less 70% × $200,000 after tax cost = $60,000. The present value, if repeated annually, adds $600,000 ($60,000/10%) of intrinsic value.

Scheduling

A "quick hit" in terms of operating performance and intrinsic value per share may be eliminating the use of weekly bucket in favor of daily bucket scheduling throughout many parts of the company. The conventions of scheduling systems and material flow practices are not an arcane detail to leave to the whims of information systems or material managers. This convention does not afford the level of granularity required to manage a lean production system. From raw materials through several steps of conversion work in process to finished goods, the minimum planning increment is one week's worth of inventory.

It is, in part, this resulting high level of WIP inventory that drives the need for detailed scheduling. For example, with weekly bucket scheduling and a simple lean three-step conversion process, there are $7 \times 7 \times 7$ (343) permutations to be scheduled. However, this number falls to 1 ($1 \times 1 \times 1$) for the same case under daily bucket scheduling.

Discontinue any remaining use of weekly bucket scheduling and move to daily bucket scheduling with nightly updates. Defer detailed scheduling initiatives until production processes are leaned and manual Kan-bans, visual queues, and so forth, are implemented. Resolve basic production and process control issues before jumping to systems initiatives. The burden of a detailed scheduling initiative or any major new systems solution runs the risks of overwhelming the floor with complexity and data requirements as well as potentially hard-coding processes and practices that need to be reengineered.

BALANCING PERFORMANCE WITH VALUE

Intrinsic value is not maximized solely through the maximization of current operations value but through the simultaneous maximization of COV and growth value.

This requires the renewal of growth value through investments in intangibles and the future and requires the conversion of opportunities into performance, via execution or operational excellence. The implications for business strategy, financial policy, and compensation are far-reaching.

Figure 2.5 illustrates a portfolio tool that maps businesses (companies, products, SKUs, customers) performance (economic margin) on the horizontal axis and valuation (growth value as a percentage of enterprise value) vertically.

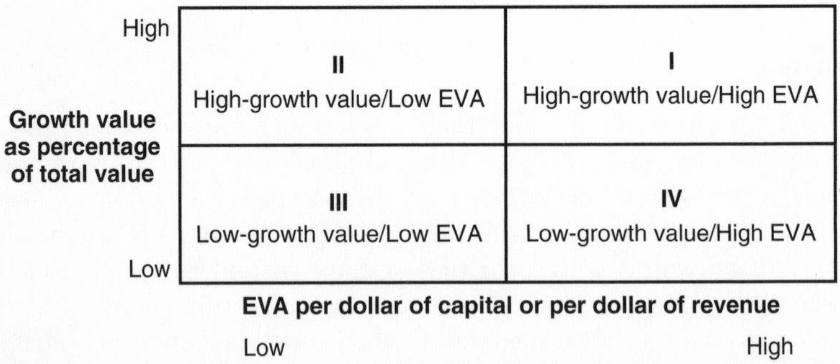

	High	II High-growth value/Low EVA	I High-growth value/High EVA
Growth value as percentage of total value		III Low-growth value/Low EVA	IV Low-growth value/High EVA
	Low		

EVA per dollar of capital or per dollar of revenue

Low   High

FIGURE 2.5   Performance/Value Matrix

Quadrant I illustrates cases where products enjoy a premium position but may have been neglected due to smaller size, traditional income-based margins, and other reasons. However, they may use little capital, creating a superior economic profit margin. They may also be highly scalable due to a global brand and ease of contract manufacture, making them an attractive story.

Quadrant II is where we find the hot businesses with high expectations for upside, or poor performers that would be worth far less except for their minimum valuation floor, often due to the threat of a takeover or breakup. Some, with negative EP contribution may be legacy brands in need of rationalization. These might be put on watch as a potential sale candidate, with those of the greatest size being the most critical.

Quadrant III are often perennial disappointments awaiting break-through change. Their economic margins need improvement before further investment. Their prospects need to be swiftly and realistically evaluated. The low growth value implies little upside and only a marginal contribution that does not justify the cost of the capacity it consumes. The low realizable value makes it a better relocation candidate.

Quadrant IV are often out-of-favor sectors, or cyclicals, facing a down-turn that require strategies to make performance more sustainable or to make costs more variable. Strategies are needed to address the root cause of the valuation constraints. They may be high performers with a valuation constraint, such as an unscalable business model, or candidates for strategic investment (strong regionals, orphaned brands, unscaled technologies). Can slow-growth markets be revived, brands repositioned, or business models and cost structures revisited to develop a more attractive and scalable value dynamic?

CHAPTER 3

Sell: Creating Value Through Divestiture

Divestitures are an essential, though often ignored, tactic in corporate portfolio management. They play an important role in actively managing the growth profile of a corporate portfolio, enabling the exit from less attractive products and markets and the reallocation of capital to more productive uses. And while acquisitions continue to far outnumber divestitures, best practice has divestitures no longer delayed by common misconceptions of book losses, market timing, and earnings dilution.

Strategic reviews and economic profitability analysis are now increasingly employed to identify divestiture candidates within portfolios where historically only acquisitions were the focus. Best-in-class, multiline businesses continuously evaluate their business portfolios to seek out opportunities to create value and shed businesses that are potentially worth more under a different form of ownership, such as businesses that have plateaued or may require considerable resources to capture their growth prospects.

Restructuring creates value through improved market transparency, resource allocation, and management incentives and accountability. Business units can be constrained on capital, strategic direction, policies, or operating procedures, which can constrain enterprise value. When businesses are freed to act in their own best interests (which may not be the same as the parent), considerable new value can be created. Divestitures tend to be viewed favorably by the market, with excess returns frequently generated both for the parent and the publicly divested subsidiary. Value creation studies show that significant value can be created through public divestitures.

A public divestiture may create value for its shareowners even if it does not raise any proceeds for the parent company. Value accrues to the shareowners, not necessarily to the parent company. The parent may even be worse off for having divested itself of a subsidiary, and the value may be lost at the parent level, but the shareowners can be better off if the subsidiary value increase more than offsets any loss in value at the parent.

Our own experience and numerous studies have demonstrated that, in general, firms that actively traded their corporate portfolios and balanced acquisitions with divestitures outperform their control groups.[1] One study cites this approach outperformed passive M&A strategies by 47 percent, and outperformed acquisition-tilted strategies by 17 percent.[2] The optimal balance of acquisitions and divestitures varies with life cycle and core competency considerations. For example, the McKinsey research found that "builders" with a tilt toward acquisitions outperformed builders that followed a more balanced approach, by five-fold. However, for "operators" a balanced strategy outperformed acquisition-oriented strategies by six-fold.[3]

Short-term excess returns of the parent company around the time of the announcement are on the order of 2 to 4 percent with a wide dispersion in outcomes, partly depending on the specific measurement period for short-term cumulative abnormal returns. Divested subsidiaries outperform their industries, with most studies reporting excess returns of about 6 percent. The most common approach to evaluating value creation from public divestiture transactions is to assess the cumulative abnormal returns around the time of the announcement. The assumption here is the semi-strong form of market efficiency hypothesis whereby, on average over time, markets will capitalize the benefits into market pricing within a few days around announcement. In fact, much of the benefit is captured in the week prior to public announcement.

We, and others, have also looked at the longer-term (typically, one-year post deal) value creation of divestitures, which is material and significant. Longer-run estimates are more contentious, but some estimates are as high as 20 to 25 percent, which is similar with findings for successful mergers and acquisitions (M&A) transactions.[4] This is consistent with the rationale of improved incentives, resource allocation, and strategic freedom. The difficulty with longer-term impact to the parents, is that these rationales reflect benefits primarily to the subsidiary businesses and because the scale of the parent and other external factors will be more significant.

Parents that succeed in their restructuring efforts more often come from industrial sectors, with generally more mature businesses, and carry a larger number of business lines. Less successful parents appear to have been less mature in terms of valuation and dividend profiles and showed greater uncertainty around their commitment to separation. Successful subsidiaries exhibit lower levels of debt and dividends and brighter future prospects.

Historically, spin-offs have been the preferred method of divestiture—both in terms of number of transactions and dollar volume—and account for 60 percent of the total. Public offerings, either in the form of initial public offerings (IPOs) or carve-outs, account for roughly one third of total restructuring activity. (A carve-out is a form of public offering in which a firm floats no more than 20 percent of a subsidiary in order to maintain the flexibility to later divest in a tax-free spin-off or split-off.) Split-offs continue to be used in special circumstances though the tracking stock trend seems to have largely passed (many former tracking stocks were either bought back or later sold). Yield-oriented structured securities promise to serve as a new and exciting option for the public divestiture of noncore business units in 2004.

Financial policies (liquidity, leverage, and shareholder distributions) and incentive compensation need to be recalibrated in the face of a restructuring.

DIVESTITURE CREATES VALUE

Studies of the value created by restructuring have found that parents' short-term cumulative abnormal returns average in the 2 to 4 percent range around the time of the announcement (Table 3.1). Divested subsidiaries outperform their industry indices by about 6 percent in their first year. The most common approach to evaluating value creation from public divestiture transactions is to assess the excess returns around the time of the announcement because markets capitalize the benefits into prices within a few days around announcement. Much of the benefit is captured in the week prior to public announcement.

Longer-term value creation of divested business is material and significant. Longer-term operating improvements have been demonstrated, supporting explanations of increased managerial efficiency and focus due to better incentives and resource allocation. Long-run estimates of value creation are more contentious, but some range as high as 20 to 25 percent. We do not focus on the longer-term impact to the parents because the

TABLE 3.1 Summary of Academic Findings

Date	Authors	Time Period	Sample Size	Short Term	Long Term
2002	Veld, *et al*	1987–1900	156	2.6%	–
2000	Elder and Westra	1984–1999	35	3.0%	–
1999	Krishnaswami *et al*	1979–1993	118	3.2%	–
1999	Desai and Jain	1975–1991	155	3.8%	–
1996	Johnson *et al*	1975–1988	104	4.0%	–
1995	Slovin *et al*	1980–1991	37	1.3%	–
1994	Cusatis *et al*	1965–1990	142	–	12.5, 26.7, 18.1%
1991	Klein *et al*	1966–1988	17	2.0%	7.8%
1984	Rosenfeld	1963–1981	35	5.6%	6.1%

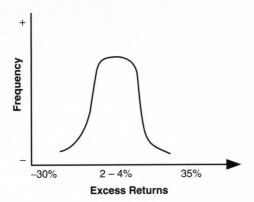

FIGURE 3.1 Distribution of Divestiture Returns

rationales reflect benefits primarily to the subsidiary businesses and because the scale of the parent and other external factors will be more significant.

Analysis of the past decade will show that spin-offs created the most value, followed by carve-outs; parent companies that chose to divest through an IPO (floating over 20 percent of their ownership) were the most prone to negative returns.

However, there is a wide level of dispersion (−30 to +35 percent) in outcomes (Figure 3.1). So, though the average return from public divestitures may not seem attractive enough to warrant the associated effort, cost, and risk, the allure of the tremendous value created by the "winners" most certainly is. The key issue is not so much if these transactions create value on average, but as how to identify and structure a transaction that will be successful. And common threads run between the winners and the "losers."

Winners

Parent companies of top performing public divestitures over the past decade have more commonly been industrial businesses, with more mature business lines, and have generally had a larger number of diverse businesses. Subsidiaries exhibited similar profitability as the losers, but with lower levels of debt and dividends; brighter future prospects capitalized into their market values (based on multiples of enterprise value to capital employed).

Losers

Parent companies of the worst performing public divestitures from the past 10 years tended to appear less mature in terms of their valuation and dividend profiles (higher price-to-book and low dividend payout ratios), but were not materially different in terms of size or leverage. Losing subsidiaries had similar margins to the winners but exhibited weaker prospects (as evidenced by lower valuations, higher leverage and dividends). Among the losers is often greater uncertainty around parent commitment to separation, as evident in the use of tracking stocks (none were employed by winners) and a higher proportion of retained control and ownership.

SOURCES OF VALUE: MOTIVES FOR DIVESTITURE

Beyond the criterion of strategic fit, many factors drive the decision to classify a business as noncore and search out divestiture alternatives. Though a portion of the value accruing to shareholders can represent a wealth transfer from bondholders due to lost collateral—parent firm credit rating downgrades are evident—these businesses are usually worth more under an alternative ownership structure.[5] The primary rationale for most restructuring is the creation of value through improved market transparency, management incentives and accountability, and resource allocation.[6]

Transparency

More frequent, granular, and comprehensive disclosure of strategies, tactics, and operating and financial performance aid the capital markets in evaluating a business and its worth. Higher market multiples (capitalization rates) result in the face of better earnings quality (cash flow certainty). Yet, competitive concerns, accounting difficulties, and administrative burden frequently inhibit better segment reporting in business units, making it more difficult to achieve this benefit without full separation.

Incentives and Accountability

Longer-term operating improvements have been demonstrated in the research on divestitures, supporting views of increased managerial efficiency due to better focus, incentives, and resource allocation. Improved transparency and line of sight (shorter distance) between management actions and results and the availability of equity incentives (stock, restricted stock, stock options), lead to an improved system of incentives and accountability. This helps attract and retain the best talent by providing better manager-owner incentive alignment and leverage for a given level of shareholder cost. Business unit compensation is frequently complicated by concerns of internal consistency within large organizations, undermining the strength of incentives and the cost of competitive pay.

Resource Allocation

Resources might be constrained due to the perception of more attractive opportunities or competing needs and interests within the portfolio of a multiline company. The "diversity discount" (also known as the conglomerate discount) of multiline companies is frequently cited as an indication of the opportunity for improved fit and focus.[7] Capital allocation and management attention in the parent and segment can be improved through the streamlining effect of a well-executed public divestiture. Various studies have found divested businesses frequently demonstrate higher levels of investment and improved profitability once freed from their parent.

Strategic Freedom

Business units are sometimes constrained on strategic direction, operating policies, or execution procedures. A parent's reluctance to embrace the business unit vision can constrain growth prospects and, ultimately, enterprise value. When business units are freed to act in their own best interests, which may not be the same as the parent's, the opportunity to generate considerable new value will often arise.

However, the subsidiary's needs may not be fully aligned with the interests of the parent company. In vertically integrated enterprises, the subsidiary may wish to sell a product to competitors of the parent company, such as Motorola's semiconductor business, GM's auto parts business, and numerous captive finance businesses. Ultimately, it must be decided if the new value created at the subsidiary level is greater than any potential loss in value at the parent level. In many cases, it is, leaving shareholders better off after a split.

Takeover Premiums

Published academic research has demonstrated that some of the value created through financial restructuring can be attributed to increased market expectations for consolidation and the subsequent receipt of takeover premium. Interestingly, the McKinsey research found that outperformance was greatest (26 percent) among the roughly one third of companies that remained independent in the long term.[8] And though part of the value created is due to an increased expectation for takeover premiums, this is insufficient to explain all of the value created. Takeover premiums account for a portion of the value created by divestitures, but operating gains have been shown to be more significant.[9]

Financial Policy

Optimal financial policies (operating and strategic liquidity, leverage and funding, dividends, and share repurchases) tend to differ between higher and lower growth businesses. Industry factors also drive different practices, leading to an opportunity to optimize business unit weighted average cost of capital (WACC) and financial flexibility (if divested), that can fundamentally justify a higher market multiple.

ALTERNATIVE METHODS OF DISPOSITION

The decision to divest is often easier than the decisions around how to divest. Divestiture tactics affect taxes, accounting, and proceeds raised as well as the fundamental degree of intrinsic value creation.

Private and Public Sale

Private sales provide quick execution but proceeds are not necessarily in cash and tax leakage can be large. Economics can be improved via competitive bid dynamics and tax efficient structures (Section §338h10 acquirer tax basis step-up; §355e Morris Trust). In practice, a dual-track process is often undertaken with one of the following methods of public disposition introduced into the restructuring plan.

In an IPO, a firm issues shares of a subsidiary to the public in exchange for cash. If a parent company continues to hold a stake in the subsidiary final separation may be achieved through secondary common stock offerings, block trades, selling down over time, or exchangeable securities.

IPOs are frequently undertaken with the goal of unlocking trapped value, while raising proceeds for the parent. Attractive businesses of sufficient size are frequently sold in the public markets at a premium to precedent transactions and trading multiples.

IPOs are often the method of choice for divesting growth businesses during hot markets when embedded tax gains are relatively insignificant and there is a strong desire to raise proceeds. Over the long term, the subsidiary in an IPO has generally outperformed the parent, indicating that IPOs are frequently used for businesses that may face more attractive opportunities than the parent.

Equity Carve-Out

A carve-out is an IPO of no more than 20 percent of a parent's holdings in a subsidiary. Parent companies retain a range of options regarding timing and tactics for further separation from the subsidiary. By maintaining at least 80 percent ownership in the subsidiary the parent company retains the option of distributing the remaining stake to its shareholders through a §355e tax-free spin-off (back-end spin). Multiple classes of stock can be used to sell up to 49 percent of the economics as long as at least 80 percent of the vote is retained. To mitigate tax implications, the subsidiary will benefit by issuing stock to the public and, subsequently, distribute a dividend to the parent.

The carve-out provides some cash proceeds in an otherwise cashless transaction. Carve-outs also allow the establishment of an equity market for subsidiaries, thereby providing better access to capital as well as provide clearer valuation information to the parent and investors, while giving an opportunity to design stronger incentives for subsidiary managers. Companies that employ carve-outs as a restructuring tactic tend to need (or at least desire) cash proceeds, may lack clarity around the subsidiary valuation, and may be uncertain about the need, sentiment, and timeframe for final separation. They can be used to facilitate the pricing of an exchange-offer as a prelude to a split-off though these transactions are rare.

Around the time of announcement, parent companies slightly outperformed the market; for the longer term, the parents faired even better. Subsidiaries generally outperform their peer groups by about 8 to 10 percent in the first year after a carve-out.

Spin-Off

In a spin-off, a firm distributes 80 percent or more of a subsidiary tax-free (§355e) to existing shareholders on a pro-rata basis. Shares of the subsidiary are distributed to the parent's existing shareholders such that their percentage ownership in the parent firm and new business entity remains unchanged. Much like a dividend, no cash is raised and the total number of shares outstanding remains unchanged. While the earnings power of each individual parent share is reduced, shareowners now own a share of the subsidiary, such that their net effective position remains unchanged.

Most companies employ a spin-off when the tax benefits are significant and they have no compelling need to raise proceeds. Companies often pursue spin-offs with the objectives of unlocking value trapped within a subsidiary and giving shareholders a chance to own the parent and the subsidiary separately.

Spin-offs have created more value than any other tactic, with parents generally outperforming the market around the time of the announcement by about 8 percent. In the first year post spin-off, subsidiaries tended to outperform by another 10 percent. For instance, over the period between 1995 and 2003, Dun & Bradstreet (DNB) spun-off a number of subsidiaries (several preceded by carve-out transactions) and earned a 14.5 percent compound return in the process (versus the S&P500's 7.7 percent return).

Split-Off

In a split-off, a firm distributes at least 80 percent of one or more subsidiaries through a tax-free (§355e) exchange offer; shareholders elect to swap parent stock for subsidiary stock, or to retain the parent stock. No cash is raised, but the number of shares outstanding is reduced, akin to a reverse stock split. The exchange ratio must be set to provide sufficient value to induce tender, but not so high as to risk excessive wealth transfer.

The split-off is a less common tactic and is usually used by companies evaluating a divestiture and desiring to reduce the number of their shares outstanding. An equity carve-out is frequently a precursor to a split-off to help establish this exchange ratio. Split-offs have been employed to retire the overhang of a large block of parent stock held by an individual shareholder or to adjust a shareholder's (or class of shareholders') investment level in a subsidiary. EDS's split-off from GM in 1984 is likely one of the best known and best performing cases. Another attractive feature of split-offs is the avoidance of "recirculation" of shares that can occur as a result of a spin-off. Since shareholders "elect" to hold subsidiary stock, they have less of a need to realign their portfolios post-deal. This may support and stabilize the stock price in the short-term period of ownership churn around a financial restructuring. The small number of deals leads to difficulty in drawing empirical conclusions regarding the success of split-offs.

Tracking Stock

A tracking stock (also known as a letter stock) represents a legal claim on the parent's assets and an effective economic claim on a subsidiary. Tracking stock can be created through an IPO, carve-out, spin-off, or split-off of a subsidiary.

The board of directors must somehow represent both the interests of shareholders in the parent as well as the interests of shareholders in the subsidiary. Historically, companies pursued tracking stocks when they hoped to retain a significant degree of influence over a business while unlocking hidden value by tracking subsidiary performance with a publicly traded security.[10] The use of tracking stock seems to have largely passed as many have performed poorly or encountered governance conflicts and have since been reacquired. For example, during Q1 2004, Sprint announced its intention to recombine its long-distance and wireless businesses (originally separated using a tracking stock structure) by exchanging 0.50 Sprint FON shares for each Sprint PCS share.

Trackers have been used by diversified companies to allow investors to capture the value of higher growth businesses (GM Hughes and EDS), as well as to launch higher-risk capital-intensive ventures (Genzyme Tissue

Repair), and include many examples of direct "e" channel plays. Some of the other more significant Tracking Stock transactions include AT&T/AT&T Wireless, US West/TCI, and DLJ/DLJ Direct. Tracking stock gained popularity in the late 1990s as a tool for conglomerates to participate in the stock market run while retaining subsidiary control.[11]

Yield-Oriented Structures

Yield-oriented structures, such as master limited partnerships (MLPs), real estate investment trusts (REITs), Unit Trusts, and "Extreme" Dividend Stocks, are public divestiture alternatives well suited to today's income-starved climate. Essentially, a public divestiture alternative to the private sale to a financial sponsor, these types of structures are appropriate for businesses with low expected future capital requirements, a strong and stable cash flow profile, and a need/desire to distribute a large proportion of this cash flow to investors.

For example, yield-oriented securities can be structured to grant holders composite ownership of debt and equity with all the appropriate rights; they may receive the same tax treatment as if they separately invested in the underlying securities (reporting interest income and dividend income for tax purposes).

Typically created through an IPO, yield-oriented structures may be created via a subsidiary carve-out, split-off, or spin-off. These structures are valued as the annual distributable cash discounted at the stated annual yield but may receive a premium valuation due to the increased certainty around expected returns and reduced governance concerns with little cash remaining in the business.

WHAT WORKS BEST FOR WHOM?

Though the various public divestiture tactics all lead toward separation, the most appropriate tactic can depend, in part, on the specific characteristics of the parent and subsidiary. General market conditions will be a factor. Interestingly, neither our own empirical research nor the published literature provides any evidence supporting size or industry as key determinants of methods employed. In general, IPOs are selected over spin-offs in the following cases:

- To dispose of more highly valued businesses
- Businesses with higher growth rates
- Businesses with a greater need for capital (Capex and R&D)

- During bull-market periods
- Where parent companies themselves exhibit lower growth profiles and more financial leverage

In the case of IPOs, rival share price reaction is often negative, implying the market may view the event as a signal of sector overvaluation or that the economic gains from IPOs are expected to accrue at the expense of rivals. In contrast, rival share price reaction to spin-offs tends to be positive, potentially a signal of undervaluation.[12]

WHAT HAPPENS LONGER TERM?

As discussed earlier, academic studies do support the notion that a portion of value created by divested businesses originated from anticipated take-over premiums.[13] But this accounts for only a fraction of the total value created as many divested businesses continue to operate as independent companies. And a significant portion of the value creation can be attributed to documented improvements in operating performance.[14]

One long-term study of spin-offs found that about half of the divested businesses have survived as viable independent entities.[15] The others have been acquired, bought back by the parent, or delisted. The surviving businesses produced the highest returns. And the most successful examples of corporate restructuring transactions are those where the subsidiaries achieve full independence over a fairly short period of time and have maintained that status longer term.

Case Study: Dun & Bradstreet (DNB)

Once a sprawling information conglomerate, Dun & Bradstreet (DNB) initiated a plan in the 1990s to unlock shareholder value through increased focus. The bulk of DNB's divestitures were completed using spin-off or carve-out/spin-off techniques. Cognizant Technology was divested using a partial public carve-out followed by a complete spin.

Not content to shed businesses, DNB acquired several related businesses. An original DNB investment would have significantly outperformed the S&P500 and led to seven new public company holdings, five of which survive to this day. The remaining two, AC Nielsen and Nielsen Media, were purchased for cash by VNU (a Dutch media and advertising conglomerate). Interestingly, VNU almost purchased another, IMS Health; however, VNU shareholders rejected the plan.

Additionally, the stock continued to trade well and DNB's valuation multiples expanded significantly, reflecting a higher attribution in the market to profitable future growth prospects. These changes in DNB were accompanied by an outflow from Value and Index style institutional holdings, into Growth At a Reasonable Price (GARP), Growth, and Hedge Fund holdings.

PRACTICAL IMPEDIMENTS TO DIVESTITURE

Despite the real opportunity for tremendous value creation, several practical impediments exist to corporate divestiture activity. We outline how earnings dilution, confusion over value creation, fear of shrinking the business, book losses, and executive compensation each play a role in inhibiting corporate divestitures.

Earnings Dilution

Many executives are reluctant to divest unwanted businesses because of earnings dilution. This is especially true for large, mature, low-growth, cash cow businesses even though they fail to earn their cost of capital and may be worth more to a different owner or under a different ownership structure. We illustrate the math of multiple expansion in the face of dilution from a divestiture. A high price-to-earnings ratio (P/E) parent divests a low P/E subsidiary, reducing earnings per share (EPS). The multiple expands because the earnings reduction is disproportionate with the reduction in intrinsic value.

Table 3.2 shows that a parent company that spins off its low multiple business faces significant earnings dilution and multiple expansion. The larger the divested subsidiary, the more likely the impact will be material in terms of earnings dilution and in terms of multiple expansion. In the case of a split-off, share count is managed through the exchange process, providing

TABLE 3.2 Divestitures and Dilution

	Parent Before	Parent Spins Low	Splits Low	Parent Spins High	Splits High
Shares	300	300	200	300	100
Income	200	100	100	100	100
Value	3,000	2,000	2,000	1,000	1,000
Stock Price	$10.00	$ 6.67	$10.00	$ 3.33	$10.00
EPS	$ 0.67	$ 0.33	$ 0.50	$ 0.33	$ 1.00
P/E	15.0	20.0	20.0	10.0	10.0

more attractive cosmetics, much in the same way that a reverse stock split would achieve if executed on the heels of the spin-off. Alternatively, the most attractive course, from an earnings accretion perspective, would be to split off the higher multiple business, achieving an even greater reduction in share count.

Shareholder value is preserved despite the lower share price, excluding taxes. In the case of a spin-off, shareholders have at least as much value but now in two stocks. In a cash sale, proceeds can be reinvested, used to enhance credit, or returned to shareholders. Furthermore, it would take only a slight extra multiple expansion (arguably due to signaling) to maintain share price in cases where the subsidiary is small although this is unnecessary because total value (remaining company plus distributed value) is preserved regardless.

Who Gets the Value Created?

Confusion around investor wealth and value creation is a second obstacle. Though corporate divestiture may create tremendous shareholder value, depending on the circumstances of the divestiture, much of this value may not remain resident within the parent company. The residual value may accrue to the shareholders in the form of another security, the repurchase of securities at a premium or a cash distribution. Though the shareholders are better off and total investor wealth is increased, the parent security may be smaller, and worth less. The market capitalization is likely to be smaller, and unless the share count is reduced (through a share repurchase, reverse split, or split-off), the parent company share price will be lower. Yet the shareholders, to whom the board owes their fiduciary responsibility, are better off.

Shrinking the Company

Many executives are reluctant to shrink the company. A divestiture is often delayed until a suitable, offsetting, acquisition candidate can be found, especially where cash proceeds are involved. The use of cash proceeds to repurchase stock, often the best course, is a last resort for many. This obstacle is partly due to the aforementioned confusion around value creation but also may be partly attributable to executive compensation design.

Book Loss On Disposition

Many companies are reluctant to sell underperforming or noncore businesses or assets because they face the prospect of a book loss on disposition, the noncash accounting entry required for the income statement to reconcile to the new pro forma balance sheet. But underperforming assets are typically worth less than the book value of capital; they are after all, underperforming. Awaiting a buyer willing to pay at least book value, these unwanted businesses often linger, decay in value, and consume resources.

We offer three compelling reasons to sell any underperforming or noncore assets now, regardless of the potential book loss on disposition:

- Market multiples reflect cash earnings
- A positive signal
- Opportunity cost of capital and other resources

Market Multiples Reflect Cash Earnings   Book values are not a reflection of the value of a business, nor are they meant to be. A company's balance sheet can be at best a measure of capital, that is, the amount of cash that was invested in the company. Whether such capital translates into value depends on a manager's success in earning returns above the cost of capital.

Countless theoretical and empirical studies have shown that extraordinary, noncash charges (e.g., loss on disposition, write-downs, and accounting changes) are economically inconsequential and certainly not deserving of the attention received.[16] Intrinsic value is unaffected by these charges because neither the company's future operating cash flows, nor its discount rate, is affected. Thus, net present value (NPV) is unaffected.

The stock market does look through the book losses by comparing the market multiples (P/E) of high book loss companies to the relative pricing inferred on low book loss companies. We grouped the 750 largest U.S. industrial companies with book losses into three groups of book loss as a percentage of earnings. If the market ignores the earnings drag of book losses, we should see correspondingly higher market multiples on companies with more book losses to offset the impact of the charge. And, indeed, we see that. The market is not fooled by the lower earnings figures from the book loss; a higher multiple is effectively assigned from the intrinsic value. We should not worry about such noncash, extraordinary charges.

A Positive Signal   Though some have called book capital a meaningless accounting artifact, many managers worry about the effects of public disclosure for a loss on disposition. Will it damage our reputation? Does it signal a mistake? What will the share price do?

But the "charge is a noncash charge." It is not an operating expense but is an extraordinary, or special, one-time charge. As we have shown, along with countless others, the market recognizes that these charges do not affect future cash flows or the discount rate nor do they affect intrinsic value.

All too often, the event is not news. We know what businesses are underperforming. We know what businesses are noncore ones. We are waiting for someone to do something about it. The recognition of a book loss on disposition can be, if anything, a positive signal. Recognizing that sunk costs are irrelevant, positive action is now being taken. Rather than risking the appearance of denial or inertia, the company positions itself as being responsive to change, confidently moving forward. Underperforming and noncore businesses are disposed, resources are reallocated, and a bold new vision is communicated.

For example, on September 27, 1999, Lockheed Martin announced the results of a strategic and organizational review that encompassed three major actions: (1) streamlining the organization and making new senior management assignments; (2) repositioning certain related high-growth businesses; and (3) evaluating divestitures of noncore businesses. Management communicated that all of the potential divestitures, if combined, would result in a decrease in net earnings of approximately $1 billion, primarily noncash.

On July 13, 2000, Lockheed Martin announced the sale of Aerospace Electronics Systems (AES) businesses to BAE Systems for $1.67 billion in cash. The company recognized a non-recurring and unusual loss, including income taxes, of $598 million related to the transaction, which was included in other income and expenses. On a book basis, the company generated $1 billion after-tax loss, primarily reflecting the goodwill incurred as a result of the high price Lockheed Martin paid for such businesses in previous years. Lockheed Martin's post-announcement shareholder return was 26.7 percent, measured over the period from announcement of sale of AES to BAE Systems (July 2000) to completion of sale in November 2000. Research analysts viewed the Lockheed Martin announcement of divestitures of noncore assets positively because of increased focus on core areas, reduced vertical integration risk, and enhanced financial flexibility.[17]

Opportunity Cost   Disposition creates value in many ways. While an underperforming or noncore business is awaiting sale, it continues to consume resources. In fact, many underperforming businesses consume a disproportionate share of resources because they are underperforming. They require more oversight and continue to tie up capital that could otherwise be deployed. A book loss on disposition often corresponds to a tax loss, a real source of cash savings that contributes to intrinsic value.

Nevertheless, these businesses often decay in value when relegated to the category of noncore or underperforming. It becomes harder to attract and retain good talent, important customers become wary and are likely to use their bargaining power, and maintenance is typically postponed.

Strategic change, major organizational initiatives, acquisitions, and other investments are also deferred.

On October 5, 1999, American Home Products (AHP) announced a restructuring of its agricultural chemical business (AgChem) with a charge of $220 million to close offices, make severance payments, and buy back unsold chemicals from dealers. The business had suffered from a weak global farm economy and intense competition from its rival, Monsanto.

On March 20, 2000, AHP announced an agreement to sell the AgChem to BASF AG for $3.8 billion in cash. AHP recorded an after-tax loss of $1.6 billion. AHP's post-announcement shareholder return was 12 percent, measured from announcement of sale (March 2000) to completion of sale in June 2000.

Research analysts viewed the business as a drag on AHP's top and bottom-line growth and the sale was, therefore, well received by the investment community. Furthermore, AHP freed up $3.8 billion in cash, which was used to support four new drug product launches and to fund the reserve, if necessary, for liability of pending diet drug litigation.

Executive Compensation

Unfortunately, we frequently find an economic incentive to preserve company size. This is due to the prevalence of company size metrics in the design and calibration of executive compensation. Company size is highly correlated with competitive pay and is frequently an input into annual executive compensation studies. The natural log of company size (ln(revenue), ln(net tangible assets) or ln(market capitalization)) is one of the best indicators of CEO total direct compensation and is frequently used to "size-adjust" executive pay data. Therefore, a divestiture could represent an effective pay cut, creating a disincentive for any material divestiture unless the Compensation Committee is alerted to this problem. At the parent company level, executives must be "made whole" in this process.

At the subsidiary level, the creation of public equity in a subsidiary can resolve an incentive compensation problem by improving "line of sight" and accountability for shareowner value. Cash bonuses and equity incentives can be more effectively linked to the performance and fortunes of the business. Subsidiary executives may hold options and shares in the parent, which would have the undesirable effect of decoupling executive fortunes from that of the newly independent company. An exchange of parent stock and options for those of NewCo is frequently employed to better align the executive incentives.

Furthermore, with full separation through a divestiture, subsidiary managers may lose the diversification benefits they enjoyed working for a conglomerate, where cash bonuses are tied to the performance of individual business units but equity-linked incentives are linked to conglomerate stock. Higher total direct compensation may be warranted if the new pay package is effectively a riskier plan.

FINANCIAL POLICY CONSIDERATIONS

In addition to incentive compensation policies, financial policies (financial liquidity, financial leverage, and shareholder distributions) may need to be recalibrated in the face of a divestiture. Furthermore, a relationship exists between financial policies and the divestiture methods employed.

Greater financial liquidity is needed for businesses with more volatility in their operating cash flows or with a weak outlook. Liquidity is more similar to comparable companies than to the parent. Subsidiary liquidity is generally higher than the parent, for cases of spin-offs and IPOs. IPO subsidiaries tend to have the highest liquidity, suggesting more disparate prospects for growth and volatility between the IPO parent and IPO sub. IPO parents exhibit lower liquidity than spin-off parents, which may partially explain the choice of IPO versus spin-off.

Financial leverage is typically less appropriate for growth. Divested subsidiaries are frequently less levered than the parent but similarly levered to comparable firms. IPO subs tend to be the least leveraged, again suggesting the most disparate growth prospects between the IPO parent and subsidiary. IPO parents are slightly more leveraged than spin-off parents, again suggesting the attraction of raising proceeds.

Shareholder distributions such as dividends and share repurchases tend to be less appropriate for growth-oriented businesses, where ostensibly, the capital should be reinvested in the growth prospects, reducing the need to raise expensive capital externally. Dividends tend to be even more inappropriate than share repurchases for these businesses because of their fixed-cost nature (at least buybacks can be suspended if need be). Subsidiary dividend payout ratios are most frequently much lower than the parent but more similar to comparable firms. In most cases, dividends are initially set to zero. This was especially true for IPOs, which presumably face higher growth prospects.

TAX CONSIDERATIONS AND STRUCTURAL REFINEMENTS

Section (§) 355 of the Internal Revenue Code (IRC) stipulates the following conditions to qualify as a tax-free event:

- The parent must have control of the subsidiary prior to distribution and must have had controlling (80 percent) ownership for at least 5 years,
- All subsidiary stock and securities owned by the parent must be distributed (with occasional exceptions),
- Continuity of historic shareholder interest (minimum 50 percent continued interest) must be maintained in the parent and subsidiary,
- Business operations of the subsidiary and parent must be continued after divestiture, and
- Subsidiary and parent may not be acquired within two years of divestiture; this feature can be used as a defense against hostile bids.

Under §338(h)(10) treatment, a stock acquisition is treated as an asset deal; subsidiary net operating losses (NOLs) remain with the parent as the cost basis of assets are marked to market. Without the §338(h)(10) election, all tax attributes of a subsidiary carry-over to the acquirer.

- In an "A" reorganization, the acquirer receives all assets and all liabilities of the target in exchange for a mix of stock (50 percent minimum) and cash.
- In a "B" reorganization, the acquirer must use 100 percent stock to acquire a minimum of 80 percent of the target's stock.
- In a "C" reorganization, the acquirer receives most (70 to 90 percent) of the target's assets (but not liabilities) in exchange for a combination of stock and cash (minimum 80 percent voting stock). Any liabilities assumed count as cash consideration.

Debt Swap with Spin-Off

In situations where a spin-off would reduce the parent's tax basis in the subsidiary below zero (which would trigger a taxable event), a debt swap for subsidiary shares (§355a1a) can provide a tax efficient distribution mechanism. To qualify the debt must have a term of at least 5 years (e.g., AT&T/AT&T Wireless).

Alternatively, debt of any term may be used if the exchange is pursuant to §361 as part of a D-type reorganization of the subsidiary (e.g., Lucent's IPO of Agere). In either case, no taxable gain is recognized on the exchange of debt for shares.

Morris Trust

The Morris Trust consists of a concurrent spin-off and merger with a smaller target company. This type of transaction may occur pursuant to §355e if parent shareholders own at least 50 percent of the vote and value of the combined company (for up to 2 years). Partial payment in cash can be used in cases where the target is too large to meet the aforementioned requirement. Furthermore, any consideration exchanged must be almost totally stock to comply with §355, and the complex restrictions of a spin/merge transaction (Morris Trust) require care. If the target is a public company, it may be most efficient to merge the SpinCo into a subsidiary of the target via a §368 triangular merger.

CHAPTER 4

Grow: How To Make M&A Pay

Almost all studies of mergers and acquisitions (M&A) show value creation in aggregate. But often the bulk, or even all, of the value creation is found to accrue to the shareholders of target firms while the shareholders of acquiring firms fair far worse. Debate continues on how much less, when, and why. Some research does show that acquiring shareholders also benefit. The equally weighted average announcement return was 1.1 percent or $5.61 of value per $100 invested. However, the dollar-weighted average announcement returns are −1.2 percent.[1] Small acquisitions by small firms create value, but large firms make large acquisitions that may produce large losses. Acquisitions in aggregate resulted in losses as large firm losses outweighed small firm gains.

But such studies obscure reality behind the law of averages and provide little actionable advice. And this is not the question to which executives need answers. Despite the mountains of rigorous academic literature on the topic, there has not been a focus on helpful guidance for executives. Though many M&A deals are unsuccessful, for a host of reasons, many do create tremendous value. A more important question for board directors and corporate executives is, "How can we make M&A add value and incorporate it as part of our growth strategy?" How to ensure a win?

We build on the newer research in this area, articulating linkages between key success factors, value creation, and the allocation of value creation between buyers and sellers. There is growing evidence to support the importance of strategic fit, target size, ownership, financing, profitability, and growth profile. We advance these findings to highlight the recurring themes evident in successful mergers and acquisitions.

M&A TODAY

Several factors in today's business environment contribute to an M&A climate that is more attractive today than it has been in several years.

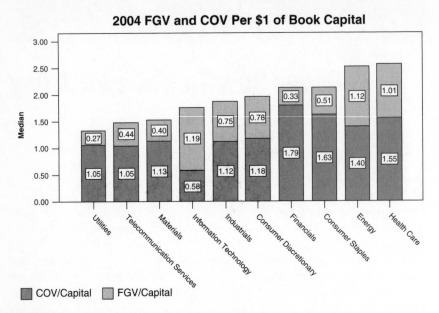

FIGURE 4.1   2004 GV and COV per $1 of Book Capital

Resurgent interest in M&A, combined with the dubious track record and the prevalence of big wins and losses, makes this an important area of study for corporate finance practitioners and academics alike. Market valuations reveal a chronic dependence on expectations for positive net present value (NPV) growth (see Figure 4.1).

"Quiet Period"

Bold strategic action had been on hold as executives and their directors sorted through a wave of inward facing initiatives, such as accounting (e.g., restatements, stock options, FAS 133), governance, and regulatory (e.g., SOX) reform. A long run of bankruptcies and corporate scandals, continued threat of terror, conflict in the Middle East, rocketing oil and steel prices, and election year politics, contributed to an overwhelming reticence toward action and slowed the stock market recovery.

An overhang on stock market valuations made sellers reluctant to sell and deterred buyers as they saw their own currency similarly devalued. The subsequent decline of "mega deals" ($10 billion+) was a principal dampener on M&A activity after the 1998–2000 peak, though we see stabilization now underway. The "quiet period" has ended; pent-up demand is sizable, and deal conditions are favorable.

Favorable Capital Markets

With the bulk of the aforementioned negative news capitalized into market prices and much of the uncertainty now clearing, equity capital markets are positioned to rebound. Low interest rates and tight credit spreads continue to make the debt capital markets compelling, even to issuers with no use of proceeds.

Though the leveraged loan market continues to be strong, high-yield and convertible bonds provide viable alternatives. Concerns over the prospect of rising rates and the attractiveness of buying duration now as rates remain low are factors that favor bonds over the bank market. And even though leveraged deals typically play well to the flexibility of bank debt, innovative call features and equity claw-backs have helped enhance the financial flexibility of bonds, a traditional concern.

The Rise of Financial Sponsors

Financial sponsors are a growing global force in M&A. Sponsors benefited from the preoccupation of strategic buyers, taking advantage of the lull in corporate activity and favorable capital markets. An increase in stapled deals—where the seller's bank arranges financing for buyers—is another trend that has fed the growth and competitiveness of the sponsor market and has supported valuations. With over $100 billion of uninvested capital, sponsors are now price-competitive with public market alternatives and are actively searching for new opportunities.

Divestitures and middle market activity, dominated by sponsors, have rebounded. An often-overlooked fact is that smaller acquisitions never disappeared. Volume is more evenly distributed in sectors with large middle markets. Sector analysis (not shown) reveals that global real estate (5 percent of total 1992 to 2004 YTD volume) and healthcare (7 percent) have seen a steady flow of M&A activity.

Currency Windows of Opportunity

Beyond potential price and financing arbitrage opportunities, a well-crafted foreign exchange (FX) policy is necessary to successfully integrate a cross-border deal. Foreign direct investment is driven more by equity market development than by currency movements. However, while exchange rates are not driving deal flow, they are an important consideration to deal timing and structuring. They can also create attractive windows of opportunity in terms of pricing and financing.

Some of the greatest recent opportunities have stemmed from USD/EUR movement, Canadian (CAD) volatility, and the Latin American currencies though the greatest window of opportunity into South America investment may have passed.

Big Business Is Back

According to Securities Data Corp (SDC) data, the importance of the "mega deal" to M&A is perhaps best illustrated by the telecom and financial services sectors, which constitute 17 percent and 20 percent, respectively, of the total $7 trillion global M&A volume of 1998 to 2000. Roughly 70 percent of these telecom and 70 percent of these financial services deals were a few large transactions (e.g. Ameritech-SBC $63 billion deal and JP Morgan/Chase Manhattan $34 billion deal). By 2003, telecom deals had plummeted 78 percent from deal volume of 2000, and financial services was 48 percent off deal volume in 2000. But now big business is back. Based on 2004 part-year dollar volumes, M&A is up 44 percent globally (34 percent in the United States) over 2003. Large strategic combinations are leading the way, with Cingular/AT&T, and Kmart/Sears just a few, obvious examples.

Sustainable Growth

Expectations for long-term growth rates are crucial to strategic and financial planning, valuation, and cost of capital estimates. Based on the past 20 years of S&P500 nonfinancials universe, sustainable growth is a difficult task. Expectations for long-term growth rates, such as top-line, operating profit, and net income, have generally declined since the heady days of the DotCom era. In an effort to provide guidance for planning purposes, we summarized our long-term growth rate findings in the following table. Although earnings growth is what is required to drive equity values, the incidence of negative earnings makes top-line analysis more helpful. Ultimately, long-term earnings growth can only be sustained through top-line revenue growth.

Table 4.1 illustrates just how difficult it is to consistently outperform "double-digit" top-line growth, near median performance for short periods but over 60th percentile performance for longer periods. For earnings growth (not shown), the "double-digit" benchmark is slightly easier. The data also show data compression over time. There is less variation in outcomes for longer periods, effectively a mean reversion.

Though some companies have grown at high rates historically, they are relatively rare. The persistence of long-term earnings growth is elusive and is not exhibited any more commonly than what we might expect to find by mere chance. The Institutional Brokers Estimate System (IBES) long-term growth forecasts are generally optimistic and add surprisingly little predictive power in identifying high-growth candidates.

TABLE 4.1 Sustainable Growth

Percentile	1-Yr CAGR Sales	3-Yr CAGR Sales	5-Yr CAGR Sales
90th	32.8%	25.3%	21.1%
75th	17.8%	15.0%	13.2%
Median	8.6%	7.6%	6.8%
25th	1.6%	2.0%	2.3%
10th	−6.8%	−4.0%	−2.5%

If we deconstruct an S&P500 valuation with a price-to-earnings multiple of 30x, it implies 6.8 percent perpetual earnings growth, or about 30th percentile earnings growth performance. Median estimates for historical real growth of about 3 percent are consistent with the real rate of growth in gross domestic product (GDP) over the same period.

The corporate implications are clear. Sustainable growth is elusive. Hurdle rates and growth rate assumptions are often too high given the evidence of history. Assuming constant growth and current dividend yields of about 2 percent we might expect long-term returns from equities of about 7 to 9 percent, a much lower cost of equity than most corporate hurdle rates would imply.

TRANSACTIONS THAT CREATE VALUE

For a host of reasons, many M&A deals are unsuccessful. But many do create tremendous value. Our objective is to understand how to incorporate M&A as part of a growth strategy to meet the value imperative. We hope to ensure the ingredients of success are incorporated at the outset of an M&A process.

Interestingly about one half of all deals have positive excess returns in the short term and about one half exhibit positive excess returns for the longer term. However, the outcomes are widely dispersed—the averages are hardly meaningful—and longer-term outcomes are more dispersed. Short-term outcomes are not as widely dispersed as longer-term outcomes but tend to be the focus in the literature because the impact is more isolated from the influence of other unrelated factors. Their usefulness is of course, predicated on a semi-strong form of market efficiency—we assume the market provides our best independent assessment of the transaction and incorporates these expectations into market prices—and the net present value (NPV) of the impact is capitalized into share price. Similar insights are often evident in both horizons because the populations overlap and short-term success tends to be correlated with longer-term success. We and other researchers have found short-term returns to be reasonably consistent with longer-term returns.[2]

Most short-term excess returns narrowly clustered within a range of between $+/-5$ percent; longer-term excess returns are widely dispersed and frequently exceed $+/-20$percent. So, acquirer shareholders are either big winners or big losers. How then can the critical business process of M&A be managed toward the "right tail" rather than the "left tail" of outcomes?

There are many common themes in the data of successful deals and successful acquirers. Based on our own empirical research as well as the existing research, key success factors include strategic fit, target size, ownership, premium, financing, profitability and growth, valuation, and to a lesser extent, financial policy considerations.

Strategic Fit

A higher degree of strategic fit leads to a more successful M&A outcome. Based on Standard Industrial Classification (SIC) codes as a rough proxy for strategic fit, acquisitions within the same industry (share 8-digit SIC) are about 50 percent more likely to be winners for the longer term than unrelated acquisitions.

Moderately related (share 2-, 4- or 6-digit SIC) and unrelated acquisitions are less likely to be successful. The weight of the literature supports the notion that related industry acquisitions outperform unrelated acquisitions.[3] One study found that acquirers that pursued transactions in unrelated industries tended to experience excess cash flow declines and valuation discounts, versus acquirers that maintained industry focus. Acquirers that pursued transactions in unrelated industries experienced excess cash flow declines of 10 percent and valuation discounts of 4 percent, versus acquirers that maintained focus.[4]

Operational synergies should be larger and easier to achieve in related industries. Post-merger integration is likely to begin sooner, advance more quickly, and achieve greater results due to a more significant overlap in knowledge, skills, and business processes. Synergies are also less likely to be overestimated in like industries, preventing the risk of overpayment by the buyer. Lastly, the buyer's competitive advantages are more likely bear relevance to the target, and may be leveraged across an increased scale of business.

However, the greater presence of cost savings can be priced into a similar industry acquisition, leading to a greater reliance on successful post-merger integration and, therefore, execution risk. For the longer term, as integration efforts bear fruit in the form of synergy cost savings, the market rewards these deals accordingly.

Profitability and Growth

Higher target profitability and growth is associated with greater success. Cases of winning targets tend to have higher levels of profitability, such as earnings before income and taxes (EBIT) margins, than cases of unsuccessful targets. Though these cases have greater earnings per share (EPS) dilution, targets with attractive product and market prospects represent the more successful targets.

Similarly, higher target growth prospects are associated with greater longer-term success. Three-year trailing top-line growth for cases of successful targets tends to be 30 to 40 percent higher than for cases of unsuccessful targets.

However, the best targets may create pain in the short term, we saw poor short-term market reactions associated with higher growth targets but not statistically meaningfully growth rates. Again, while repositioning into more attractive markets proves successful for the longer term, it is not without risks in the short term and can be subject to considerable execution risk. For this reason, the market may take a wait-and-see approach. We find similar results with valuation.

Valuation

Higher multiple targets tend to outperform lower multiple targets for the longer term. The cases of winning targets exhibit valuation multiples that are roughly 50 percent than the valuation multiples of the cases of unsuccessful targets, indicating that growth strategies are more likely to outperform "cost synergy" strategies.

Consistent with our findings around target profitability and growth, acquisitions of more attractive targets are more likely to be a longer-term winning strategy; for the shorter term, this comes with increased execution risk and a potential for negative market reaction around the time of the announcement. Without a demonstrated track record of similar success, the markets tend to await milestones indicative of a successful execution before fully capitalizing the expected benefits into share prices.

Absolute and Relative Size

The critical post-merger integration process is easier for smaller deals, that is, a less significant resource drain, more manageable assimilation logistics, and greater speed of execution. In our experience, small deals tend to be held to a higher standard in pricing and approval, garnering less visibility and less likely to receive special accommodation within the approval process than larger, strategic acquisitions. Bargaining power is more likely to favor the buyer in cases where the deal is less significant to the seller. For these reasons, the risk of overpayment is lower for smaller targets. Smaller deals are more likely to be private companies or business units of larger enterprises, which can attract lower prices.

Smaller deals tend to outperform larger deals. Smaller deals are more frequently associated with successful announcements and the top 500 successful deals of the past decade ("winners") average only three-quarters the size of the bottom 500 unsuccessful deals ("losers"). One study found that 66 percent of deals under $5 billion created value for the acquirer's shareholders, and about 66 percent of deals over $5 billion destroyed or did not create value for the acquirer.[5]

However, relative size is a more complicated issue, in part because smaller acquirers tend to outperform larger acquirers. Interestingly, smaller firms tend to be more successful in making acquisitions, presumably due to their discipline with respect to strategic fit and pricing. A study of 12,000 acquisitions from 1980 to 2001 found that small acquirers (market capitalization below the 25th percentile of New York Stock Exchange (NYSE) listed firms in the year of acquisition; today this would be $700 million) systematically outperform.[6] Therefore, on a relative basis, it may come as no surprise that we found the larger relative sizes (targeting at least 50 percent acquirer revenue) to be slightly more frequently associated with winners. One study of public deals found that deals, where the target capitalizations were less than 5 percent of acquirer, outperformed larger deals where the target was at least 25 percent as large as acquirer. In this study of public deals, small relative deals demonstrated positive excess returns of 0.3 percent in the two days before and after the announcement date; larger relative acquisitions had −1.5 percent returns for the same time period.[7]

Ownership

Private targets tend to outperform public targets. Private targets (including units of publicly traded companies) have been more than 50 percent more likely to be among those immediately viewed positively as negatively. And while our own longer-term findings were inconclusive, the literature tends to favor private targets. One study of serial acquirers (defined as five or more acquisitions/divestitures) reports that excess returns are higher for firms acquiring private companies than for firms acquiring public companies. This study indicated that within three days of the announcement date bidder shareholders gain 2.1 percent when buying a private firm or subsidiary but lose 1.0 percent when purchasing a public firm.[8]

Private targets are likely to share all the benefits of smaller targets: more disciplined evaluation process, easier post merger integration, advantageous bargaining power. But even controlling for size, private targets still generally outperform their control group.[9] Private businesses have no definitive starting value to assign a premium, which may lead to lower prices paid. Other factors that can lead to a motivated sale situation include succession issues, liquidity, estate planning, and tax considerations.

Premium

Premiums are not indicative of either short-term or longer-term success. Successful deals demand a disciplined acquirer, yet premiums do not differentiate winners from losers. There is not a statistically significant difference in premiums paid by short-term winners and losers or longer-term winners and losers; in fact, longer-term winners average slightly higher premiums.

Premiums are influenced by too many factors to be a reliable indicator of success, including historical market values, strategic considerations, and estimated synergies. One study concluded that mergers achieve cost synergies more often than revenue synergies; 25 percent of mergers failed to achieve 30 percent of stated revenue synergies, and more than 60 percent of mergers realized close to 100 percent of stated cost synergies.[10]

M&A FACT AND FALLACY

Today's M&A environment seems more challenging than ever. But potential buyers have generally restored their debt capacity, are building surplus cash, and face increasing pressure to renew their growth options.

Since early 2000, the market has seen a steady decline in profitability, returns on capital, valuations as well as actual and expected growth rates. The proportion of enterprise value predicated on profitable growth for the S&P500 had declined from 72 percent in December 1999 to 56 percent in March 2003, almost a 50 percent decline from $8,550 billion to $4,350 billion.

However, not all acquisition strategies are created equal. Companies that actively managed their portfolios have outperformed those that did not. Acquirers outperformed divestors but lost to companies that balanced acquisition programs with a healthy dose of divestitures.[11]

The current environment of low interest rates and reduced valuations offers an opportunity for many companies to renew growth options. Yet we find three recurring issues that stand in the way. We will address these pitfalls that commonly impede transactions:

1. Goodwill
2. Market timing
3. Earnings dilution

The Goods on Goodwill

Under the pooling method, goodwill had been ignored with no record on the balance sheet of the accounting premium—the excess purchase price over book value—and no associated amortization expense postdeal. The exclusion of the accounting premium allowed for a higher level of earnings, return on capital and economic profit(EP) or economic value added (EVA). In 2001, the Financial Accounting Standards Board (FASB) eliminated the pooling of interests method.

Many companies are now reluctant to pursue acquisitions that depress returns on capital employed or are dilutive to economic profit (EP). However, most business values are generally higher than book capital, in that any acquisition will initially depress return on capital employed. The transaction capitalizes preexisting value, suddenly recognizing it in book capital for accounting purposes, a mark-to-market event.

But book values are backward-looking accounting artifacts, a view shared by academics and Wall Street practitioners alike.[12] Intrinsic value is forward looking premised on the present value of future cash flows. Any attempted reconciliation between market and book value is an exercise of questionable value.

A more important premium to enumerate and track is really the excess purchase price paid over fair market value, the economic premium. A strategic buyer should be focused on business case rationale, strategic fit, synergies, and integration, rather than the justification of preexisting market values. This is the job of institutional investors, traders and financial buyers. With respect to stand-alone valuation, a good starting point should be a fairly valued asset in a reasonably efficient market. A purchaser should feel compelled to justify, and earn a return on, any economic premium over fair market value rather than focus on the difference between the market and book value of accounting capital.

The opportunity cost of any business's market value is equally important, but only the acquired ones are recognized under generally accepted accounting principles (GAAP). Yet the decision to acquire is the same as the decision not to divest. Organically grown business values are left off-balance sheet and their opportunity cost is ignored; most of the soft costs made to build these businesses (investment in R&D, human capital, etc.) are expensed rather than capitalized.

On December 17, 2001, Amgen announced acquisition of Immunex for $16 billion in cash and stock. The deal was a case of a company looking to buy into growth but Amgen's return on capital employed (ROCE) would decline from 22 percent (18 percent on a pro forma basis) due to the high growth value (GV) embedded in Immunex's share price. The acquisition would add a third therapeutic area (inflammation) to Amgen's leading positions in oncology and nephrology. Additionally, Immunex's research expertise in immunology and oncology was expected to strengthen Amgen's research capabilities to build a strong product pipeline. The transaction was well received by research analysts. And upon announcement of the transaction, Immunex shares climbed 13 percent and Amgen shares rose 6 percent, measured over the period from one day before announcement to announcement date.

Goodwill is most inhibiting in the cases of companies looking to buy into higher margin or higher growth sectors, where dilution to returns on capital and EVA will be the greatest. Unfortunately, these are the sort of strategic actions that many businesses need to consider to reposition themselves.

Market Timing

Many acquisitions, and even more dispositions, are postponed in an effort to time the market better. Growth initiatives are postponed to await lower multiples as dispositions are delayed on the prospect of higher market multiples. Market timing is premised on the notion of fundamental market inefficiency. But the market for corporate assets is surprisingly efficient, and other imperatives play into the decision process. We offer three reasons not to attempt timing the market:

1. Offsetting multiples
2. Destruction of delay
3. Now is the time

Offsetting Multiples   Acquisitions and the divestiture of underperforming or noncore assets are postponed by a reluctant parent committed to the sale but hoping to execute at a time when market conditions and business earnings are at their most favorable levels. Unfortunately, attractive earnings levels and market multiples typically do not coincide. Likewise, we often discuss acquisition targets that offer compelling rationale and strategic fit but are delayed by the buyer in the hopes of achieving more favorable market pricing.

The market is surprisingly efficient. Market troughs are typically characterized by poor earnings and relatively high market multiples. Market peaks are typically characterized by record earnings and relatively low multiples. The two effects generally cancel with the net effect of enterprise values being reasonably indifferent to the vagaries of the business cycle.

Table 4.2 shows the futility of delaying transactions to time the market. We show Global Industry Classification Standards (GICS) 151010

TABLE 4.2 Chemical Sector Earnings Offset Market Multiples

	GICS 151010 Chemicals						
$s in MMs	1994	1995	2001	2002	2003	2004	2005
P/E (x)	118.8	10.4	58.4	111.6	189.8	129.6	33.4
Net Income	1,087	12,982	2,827	1,384	1,007	1,734	6,416
Market Capitalization	119,344	134,370	164,143	152,675	186,373	220,115	213,177

(Chemicals) over the past decade; higher earnings are offset by lower multiples, and higher multiples are offset by lower earnings.

Destruction of Delay A second and perhaps more important argument against market timing is the destruction of delay. Delayed acquisitions hold up execution of your growth strategy. Growth opportunities deferred may fade away or the window of opportunity may pass. Alternatively, the target may become less competitive as it sits held for sale, with an uncertain future.

A business held for sale, or with an uncertain future, declines in value rapidly as it is targeted by competitors using the opportunity to steal customers and employees. The products or services holding an explicit or implicit need for future support will be more difficult to sell for a business in limbo. Important customers will become wary and use their increased bargaining power. Attracting and retaining good talent also becomes harder. Investments and maintenance get postponed. Delay will destroy value.

Now Is the Time Balance sheets have been mostly repaired, liquidity is generally restored, and in many cases, cash balances are running at an all time high. The capital markets remain receptive to issues. Interest rates are low and pricing is strong. The cost of capital is at a historic low. Financial sponsors are eager for deals and have generally lowered their required rates of return. Stapled financing is generally available on favorable terms; target financial advisors offer stapled financing, or commit money, in the form of debt, to lend to potential buyers in a buyout deal. With funds readily available and shareholders anxiously awaiting an inflection point, now is the time to act.

Earnings Dilution

The acquisition of an attractive business and the divestiture of an unattractive business will generally lead to earnings dilution. Yet despite modern corporate finance theory and a large body of empirical evidence, many attractive businesses are not acquired or unattractive ones not divested, due to concerns of earnings dilution. Though close to 50 percent of all deals are dilutive, the number should likely be higher.

The aversion to earnings dilution is an impediment to any acquisition, but the obstacle is greatest in the case of companies that hope to reposition into higher margin and higher growth end markets, where earnings multiples are consequently higher than their own.

Strategically, dilution is a fact of life for any company hoping to transition into a portfolio of higher margin, higher value-added businesses with better end markets and improved growth prospects. Boards and corporate strategists will need to understand that the requisite for multiple expansion strategies will most certainly be near-term earnings dilution.[13] Empirical support exists for multiple expansion, the mathematical corollary to near-term earnings dilution. One study found that dilutive deals outperformed accretive deals. Nearly one half of all companies with one-year excess returns greater than 10 percent resulted from dilutive deals, yet only a third of such deals were from accretive transactions.[14]

The conventional accounting framework around valuation implies stock prices are a function of normalized current EPS, capitalized at an appropriate price-to-earnings (P/E) capitalization factor, or P/E multiple. Many extrapolate from this framework that if a company typically sells at 10 times earnings, and earnings per share falls from $1 to 80 cents, then share price will fall from $10 to $8, no matter what the cause or however temporary the downturn.

But P/E multiples change all the time; they are the result of the market's valuation and not an input to it. The quality of current earnings and expectation for future earnings changes all the time. Multiples change as a result of a change in underlying earnings, in the wake of changing prospects, as a consequence of acquisitions and divestitures, and after changes in financial policy or accounting methods. Intrinsic value is a function of core earnings and the appropriate capitalization factor, and this translates to estimating normalized current cash flows and their appropriate growth and discount rates.

Consider an acquisition in which a company selling for a low P/E multiple (10x) buys a firm selling for a high P/E ratio (20x) to enhance its growth prospects in an all stock deal to guard against excessive leverage and a possible ratings downgrade. For simplicity, we assume no synergies (Table 4.3).

Low must issue 200 shares at $10 to retire all 100 of High's $20 shares. Because more of the low P/E shares are needed to retire all the outstanding high P/E shares, the buyer's EPS will always decrease. Many would be reluctant to do this deal because EPS dilution signals bad news for the shareholders. But if we reverse the transaction so the high P/E firm

TABLE 4.3 Acquisitions and Dilution

	High		Low		Low Buys High		High Buys Low
Shares		100		100		300		150
Income	$	100	$	100	$	200	$	200
Value	$	2,000	$	1,000	$	3,000	$	3,000
Stock Price	$	20.00	$	10.00	$	10.00	$	20.00
EPS	$	1.00	$	1.00	$	0.67	$	1.33
PE		20.0		10.0		15.0		15.0

buys the low-multiple company, then the buyer's EPS must always increase; only 500 of the high P/E shares at $20 are needed to retire all 1,000 of the outstanding low P/E shares ($10). Many think that is good news for the buyer's shareholders. When Low buys High, it is dilutive to EPS but the multiple expands. When High buys Low, it is accretive to EPS but the multiple fades. Low-High is just High-Low with a two-for-one stock split. Regardless of which company buys or which company sells, the merged company will be the same, with the same assets, products, prospects, and value.

Any company hoping to transition into higher margin, higher value-added businesses and improved growth prospects will need to get comfortable that the corollary to multiple expansion will most certainly be near term earnings dilution.

RX FOR THE "CONGLOMERATE DISCOUNT"

Much has been written of the conglomerate discount (also known as the diversity discount). We summarize the main findings of the literature. We will also speak to the fundamental shift in strategy that is required to cure the conglomerate discount. Many studies have replicated findings that diversified firms trade at a 10 to 15 percent discount to pure plays. One found that firms making refocusing announcement gained about 7 percent in excess returns and this return was significantly related to the value reduction associated with refocuser's diversification policy.[15] We outline the primary causes below.

Selection Bias

The discount may simply reflect a selection bias—pure plays are often better businesses to start with—and better performance and valuation is due to better products, markets and opportunity. New econometric techniques for "casual inference" suggest the act of diversification does not destroy value and that after controlling for these other factors, conglomerate ownership leads to a premium rather than a discount.[16] Successful acquirers must overcome the pervasive reluctance among multi-industrials to pay for better businesses with better prospects.[17]

Performance

Postacquisition cash flow declines have been known to drive diversification discounts; bidders acquiring unrelated targets experience larger cash flow decreases and valuation discounts.[18] Post spin-off, there is typically a significant increase in investment efficiency and a subsequent elimination of the diversity discount.[19] Resource allocation is greatly enhanced outside the umbrella of a diversified firm.[20]

The conglomerate discount of multiline companies is frequently cited as an indication of the opportunity for improved fit and focus; capital allocation and management attention in parent and segment can be improved through the streamlining efforts of a restructuring. Successful acquirers can overcome the performance problem with targets that demonstrate a stronger fundamental strategic fit, as well as market-oriented strategic planning and capital allocation.

Governance

Some studies have suggested that weaker incentives and other pay and profile issues make it more difficult to attract and retain the best managers for diversified businesses. Weaker incentives, line of sight, and capital market discipline make the agency costs of diversified businesses greater.[21]

Stronger incentives and accountability can overcome governance issues. Improved transparency and line of sight (shorter distance) between management actions and results, and the availability of equity incentives (stock, restricted stock, and stock options), lead to a stronger system of incentives and accountability. This helps attract and retain the best talent available and provides better manager-owner alignment and leverage for any given level of shareholder cost.

Transparency

One study found spin-offs improve the quality of information managers and investors can infer, leading to an increase in the expected price of equity.[22] Another found that businesses can be undervalued if the market cannot observe the cash flows of each division in the firm.[23] Competitive concerns and administrative burden frequently inhibit better segment reporting.

Successful acquirers must provide transparent reporting, especially with respect to lines of business. More frequent, granular, and comprehensive disclosure of strategies, tactics and operating/financial performance aid the capital markets in evaluating a business and its worth. Higher multiples (capitalization rates) result in the market in the face of better earnings quality (cash flow certainty).

EVA AND M&A

In the wake of accounting scandals and governance reform, we have witnessed a back-to-basics renaissance in security analysis and corporate financial management. Value-based management is back in fashion, and business development professionals are again wrestling with the practical difficulties of making it work for mergers and acquisitions. We outline some requisite adaptations, based on our own experience with EVA and mergers and acquisitions.

The heart of most problems is that accounting book capital serves as the basis for returns. Economic profit (EP), return on equity (ROE), and ROCE are all return-based measures where book capital forms the founding basis for returns.[24] Market values remain detached from book values and unrecorded unless there is an acquisition.

Acquisitions force a mark-to-market event by creating goodwill. Accounting goodwill recognizes the full market value plus premium paid over historic book capital, capitalizing this onto the balance sheet. The higher capital employed does not imply any fundamental change in assets or business process, just recognition of preexisting value. This records acquired assets on a different basis.

Acquisitions mark up the capital base for EVA and other return-based measures even if no acquisition premium is paid. Therefore, EVA, ROE, and ROCE will always be diluted even though there is no change in assets or underlying economics, only an exchange in ownership at a fair market price. Therefore, organic growth will always be favored over acquisition growth under this framework because market premiums over book capital are never recognized in EVA, ROE, or ROCE.

Attractive markets are the most disadvantaged. The mark-to-market event of an acquisition is least significant for low-growth, low profitability businesses where price-book ratios are near one, or even below one. The least attractive markets will fare the best with a simplistic EVA, ROE, or ROCE. High-growth, high-return businesses, brimming with strategic potential, will be the most disadvantaged. In an efficient market, price-to-book ratios will be highest, and thus, EVA, ROE, and ROCE dilution will be the most severe for the most attractive targets.

Many acquisitive companies that use EVA will reference a longer window, say three years, to achieve EVA accretion, an attempt to overcome this mark-to-market problem and its impediment to acquisition growth when using EVA, ROE, and ROCE.

However, this solution is most commonly employed by turnaround acquirers for value-oriented targets in low-growth industrial markets. More attractive targets and markets are likely to involve much higher price-to-book ratios. And as we have shown, these are precisely the targets that perform best for the longer term. The dilution impediment must be removed to execute successful growth strategies.

We propose economic goodwill, not accounting goodwill, be included as capital employed in the EVA, ROE, and ROCE evaluation of acquisition targets. Economic goodwill is the premium paid over market value, as consideration. This eliminates the systematic bias of EVA against acquisitions and against high growth, high margin markets, and it records the capital of all businesses on an equal basis.

The justification of the stock market's capitalization is best left to market makers. Inorganic growth should be held to the same standard as organic growth and old businesses to the same standards as new businesses.

Value-Based Measurement of Postacquisition Performance

With M&A activity and the awareness of governance issues on the rise, a key issue facing executives, investors, and Board of Directors is how to evaluate postacquisition performance. The two most commonly employed approaches, market reaction and accounting impact, have serious flaws.

Although stock market reaction to the announcement is an unbiased and forward-looking perspective, it does not provide a benchmark for evaluating post merger operating results.

The financial impact to accounting statements and metrics lacks clarity due to accounting conventions and a focus on historical data that becomes increasingly irrelevant over time, especially after an acquisition, due to the noise created by various accounting treatments.

Value-based measurement of postacquisition performance provides a simple and direct approach to evaluating premiums paid against actual operational performance and provides a link between the market and operating performance. This approach uses information from the market to forecast the minimum level of incremental operating performance required

Step 1	Step 2	Step 3	Step 4
Define current operations and growth values	Determine the expected return on growth value	Derive expected annual EVA growth	Compare actual versus expected EVA growth values

FIGURE 4.2 EVA-Based Postacquisition Audit

TABLE 4.4 Derivation of Requisite EVA Growth

A	Growth value	$ 1,000
B	WACC	8%
C	Return on growth value (A × B)	$ 80
D	EVA growth cap factor (1 + 1/B)	13.5
	Annual EVA growth required (C/D)	$ 5.93

to justify any premium paid.[25] This predetermined benchmark is used as a measure of success or failure against the actual operational performance of the combined entity.

Per Figure 4.2, start by defining the improvements in performance over and above those that were already expected by the market, from the combination of the two businesses. Separate the market value into current operations value (COV), or present value of the pro forma net operating profit after tax (NOPAT) capitalized as a perpetuity and the GV or any remaining market value, which we attribute to the present value of EVA growth). The combined company can provide adequate returns on its COV by maintaining the current level of NOPAT. Returns on the GV can only be achieved through EVA growth (NPV-positive growth in volume, margins, utilization).

The final step in the process is to estimate the required annual EVA growth (Table 4.4). This is the benchmark that will be compared against any actual EVA growth achieved. The present value of the annual growth can be capitalized by dividing it by the capitalization factor (1 + 1/WACC). This is the total wealth created, or destroyed, by the merger that can be compared with the initial market reaction.

HOW "SERIAL ACQUIRERS" CREATE VALUE

Markets reward serial acquirers for their growth strategies, providing further empirical support for the advantages of a dynamic M&A strategy over the longer term. We define serial acquirers as companies that executed more than five M&A transactions, including divestitures, from 1992 to 2004; we define one-time acquirers as companies that executed only one M&A transaction, including divestiture. Serial acquirers outperform one-time acquirers across longer-term time horizons.

Successful serial acquirers tend to incorporate many of our previously discussed key success factors in their acquisition strategy. For example, serial acquirer acquisition tends to be more attractive. Their targets demonstrate higher growth, profitability, and valuations. Serial acquirers are twice as likely to make acquisitions of targets with revenue less than 25 percent of their own revenue when compared to one-time acquirers; though in absolute terms, they were similar.

One study of sample serial acquirers found that 82 percent of all acquirers chose targets that had a relative size of less than 20 percent, that 76 percent used cash (hybrid deals are included in cash), and that 85 percent acquired private companies (includes sale of subsidiary).[26] Other studies found that serial acquirers tended to buy targets with faster revenue growth.[27]

Serial acquirers exhibit more conservative financial policies, providing increased financial strength to support business growth. Serial acquirers generally have higher liquidity relative to other acquirers, and similar financial leverage, but stronger credit quality (in part due to size and qualitative factors). Serial acquirers tend to maintain lower dividends and share repurchase program levels, likely due to the availability of reinvestment opportunities.

Active Portfolio Management Case Study: Danaher

Danaher (DHR) is one of a select few stocks that has outperformed Warren Buffett's Berkshire Hathaway over the past many years. This $19 billion diversified industrial company, has employed a mix of acquisitions and selective divestitures to beat market indices by a wide margin. The company complements organic growth (4 to 6 percent compound annual growth rate or CAGR) with an active portfolio approach that balances divestitures, bolt-on acquisitions, and new platform acquisitions to achieve total compound annual revenue growth of 15.5 percent from 1987 to 2004. M&A activity over the last 10 years exceeded 60 acquisitions and divestitures, totaling about $12 billion, which comprises businesses acquired in the last five years constitute over 60 percent of 2003 revenue.

DHR has employed a disciplined strategy for creating value for the longer term. The majority of DHR's acquisitions have been in the same, or similar industries, allowing the company to apply its business processes to achieve revenue and cost synergies quickly and successfully.

TABLE 4.5   Select DHR Transactions

Announcement Date	Business	Value	% of Market Capitalization
March-04	Kaltenbach & Voigt	425	3.0%
December-03	Gendex	100	0.8%
December-03	Radiometer	640	4.9%
November-02	Willett International	110	1.1%
September-02	Thomson Industries	165	1.9%
February-02	API Heat Transfer	65	0.7%
January-02	Videojet	400	4.5%
December-01	Gilbarco	325	3.8%
December-01	Viridor Instrumentation	150	1.6%

Bolt-on acquisitions are focused primarily on smaller, complementary, and synergistic targets that can be immediately integrated into the company. DHR's recent acquisitions (Table 4.5) have been less than 5 percent of the company's market capitalization.

Platform acquisitions are attractive product and market opportunities with superior growth and profitability characteristics. Consistent with our own findings and with our discussion of dilution, DHR does not shy away from higher value target opportunities. It has recently used M&A to establish a new platform in the medical technology industry although it classified the venture as an expansion of the larger process and environmental controls platform. Other recent acquisitions, like Radiometer in 2003, also had higher margins.

Financing has come largely from internal cash generation and the company makes it a priority to maintain its "A" credit rating. DHR plans to continue its successful portfolio strategy.

"Real Options In M&A" Case Study: Anheuser-Busch

Anheuser-Busch (BUD), the world's largest brewer, has earned a total shareholder return over the past 10 years of 16 percent (versus 11 percent for the S&P500). This $40 billion giant has defied convention by delivering strong returns (compound average growth in net operating profit after tax of 5.5 percent, with international income growing 400 percent since 1998) in an ostensibly low-growth business. Revenue (78 percent domestic) growth over the period averaged 1.9 percent.

Almost 10 years ago, BUD initiated a bold new strategy. BUD divested a diverse set of unrelated businesses, including a baseball team and stadium. After briefly shrinking the company, BUD initiated a series of investments in emerging markets (e.g., Brazil, Chile, China, and Mexico) with ostensibly better growth prospects than the domestic market but with more risk. BUD typically bought minority equity stakes, through joint venture vehicles, with cash, technology, access to the company brands, and U.S. distribution. In return, it gained access to growth and more brands for its portfolio. This new strategy represented an application of "real options thinking" in mergers and acquisitions.[28] BUD was developing three types of valuable real options: call options on growth, nested options to stage or defer, and put options to abandon.

BUD created a series of nested call options on growing emerging markets. The company could test the waters, learn the local markets and refine the execution of its company strategy for the local market accordingly, before committing more capital. A conventional market entry would require a $2 billion initial investment. The company could "call" or exercise the option, if the present value of expected future cash flows exceeded the cost of the investment, by buying out the remaining equity.

Options to stage or defer capital investment, through the use of the joint venture vehicle, avoided the large opportunity cost and risk of "lumpy" capital investments. Smaller discrete investments could be metered in, subject to an on-going evaluation of capital cost and availability, market opportunity, joint venture economics, and perceived risk.

BUD created valuable put options to exit more easily and cost effectively (which it exercised in Brazil and Chile). Minority investments limit the downside exposure to the initial option cost (a few million dollars) rather than the full cost of underlying assets (a few billion dollars). Furthermore, they create an opportunity for capital recovery (without creating a new entrant to the market) by selling back to the existing local partner, if required.

The market has recognized the real option value created, with total shareholder return (TSR) outpacing profit growth, multiples expanding, and the proportion of BUD's enterprise value predicated on growth expanding from 23 percent in December 1994 to 59 percent in December 2004.

FINANCIAL POLICY CONSIDERATIONS

Financial policy appears to be a second-order issue, in terms of what types of policies are most consistent with winning strategies. Optimal financial policies (financial liquidity, financial leverage, and shareholder distributions) tend to differ between higher and lower growth businesses. Industry factors also drive different common practices between sectors, leading to opportunity in WACC and capitalization rates.

Although financial liquidity might affect the incidence of deals for a company, liquidity is not a meaningful factor in success. There is no statistically significant difference in the liquidity profiles of winners or losers, long-term or short-term, with a wide dispersion in the data.

With respect to financial leverage, lower leverage is associated with longer-term success, where the difference is more meaningful. Lower levels of financial leverage provide an advantageous bargaining position and an increased financial strength to execute an acquisitive growth strategy. The lower levels enhance the ability to use cash and debt, factors associated with success. Interestingly, highly leveraged targets tend to fare poorly because they tend to be less profitable and more likely to involve stock. Shareholder losses in diversification are partly a function of firm leverage.[29] Industry factors drive different practices, where suboptimal capital structures increase WACC and reduce value. Though independent capitalization of different businesses may lead to more appropriate capital structures, advantages can be offset due to the significance of size in credit quality and cost.

Statistically, dividend policy is only a marginally meaningful factor in success.

FINANCING GROWTH

Financing growth typically raises all of the same questions as when refinancing or contemplating optimal capital structure—debt versus equity or equity-linked, term structure, fixed versus floating, currency, seniority, optionality, and so forth. We see three common pitfalls that confound the deal financing decision and interfere with the investment decision:

1. To view the structure as a separate and distinct entity, apart from the context of the buyer's existing capital structure
2. To assume new financings are the only method to affect change toward the optimal or most appropriate capital structure
3. To view the value of an acquisition as being dependent on how it is to be financed, with the benchmark for value being the WACC

Though incremental analysis is the foundation to any discounted cash flow (DCF) or NPV analysis, liability management and the entire field of risk management require us to look at any situation in its entire context. Ideal acquisition funding depends in part on the existing capital structure plus any debt being assumed as part of the deal.

For example, if credit rating targets are a concern, possibly a constraint, for deal financing, then pro forma ratios will be critical to the amount and sources of cash that can be used to minimize stock in the structure. Quantification of existing excess cash plus the cash available from operations 12 to 18 months postdeal will depend on the total company.

If coverage appears to be the ratings constraint, then low coupon, even zero coupon, funding might be employed, such as commercial paper (CP), samurai bonds, and convertibles. If leverage is more the concern, then perhaps a high-equity hybrid, mandatory convertible, or a 100-year bond could be employed.

Commercial paper might be employed if funds from operations are intended for debt reduction to achieve certain ratios within 12 months postdeal. CP and bank debt facilitate debt amortization. Optimal incremental floating rate exposure depends in part on the amount, term, and type of existing floating rate exposure.

Changes to the fixed-floating mix need not await, or be linked to, issuance. Swaps, swap settlement, mirror-swaps and T-locks can be employed in an accounting-friendly manner (hedge accounting compliant) to alter the duration and the fixed-floating mix irrespective of issuance.

Acquisition financing terms are typically on-the-run maturities (i.e., 5-, 10-, and 30-year terms) for straight debt to avoid complication and ensure timely and efficient execution. However, because convertibles tap alternative pools of capital, they might be employed for off-the-run maturities (e.g., 3 and 7).

The existing capital structure is an important consideration to avoid maturity gaps and maturity towers to reduce refinancing risk and optimize the term structure of the liability ladder. Maturities and put dates should target existing maturity gaps and avoid existing maturity towers. Avoiding call options to reduce cost is safer than adding puts from a liquidity management perspective. However, symmetrically matched puts and calls can be employed to truncate the tenor of a long-dated convertible.

Empirically, cash deals tend to outperform stock deals. Longer-term cash deal outcomes were more likely to be winners, and our short-term stock deal outcomes were less prevalent among our winners. Studies corroborate the association between cash deals and success.[30] Announcement returns are positively related to the proportion of bank debt in a deal. One study of acquisitions found that banks extend financing in 70 percent of the tender offers and finance the entire tender offer in half of these takeovers. The three-day announcement returns for cash tender offers financed entirely by banks average 4 percent and are statistically significant. In comparison, cash tender offers financed partially by banks or those financed entirely by financial slack are associated with small and statistically insignificant announcement returns. The authors suggest that bank debt performs an important certification and monitoring role for acquirers in tender offers and are most important for poorly performing acquirers and acquirers facing substantial informational asymmetries.[31]

While the use of stock may signal a belief by managers that their stock is fully valued, the use of cash and debt signals confidence in future cash flow and promotes increased discipline. The cash cost of servicing debt creates an explicit hurdle, whereas equity introduces a hurdle rate that is merely an opportunity cost.

However, acquirers with strong, long-run stock performance are more likely to use their stock as an acquisition currency; acquirers with weaker stock are more reluctant to use their stock and instead opt for cash. And stock deals hedge the stock market values and execution risk. Cash transactions require acquirer shareholders to take the entire risk of realizing synergies, while stock transactions syndicate this risk across both shareholder bases. Thus, the decision between cash and stock financing directly affects the distribution of post M&A synergy benefits.

CHAPTER 5

Cash and The Optimal
Capital Structure

Global cash and near-cash balances are at record levels and continue to grow, topping $2,700 billion for all NYSE and NASDAQ listed companies and growing 24 percent annually. U.S. exchange listed cash holdings are up 770 percent since 1994. On an industry sector basis (not shown), the largest increases came from media (1,700 percent), power (1,360 percent), and telecommunications (1,300 percent). Cash and cash equivalents constitute a record proportion of corporate balance sheets, now at 17 percent of total corporate assets, about 20 percent as large as aggregate corporate revenue. This "problem" is pervasive across most industry sectors, attracting research analyst scrutiny in the Americas, Europe, and Asia.

And until recently the debt and equity markets seemed united in their support of excess liquidity insurance against risk and dry powder for growth. But with balance sheets largely mended, volatility easing, and the outlook for corporate cash flow on the rise, the need for (and benefit of) excess liquidity has been reduced.

Historically, much of this cash was "trapped" overseas for tax reasons but in United States, passage of The American Job Creation Act of 2004 has created a one-time window of opportunity to redeploy capital to more productive uses.

Increasingly, the optimal capital structure question is expanding to include the left-hand side of the balance sheet. *It is now as much a question of cash balances and pension assets as it is about financial leverage.* Amidst the prospect of rising capital costs, debt and equity, the opportunity cost of being overcapitalized will be a greater burden to financial performance (ROE, ROCE, and EVA) and an overhang on intrinsic value (net present value or NPV) and market multiples.

We propose a decapitalization strategy that balances the competing needs of all stakeholders, that is, maintaining sufficient operating liquidity and dry powder for growth, while enhancing both credit profiles and stock returns. *Balanced decapitalizations*—a reduction in capital employed that is funded from a balanced blend of both debt and equity to produce the desired financial strength—now offer compelling economics.

Much momentum is occurring for decapitalizations, triggered by analysts and investors, distribution actions by other companies, and a general public concern around corporate governance and the stewardship of capital. Since the highly anticipated Microsoft announcement in July 2004, we have witnessed boards worldwide and across industry sectors review this issue. Optimal capital structure has never been so passionately debated since the issue has been broadened to encompass the left-hand side of the balance sheet.

TRENDS AND IMPLICATIONS

Many factors have contributed to the current condition. High volatility and a difficult operating environment created the need for excess liquidity. Ratings agencies and analysts have been vocal advocates of excess liquidity after having been burned by many high-profile corporate liquidity crunches. And historically low interest rates reduced the opportunity cost of being overcapitalized. But the tides have shifted and new economic forces have created the impetus for change.

Balance Sheets Mended

Leverage and credit quality are on the mend. A reduction in financial leverage creates less need for balance sheet liquidity. Total adjusted leverage for all NYSE and NASDAQ listed companies declined from 51 percent debt/capital in 2002 to 39 percent in 2004. Global speculative grade defaults fell from 8 percent to 1 percent.

And while American issuers are evaluated on a gross debt basis, European and Asian issuers are frequently evaluated on a net debt basis, which would give an even more striking view. On a net debt basis, NYSE and NASDAQ net leverage was down from 33 percent to 13 percent debt/capital over the same 2002 to 2004 period.

The spike in financial leverage at the start of the decade was exacerbated by additional obligations of unfunded postretirement health benefits and underfunded pension plans. Many ratings agency analysts more formally adopted methodologies that explicitly adjusted financial ratios for these obligations.

Pension underfunding, a considerable overhang on credit ratings in recent years, has improved tremendously from voluntary contributions, a rebound in the equity markets, and reduced pension liabilities (due to higher discount rates). One rating agency report estimates the aggregate pension position has improved by 50 percent from its lowest position in 2002, but has still not recovered to the level of the prior decade.[1] Postretirement health benefits have been reduced through curbs in benefits as well as the effects of higher discount rates in the calculation of accumulated projected benefit obligations.

Volatility Down

In addition to financial leverage, cash flow volatility is also down, reducing the need for excess liquidity. The U.S. equities implied stock volatility index (VIX) is down, illustrating the broad reduction in volatility (down roughly 70 percent from its 2002 peak) that is analogous to the reduction in corporate operating cash flow volatility that is well underway.

Prospects Up

Not only has cash flow volatility declined, but the prospects for future corporate cash flows have also improved, again reducing the need for excess liquidity. For example, consensus earnings estimates for 2004 are up 550 percent over 2002 levels, and 2005 is estimated to be up an additional 15 percent. The combined effect of reduced leverage, reduced volatility, and enhanced future cash flows is a dramatically lower cash balance required for adequate operating liquidity.

Rising Rates

While the need for excess liquidity has declined, the cost of excess liquidity has risen. With Treasury rates already rising and widely expected to continue to rise, the cost of capital is climbing. For example, 10-year Treasuries, after bottoming out at 3.1 percent in June 2003, are nearing 5 percent and approach 6 percent a few years out on the forward curve. Though interest income on LIBOR-based excess cash will also rise, the negative carry between WACC and after-tax interest income will worsen. The opportunity cost of excess capital creates a large and growing drag on returns on capital, economic profits (EPs), and net present value.

Stock Price Pressure

With many stocks languishing and investors getting restless, investors and research analysts have been vocally calling for large returns of capital, a pervasive phenomenon across industries and countries. With the invisible hand at work, capital is a scarce resource that must be freed to seek out its most productive users and most promising uses. We are witnessing a pervasive trend of new or upsized share repurchase programs, increased dividends and dividend initiations, and even a return of the one-time special dividend, to eliminate historically large cash balances that accumulated in the wake of the recent period of difficult economic conditions.

HOW MUCH IS TOO MUCH?

Corporate cash and cash equivalents is a large and growing number on most balance sheets today. But many analysts are now suggesting that this is a large and unmanaged number. Only recently have we seen such interest in determining the right level of cash. The search for optimal capital structure has been expanded to include assets, such as cash and marketable securities and corporate pension assets.

Cash balances vary widely. Domestic cash balances of U.S.-listed companies range from $3 million at the 10th percentile to $930 million at the 90th percentile, with a mean of $691 million. Even after adjusting for variation in company size, cash ranged from about 1 percent of revenue at the 10th percentile, to 143 percent at the 90th percentile. On an industry sector basis, the largest cash to sales positions are in healthcare (724 percent), technology (73 percent), and media (48 percent). We obtain similar insights with other size criteria, such as cash as percentage of assets or enterprise value.

To manage cash balances better as part of the optimal capital structure solution, companies have started employing methods to determine acceptable, if not optimal, cash balances, that is, cash positions within industry norms. Typical approaches involve industry benchmarking and rules of thumb plus whatever guidance is made available by ratings agencies and analysts. We refine both of these approaches, adding multivariate regression and simulation-based liquidity models to provide guidance and facilitate management of cash balances.

Benchmarking and Heuristics

The most common approach to managing cash balances is to benchmark against industry comparables. This approach implies that cross-sectional average industry levels are at a rational level. Industry surveys, often highlighted in trade magazines, are a perennial source of this type of information. Conventions, often industry-specific or company-specific, fall into this category; 2 percent of revenue, six months of fixed cost, 12 months of R&D, $1 billion, or the cost of two fabrication plants. Though the original source of these heuristics is frequently unknown, and the underlying logic often weak, they remain the traditional complement to industry benchmarking.

REPATRIATION POLICY

In the case of many American large-cap technology, industrial and healthcare companies, a large proportion of excess cash has been trapped overseas as earnings that have not been economically viable to repatriate due to prohibitive taxes. These funds remained parked overseas, awaiting foreign investment opportunities.

But recent U.S. tax reform effectively created a one-year window to repatriate funds at an effective U.S. federal income tax rate of 5.25 percent. The American Jobs Creation Act of 2004 is estimated to provide $137 billion in tax reductions, over the next ten years, for businesses and individuals. The Act, signed into law October 22, 2004, is comprised of four elements:

- Tax relief for U.S.-based manufacturing activities ($77 billion)
- Reforms of multinational businesses ($43 billion)
- Four dozen more targeted items of business income tax relief ($10 billion)
- Individual tax cuts and excise tax reforms ($7 billion)

The Act allows a U.S. corporation to elect to deduct 85 percent of certain cash dividends it receives from its controlled foreign corporations (CFCs), either during the taxpayer's last tax year, which begins before the date of enactment, or during its first tax year which begins during the one-year period beginning on such date. Cash dividends includes cash amounts treated as dividends under sections 302 or 304 of the Internal Revenue Code (IRC). The dividend must meet several criteria to be considered deductible.

For example, if the dividend is paid directly or indirectly from funds borrowed from a related person (other than another CFC), such as the U.S. shareholder, the net increase in CFC indebtedness to such lenders reduces the deductible amount of the dividend. A CFC cash dividend received by the shareholder during the election year is eligible only to the extent it exceeds an average of the annual sums of dividends received during the base period. The base period generally is comprised of the five taxable years ending on or before June 30, 2003, discarding the years with the highest and lowest annual amounts. Eligible dividends generally cannot exceed $500 million unless described as permanently reinvested outside the United States in the corporation's audited financial statement filed with the SEC on or before June 30, 2003. If the applicable financial statement does not specify the amount of earnings permanently reinvested outside the U.S. but does specify a tax liability attributable to such earnings, the amount eligible is the amount of the tax liability divided by 35 percent. Specific rules govern allowable foreign tax credits and deductions and the computation of the alternative minimum tax. The minimum floor for taxable income is fifteen percent of the dividends.

One important area is that of allowable uses of repatriated funds. The amount equal to the dividend must be invested in the U.S. pursuant to an approved domestic reinvestment plan before the dividend is paid. The domestic reinvestment plan must provide for the reinvestment of the dividend in the United States (excluding executive compensation), including the funding of worker hiring and training, infrastructure, research and development, capital investments, or financial stabilization for the purposes of job retention or creation.

Financial stabilization is generally expected to include bond repurchases, but ideally ought *to have also* included stock repurchases. Just as bond repurchases enhance a credit profile and provide demand for market supply in the debt capital markets, stock repurchases enhance an equity profile and provide demand for market supply in the equity capital markets. Liquidity and adequate returns are essential to orderly debt and equity capital markets.

Stock repurchases help to avoid overcapitalization, and thus improve return on equity (ROE), return on capital employed (ROCE), economic profit (EP) and fundamental intrinsic value. The market multiple of the firm will rise as returns on equity and total capital employed rise. A more highly valued firm will be more competitive and better positioned for growth in the competitive global business landscape.

Finally, stock repurchases are required if optimal capital structure is to be maintained while repurchasing bonds. Businesses require the ability to perform both debt and equity repurchases to achieve and maintain optimal leverage and keep the weighted average cost of capital optimized and at a competitive level.

Multifactor Models

Multivariate regression models are a more tailored form of industry benchmarking that control for variation among companies of significant factors empirically known to be determinants of corporate cash holdings.

For example, company size is a key determinant of cash holdings. Larger companies don't require as much cash, because their cash flows tend to be more diversified, reducing volatility, and the need for operating liquidity. They are more likely to have more opportunities to find deferrable costs internally, reducing the need for external financing. Larger companies can typically raise capital more easily and cost effectively, reducing the need for excess liquidity. Larger companies also tend to be stronger credits, again making financing easier when needed.

To account for variation in company size, we tend to benchmark cash as a percentage of revenue, rather than absolute dollar amounts (although this information can be useful, especially with respect to dry powder for acquisitions). But there are diminishing returns to scale, and empirically, a natural log (Ln) function more appropriately controls for the size effect than any linear factor, whether it be a percentage of revenue, assets, or enterprise value.

Multivariate regression models provide a form of benchmarking that controls for the numerous key determinants of corporate cash holdings (e.g., size, growth prospects, R&D intensity, competitive dynamics, volatility, and financial leverage).[2] However, because these types of models predict an average level of cash, they assume that what companies are doing (albeit after controlling for various factors) is optimal. Therefore, we recommend a multiyear data set, rather than any cross-sectional snapshot. A sector may drift into periods of overcapitalization and undercapitalization but is more likely to mean revert toward optimal levels over time.

Agency Guidance

Rating agency guidance on cash balances has lagged behind that which is available for leverage. There is little information, it is not specific or actionable, little is quantitative, fact-based, or data-driven, and the conceptual frameworks are not fully developed. Short-term ratings, though primarily focused on obligations, look to cash balances as an important factor to determine ratings. An issuer's operating cash flow, current and anticipated cash balances, internal resources, alternative sources of liquidity, and cash flow projections are all central to the analysis of short-term credit.[3]

Recognizing the need for more guidance, the agencies have targeted this area for continued development.[4] Speculative grade liquidity ratings are a good first step, with a conceptual framework that defines adequate operating liquidity as the cash buffer required to ensure no need for external sources over the next four quarters. Speculative grade liquidity (SGL) ratings reflect the issuer's ability to generate cash internally and the reliance and availability of external resources, additionally SGL ratings are not mapped to long-term ratings; therefore, issuers with similar senior implied ratings might have different SGL ratings.[5]

Anecdotal guidance is most prevalent in technology where large cash balances are encouraged. For example, we have heard some suggest that cash balances must exceed total liabilities for A-rated technology credits. In one case, the indicated cash balance is many, many times larger. The apparent logic is that higher business risk warrants a large permanent cash balance to provide offsetting cushion. But there is neither rationale for how large, nor can we find empirical evidence to support any discernable impact on risk from cash holdings. In fact, our analysis found no empirical evidence of a dampening effect on industry specific asset Betas deriving from large cash holdings. For example, in the biotechnology sector we find a near zero correlation between cash and sales and asset Beta ($R^2 = 0.5$ percent, Standard Error $= 0.32$). And finally, this rationale overlooks company-specific factors, such as backup lines and facilities, equity crossholdings and other potential sources of liquidity, and the nature of discretionary or variable capital and expenses.

Stress Testing and Liquidity Models

Stress testing is an attempt to quantify, from the perspective of the company and its cash flows, how much cash is required to provide adequate operating liquidity, and to potentially prefund any near-term needs (commercial paper and near-term maturities, puts, near-term capital expenditures, near-term cash acquisition opportunities). Cash flow projections, typically based on the consensus outlook, are stressed with worst-case scenarios to evaluate the need for additional cash reserves. Under most cases for evaluating liquidity, the time horizon is four quarters, and we assume capital markets may be accessed for longer-term needs.

Monte Carlo simulations effectively automate our normal course sensitivity analysis, developing thousands of cash flow scenarios, based on a few reasonable assumptions. Building on the speculative grade liquidity rating concept, Monte Carlo simulations can estimate the required cash holdings for self-sufficiency at any given statistical confidence interval, or to predict the probability and severity of cash draw for any given level of operating cash balance.

For example, in Figure 5.1 we simulated quarterly cash flows from a consensus outlook with 14 percent volatility in top-line growth and 6 percent earnings before interest, tax, depreciation, and amortization (EBITDA) margin volatility (both normally distributed and based on an analysis of historical company and comparable data). In this instance, we found that a target cash balance of roughly \$1 billion (4 percent of revenue) provided this company with adequate operating liquidity with a nearly zero probability of draw (at 99 percent confidence).

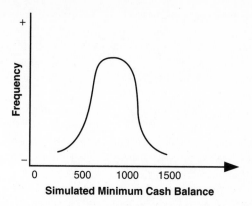

FIGURE 5.1   Stochastic Solution to Requisite Operating Liquidity

There are many important practical limitations to this framework and its application. Competitive dynamics (e.g., competition for acquisition targets; customer, supplier, or labor bargaining power) and other strategic considerations may well warrant larger cash positions than what is required for normal operating liquidity. Many companies with limited access to the capital markets, therefore, require more capital prefunding (e.g., cases of extreme leverage, early stage profitability, or constraints imposed by insiders).

The nature of volatility assumptions is such that catastrophic scenarios well outside the boundaries of historical outcomes will be understated by simulation analysis. Therefore, manually developed shock cases remain the best way to stress test cash flows and develop contingencies for catastrophic loss.

Finally, in the case of smaller companies (e.g., less than $100 million revenue) or newer companies (e.g., fewer than 20 quarters of relevant public financial statements), the necessary consensus outlook and volatility assumptions will be insufficiently robust to provide reliable guidance. In these cases, simple cash flow modeling and stress testing, supplemented with benchmarking time series data for close comparables, will provide the most reliable and intuitive guidance.

THE COSTS AND BENEFITS OF EXCESS CASH

The costs and benefits of excess cash are highly variable. Though the costs are opportunity costs, they can be quantified. Many of the benefits are strategic in nature and, therefore, difficult to quantify.

Operational and Strategic Benefits

The presence of excess cash and liquidity has more recently become recognized for its advantages by investors, rating agencies, and debt and equity analysts not only in the technology sector, but also in healthcare, industrials, and others.

Cash provides an important buffer against operating volatility and unexpected operating cash flow shortfalls, to lower the probability of financial distress and to ensure self-sufficiency and the ability to invest in growth through difficult quarters. Excess cash balances may be used as a buffer against uninsurable shortfalls.

Cash provides dry powder for acquisitions and other growth investments, which can be important in consolidating industries or for highly acquisitive companies, especially where cash deals predominate.

Enhanced financial strength have other strategic advantages, including competitive advantage against market entrants through a greater ability to engage in aggressive pricing, increased bargaining strength with suppliers from a greater threat of vertical integration or switching, and increased bargaining strength with labor through a greater capacity to sustain prolonged labor action.

Some research suggests that excess cash signals the presence of excess opportunity and the ability to exercise these real options in the future.[6] Thus, any action to reduce excess cash position should be carefully positioned with the capital markets to avoid any negative signal regarding future investment opportunity.

Finally, excess cash can be a substitute for expensive outside financings, thereby reducing transactions costs. Companies tend to use cash to manage the significant fixed costs associated with capital raising activities.

Agency Costs

The risk that excess cash will create a tempting source of funds for badly considered acquisitions or ventures is a well-documented one—the subsequent economic cost has been coined agency cost.[7] And consistent with agency cost arguments, persistent excessive cash holdings have been shown empirically to impair operating performance and lead to a greater risk of investment in negative NPV projects. The loss in value attributed to overinvestment is caused by the cash holding being easily turned into bad acquisitions or investments thus pointing on the dark side of liquidity; greater asset liquidity increases the potential conflict between managers and shareholders.[8] This is another reason why excess cash tends to draw the attention of hostile bidders.

Our own investigation found the strongest correlation between sustained levels of excess cash and underperformance to be in the energy and utilities sector, as well as the broad category of technology-media-telecom (weighted toward telecom).

Interestingly, we found the opposite to be true in the healthcare sector that is, higher levels of performance were associated with sustained levels of excess cash. This offers clear support for our preceding rationale of the importance of strategic liquidity. The higher organic growth prospects, acquisition growth, and R&D intensity associated with this sector seem to make our results especially intuitive.

Opportunity Cost

Despite the strategic benefits, textbook theory suggests corporations should seek to minimize excess cash to minimize the opportunity cost of capital employed and maximize shareholder value. The after-tax returns on cash are insufficient to meet the required return on capital, the WACC, and represent a negative NPV investment. And as interest rates climb, the gap between the returns on cash and weighted average cost of capital will widen. Not only does excess cash not earn the corporate WACC, but we also found no evidence to support the use of a lower hurdle rate for this asset class. The cost of cash equity is as high; we found no support for the notion that prolonged periods of excess cash holdings lead to lower levered betas.

For example, among the 180 listed biotechnology companies there is no empirical evidence of a dampening effect on industry specific asset betas deriving from large cash holdings. This is based on last twelve months (LTM) figures for cash and cash equivalents, revenue, market value of equity, debt/enterprise value, Barra betas and an assumed marginal tax rate of 35 percent. Company-levered betas may be adjusted for debt but there is no evidence of the need to make a similar adjustment for cash. In the biotechnology sector there is zero correlation among cash and sales and asset beta.

Nor is the amount of equity appreciably lowered. There is no support for the notion that excess cash holdings increase debt capacity (there should be little equity required to back this low-risk asset class) when credit analysis is focused on gross leverage ratios. The rating agencies in United States tend to focus credit analysis on a gross debt basis rather than a net debt basis. As share repurchases grow in Europe and Asia, we expect this view to grow internationally. Finally, though the matched maturity cost of low-duration, low-risk funds is low, this overlooks reinvestment risk and the overall weighted average cost of capital.

We conclude that there is no reason to believe excess cash should be held to a lower hurdle than WACC, and that in the absence of strategic and operational benefits, represents a negative NPV investment. Therefore, actions to reduce excess liquidity, such as the two recent self-tenders by The Limited, have been well received in the market and should give cause for consideration. Companies that have taken action to reduce excess cash tend to receive positive market reactions especially if the distributions are large, one-time events.

Case Study: High Rating Or "High Yield" Strategy?

On July 11, after an exhaustive review of its strategic alternatives, Citizens Communications (CZN) announced its intention to dramatically alter its financial strategy, with a special dividend of $2 per common share and the initiation of a regular quarterly dividend of $0.25 per share (73 percent payout ratio, 21 percent yield).

Though CZN's annual dividend represents a free cash flow payout of approximately 73 percent, the payout in 2004 rises to an even higher 207 percent including the special dividend.

Upon announcement, S&P lowered CZN's senior issuer rating two notches from BBB to BB+ (from investment grade to speculative grade). The downgrade was based on reduced financial flexibility due to the increased fixed charge servicing and an expectation that any further deleveraging would be difficult.

However, postannouncement, CZN total shareholder returns (21 percent) have outperformed both A-rated telecom peers (13 percent) and the S&P500 (0.7 percent), begging the question of whether a high-yield strategy might be better than a high-rating strategy, at least in this business.

HOW THE MARKET VIEWS EXCESS CASH

Little empirical evidence exists on the valuation effects of excess liquidity. The few working papers and published studies on corporate cash holdings tend to focus on the determinants and consequences of cash holdings from an operational perspective rather than a capital markets perspective. However, one study cited a stock market valuation premium: Companies with persistent excess cash levels were associated with higher excess enterprise values.[9] We have observed similar results but suggest this effect is most pronounced during challenging economic periods and in certain industries with significant growth prospects that are more often challenged by the effects of business cycles and exogenous volatility.

Where Too Much Is a Good Thing

Valuation effects are most pronounced within the industrial, telecom, and media sectors, where the companies that sustained excess cash holdings enjoyed a substantive premium valuation over the valuation of median cash holders in the same industry. These sectors are characterized by higher volatility and business cycle exposure, larger capital requirements, and more significant growth prospects than the sectors where pervasive excess cash holdings do not lead to valuation premiums (power, energy, and consumer).

The 15 to 45 percent premium enjoyed by excess cash holders supports earlier research that found the market will, at times, reward excess liquidity. But this is not true in every industry; however, with several sectors receiving a valuation discount for holding excess cash.

Where Too Much Is a Bad Thing

Furthermore, the research to date has focused on data drawn from recessionary periods where the market is more likely to reward excess liquidity. This effect is likely due to the protection against financial distress and the strategic value attributable to cash during times of economic difficulty. Future areas for study should include periods of strong economic growth.

However, anecdotally, the positive excess returns associated with the recent spate of decapitalization announcements would suggest that the market premium on excess cash has faded and may have completely disappeared. We expect that as economic conditions recover, the marginal premium awarded to excess cash holders will diminish as the insurance premium and strategic values become less important.

Companies and sectors that trade at relatively high valuation multiples are most likely to benefit from a financial policy that, during periods of economic uncertainty and challenge, directs more capital to excess liquidity to capitalize on the insurance value of excess cash holdings. But in periods of economic recovery and growth, these same companies and sectors are the ones that will benefit most from actions to redeploy this capital, ideally in the business where it can create the most value. Alternatively, in the event of no near-term uses, a balanced decapitalization of debt reduction and share repurchases can also offer compelling economics.

OPTIMAL CAPITAL ALLOCATION

An optimal allocation of capital considers and balances the competing needs and objectives of all stakeholders within the enduring value maximization objective. Analysts, investors, and other stakeholders will all seek to determine whether the company has appropriately considered and balanced their needs to support its strategy. The existing capital structure must be evaluated to determine the appropriate prioritization and scaling of needs, including operating liquidity, dry powder, pensions and leverage, dividends, and share buybacks.

Operating Liquidity

As discussed, a certain level of cash work-in-process (WIP) buffer is required to fill the system and provide adequate operating liquidity, normal course funding self-sufficiency to ensure continued operations without undue risk of financial distress. Operating liquidity needs are increased by higher operating volatility, lower expected operating cash flows, and higher fixed costs, including dividends and debt servicing.

Dry Powder

With valuations predicated on profitable growth, growth capital represents the use of cash with the greatest potential upside for many companies. Dry powder can provide backup liquidity for event risk. However, prefunding growth opportunities by holding excess cash creates a drag on ROCE, economic profit, and NPV; that is likely to worsen as rates rise and cash balances grow. Furthermore, though operating liquidity needs may be estimated with cash flow simulation analysis, there is no analytic framework to quantify optimal holdings for dry powder. Dry powder needs are increased by larger growth expectations and prospects, or greater anticipated challenges associated with capital raising when opportunities arise.

Leverage and WACC

Similar to holding cash for growth, debt reduction creates a source of dry powder by freeing debt capacity and improving financial strength. In the current interest rate environment, this can be less NPV negative than holding idle cash. However, debt reduction faces practical constraints, such as illiquid or noncallable debt, potential book losses, and the additional cost of swap unwinds. Moreover, many companies have taken advantage of a prolonged low rate environment and refinanced their most uneconomic debt with new debt at attractive terms. Debt reduction can also face diminishing returns due to potential credit ceilings on the rating, due to size, industry, and other qualitative factors. Finally, where net debt treatment is enjoyed, debt reduction from excess cash offers no credit enhancement and eliminates the real option to use the cash for other purposes.

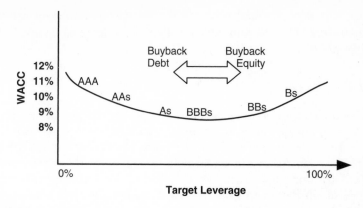

FIGURE 5.2 WACC Considerations

Optimally capitalized companies should balance share repurchases with debt reduction to maintain their optimal mix of debt and equity. Figure 5.2 illustrates corporate WACC as a function of financial leverage, that proportion of enterprise value capitalized with debt. Assuming the starting point for most companies today is their optimal capital structure, if debt reduction outpaces share repurchases, the company moves (to the left) toward a stronger credit profile but incurs a higher weighted average cost of capital due to the larger component of higher cost equity. Similarly, if share repurchases outpace debt reduction, the company moves (to the right) toward a weaker credit and incurs a higher weighted average cost of capital due to the fading expected value of the tax shield and the costs associated with a higher risk of financial distress.

Similarly, overleveraged companies should overemphasize debt reduction in their mix of bond and stock repurchases, while underleveraged companies should be overemphasizing stock repurchases in their mix of bond and stock repurchases to advance the company toward optimal capital structure through a balanced decapitalization.

Pension Funding

Though pension funding has been greatly restored from the many factors discussed, this potential use of proceeds may still be attractive in some jurisdictions. In some cases, prefunding is tax deductible. In many cases, it will reduce an overhang on the credit profile, creating a tax efficient route to store dry powder. Furthermore, accounting changes are underway to include net underfunded pension positions as debt rather than a mere footnote. Though clearly any degree of overfunding is generally undesirable, rating agency dialogue can be most problematic when funding is below the 80 percent level. However, in some jurisdictions, such as Germany, pension liabilities are typically not funded.

Share Repurchases

Share repurchases offer an efficient mechanism for redeploying excess capital that does not earn its cost of capital, and is not otherwise immediately needed. They are an efficient way of making changes to the capital structure. Share repurchases can signal fiscal discipline to the capital markets and confidence in future earnings. Self-tenders allow timely retirement of a sizable number of shares but are less flexible than open market repurchases and typically require a substantial premium to the current market price.

Dividends

Dividends are typically the first point of discussion when a company decides it has too much cash, especially in today's more dividend-friendly tax regime. But dividends are a slow, inefficient method to redeploy excess capital and they commit the company to a higher fixed cost burden to cover. The fixed cost burden makes regular dividends less appropriate for highly cyclical or volatile sectors or companies.

Notwithstanding media attention and apparent investor interest, we have found that the excess returns associated with most dividend increases are small, about 1 percent. However, we have found that the announcement of dividend initiations and major increases produced excess returns under certain conditions.

We found significant excess returns associated with large increases from companies with low volatility, low valuations, high margins, and had dividends well below their closest comparables. Dividends are also a useful means of distribution in cases of small public float and poor stock liquidity.

Special dividends are most common in cases where poor stock liquidity makes share repurchases problematic, where tax and regulatory reasons prohibit self-tenders or where a founder wishes to receive cash while maintaining proportionate ownership.

We recommend calibrating dividends not to exceed that portion of quarterly free cash flow that is recurring and stable, while volatile or uncertain excess cash flows are being distributed through share buybacks. Issuers should note, however, that large dividends reduce the value of stock options and convertible bond warrants, and impair operating liquidity and credit quality.

Case Study: Economic Impact Of Strategic Decapitalization

To illustrate the economics of a balanced decapitalization, we model and compare the impact of a leveraged share repurchase, a smaller share repurchase funded from excess cash, and a balanced use of proceeds for the excess cash that both reduces leverage and repurchases shares (Table 5.1).

The leveraged buyback, commonly promoted by today's hedge funds, offers the least compelling impact. The balanced decapitalization offers superior value creation in terms of intrinsic value, while simultaneously enhancing financial strength and credit profile. Our hypothetical company begins with a $1 billion of market capitalization, $325 million of debt, and $100 million of cash. We assume $20 million of cash is required for normal operating liquidity and strategic reserve, leaving $80 million of cash available for redeployment. The opportunity cost of excess capital creates a

TABLE 5.1 Illustration of Strategic Decapitalization

		Status Quo		Leveraged Buyback		Decapitalization		
						Equity		Balanced
Stock Price (implied)	$	20.00	$	20.69	$	19.91	$	19.74
Premium		0%		10%		5%		0%
Offer Price	$	20.00	$	22.00	$	21.00	$	20.00
Initial Shares		47,500		47,500		47,500		47,500
Shares Repurchased		–		6,158		3,810		2,000
Ending Shares		47,500		41,342		43,690		45,500
Repurchase Size		0.0%		13.0%		8.0%		4.2%
Cash Yield		3.0%		3.0%		3.0%		3.0%
Cash		100,000		100,000		20,000		20,000
Interest Income		3,000		3,000		600		600
Tax Rate		30%		30%		30%		30%
A/T Return on Cash		2%		2%		2%		2%
WACC		8%		8%		8%		8%
NPV of Cash		26,250		26,250		5,250		5,250
Value Saved		–		–		59,000		59,000
Market Cap		950,000		855,174		870,000		898,000
Incremental Debt		–		135,466		–		(40,000)
Total Debt		325,000		460,466		325,000		285,000
Incremental Tax Shield		–		40,640		–		(12,000)
Intrinsic Value		1,275,000		1,315,640		1,195,000		1,183,000
Distribution/share	$	–	$	–	$	1.83	$	1.76
Investor Return		0.0%		3.4%		8.7%		7.5%
Debt/EV		25%		35%		27%		24%

large and growing drag on the company's ROCE, EVA, and NPV, whereas the value proposition of debt, via increased tax shield, is less meaningful.

Similar to holding cash for growth, debt reduction creates a source of dry powder by increasing debt capacity and financial strength. Debt reduction in this case enhances debt/EBTIDA and interest coverage while and reducing debt/EV from 25 percent to 24 percent.

The share repurchase increases ROCE and EPS but financial leverage (especially on a debt to capital basis) also climbs. A combined action of debt reduction and share repurchases improves both financial leverage and financial performance.

Managing the Right-Hand Side of the Balance Sheet

An Executive's Guide
to Credit Ratings

C redit ratings and rating agencies are mentioned only in passing in most business schools and remain one of the most understudied aspects of modern corporate finance. Evolution within the agencies, the emergence of new agencies and agency alternatives, conflicting signals from the agencies, conflicting signals between the agencies and the markets, and several high-profile agency miscalls are all factors that highlight the need for more study in this area.

Though rating agencies have been under fire in recent years, their position as gatekeepers to the capital markets remains firmly in place. Finance executives must determine their optimal capital structure balancing business and financial risk with the need to access capital at a reasonable cost. In doing so, they must determine which ratios matter, how to incorporate industry-specific considerations, the impact of today's capital market outlook, and how to best manage an increasingly difficult rating climate.

The provision of credit, particularly in the United States, has shifted away from commercial banks to the rated capital markets. Bonds are less frequently purchased by buy and hold investors but traded to optimize portfolio risk/return profiles. The investor base has broadened and diversified (banks have become more cautious about borrowers, and other investors are ready to take risk at attractive terms), making public debt ratings generally more important to issuers than in the past. At the same time, bank markets have evolved into a rated market.

TRENDS AND IMPLICATIONS

Many factors have complicated the task of determining an optimal capital structure: a low but rising rate environment, market volatility, increased credit complexity, more aggressive corporate financial policies, and a back-lash from investors and agencies. As a result, many corporate finance executives find navigating the changing environment challenging.

Rising Interest Rates

Since January 2001, the Federal Reserve Board moved repeatedly and aggressively to lower the Fed Funds target rate, from 6.5 percent in May 2000 to a 40-year low of 1 percent in June 2003. Ten-year treasury yield fell 330 bps from 6.4 percent to 3.1 percent over the same period. Poor economic growth and employment figures during this period, as well as lagging capital markets, signaled the need for a low rate environment.

Lower interest rates and a soft equity market made debt the obvious choice for many financings in recent years. Commercial paper (CP), convertible bonds, and higher levels of floating-rate exposure have all made the cost of servicing debt appear less expensive. A steep yield curve and tight credit spreads have helped keep financing costs low, especially helpful in this period of weak operating margins.

But Fed's actions with a measured pace of 25 bps in June and August of 2004, concurrent with rising corporate yields, suggest the bottom of the rate cycle has been tested. The economy has shown sporadic signs of improvement since the 8 percent jump in GDP growth in Q3, 2003. Interest rates have since normalized and may creep higher. With rates on the rise, coverage ratios are poised to fall. (Coverage ratios are most meaningful for speculative-grade credits where the calculation commonly produces ratios of only a few turns of coverage. The statistical correlation is strongest for coverage ratios with speculative credits.)

As rates rise, noninvestment grade issuers will be forced to reduce debt or to offset rising funding costs through increased floating-rate exposure, securitization, collateralization, or selling optionality (e.g., convertibles and puts).

Reduced Credit Quality

Shareholder activism and a heightened focus on shareholder value in recent years have led to corporate financial policies that, though good for shareholders, are less desirable from the perspective of creditors. The past decade has been characterized by a trend toward more aggressive financial policies.

For shareholders, this has generally been a good thing but default rates for corporate securities have increased vis-à-vis other types of securities, such as mortgage-backed securities, asset-backed securities, and public sector debt. For example, speculative-grade defaults rose from their historic norms of about 2 percent, to nearly 10 percent in 2001 and 2002. Default rates have since moderated but remain modestly elevated.

Much of the growth in the pool of rated credits has been speculative grade, which rose 320 percent over the past decade. Not surprisingly, the stature of these analysts has been growing within the rating agencies. Growth of the speculative grade has been facilitated by generally abundant liquidity, an accommodative monetary policy, and a growing willingness to accept risk among investors in return for yield. After a number of years of reduced activity, speculative-grade issuance came back in 2003 with a roar. But growth in lower-grade issuance can serve as an early warning of renewed default pressure ahead.

Though investment grade issuers remain reluctant to slip below investment grade, many highly rated issuers have migrated toward A and BBB levels for more financial flexibility and a lower weighted average cost of capital (WACC). In today's low interest rate environment, the benefits to WACC from increased leverage tend to be quite small and subject to the vagaries of high-yield market credit spreads, with financial flexibility and other strategic rationale generally more important considerations to the determination of optimal leverage. This has largely been accomplished with increased financial leverage, greater use of share repurchases, and more cash or debt used to finance acquisitions.

The aggregate leverage for most ratings categories has remained relatively unchanged over the past decade. The highest, or elite ratings, require the most conservative and restrictive financial policies. Consequently, issuers at these levels should have a strong strategic rationale or competitive dynamics that demand such a position. The number of investment-grade companies with AAA or AA ratings has declined, from 21 percent to only 9 percent of the continuously rated companies.

The BBB category is the most popular investment-grade rating, representing more than half of all investment-grade companies. Of the pool of 656 continuously rated companies between 1993 and 2003, the share of investment-grade issuers slightly decreased to 68 percent from 72 percent. Seventy-two issuers left the investment grade, and 48 issuers were upgraded to investment grade.

Overall leverage of the same company pool has been relatively stable for investment and speculative grades, and slight fluctuations has synchronized with the economic cycle. Coverage has been consistently improving as a reflection of declining interest rates. With the exception of the B rating, the

S&P-rated U.S.-listed nonfinancials have exhibited relatively stable levels of debt/EBITDA and debt/enterprise value ratios within ratings.

The Volatility of Volatility

The unforeseen collapse of investment-grade issuers, such as Enron and KMart, put investors, analysts, regulatory bodies, and rating agencies on edge. The market responded by demanding and getting increased financial reporting transparency, improved corporate governance, and more intensified scrutiny. However, uncertainty continues to stem from conflict in the Middle East, volatile energy prices, corporate scandals, election year politics, and the incessant push of government prosecutors. Accounting changes (e.g., stock option expensing, pensions and other actuarial obligations, and convertibles) add to the unease amidst this sea of change.

Investors, analysts, and agencies have ample reason to continue to view the credit environment with skepticism though the worst is likely behind us. The average credit spread for investment grade securities peaked at 200 bps in Q4, 2002, but had declined to 64 bps by Q3, 2004. The average credit spread for speculative grade securities peaked at 890 bps in Q4, 2001, and had declined to 356 bps by Q3, 2004. The volatility of volatility is still higher than ever, making capital structure an important underpinning to viable growth strategies in today's uncertain world.

Credit-sensitive triggers (e.g., material adverse change clauses), pricing grids, and regular marking-to-market can lead to a chain reaction that weakens a corporate credit if quality declines, sometimes leading to a liquidity death spiral.

Unlike the high rate days of many of our finance textbooks, in today's low rate environment, the WACC is less sensitive to changes in financial leverage within the relevant range of potential leverage choices. The sweet spot (minimum) is more likely to be of investment-grade leverage.

Though financial flexibility can be more important than cost of capital, rating targets may not be the simple answer. Corporate financial policy can more easily target controllable drivers, such as leverage ratios consistent with the profile of a target rating and can gauge the success of these policies from credit spreads versus specific rating outcomes.

For example, practitioners may look more to corporate bond spreads and the credit default market than to rely on the information content of ratings.[1] The quality of external credit ratings, in one study, provided evidence that S&P ratings do not fully incorporate the information content of all public information, the performance of some different ratings categories are statistically indistinguishable, and ratings methodology were not fully adjusted to business cycles. Bond price approaches can improve the classification of bonds, spread risk forecasts, and detect rating anomalies. Ratings can also be notoriously sticky as they seek to reflect the agencies' assessment of an issuer's risk qualitative and quantitative profile through the cycles.

Increased Credit Complexity

Though recent accounting changes have moderated their use, off-balance sheet products and structured solutions have complicated the optimal capital structure equation. From the mundane to the exotic, debt hybrids have convoluted the simple task of determining debt and capital (e.g., operating leases, guarantees, letters of commitment, securitized receivables, convertibles, trust preferreds, debt in unconsolidated subsidiaries, put programs and equity forwards, and underfunded pension and postretirement benefit obligations), let alone defining an optimal capital structure.

The accounting changes have also complicated credit analysis—the measurement of leverage, coverage, and profitability—with income and book equity capital facing more distortions (e.g., goodwill, mark-to-market accounting, bifurcation, and stock option expense). The combination of uncertainty and complexity is certain to lead investors, analysts, and agencies to opt for the most conservative interpretation possible for each degree of freedom in the evaluation of the credit, thereby disadvantaging issuers.

Issuers should seek to simplify their own capital structure and credit story wherever possible and clarify whatever complexity remains. Provide the detail and the analytics to avoid the risk of unnecessarily conservative interpretations. For example, the present value of operating lease commitments is generally a much lower figure than implied by the shortcut capitalization factors (e.g., 8x). Unfortunately, few companies make the present value number available. Providing this detail could help prevent the more onerous approximation of leverage.

Agency Backlash

Though much has been written on disintermediation, the shift from institution-based lending to capital market-based funding, little mention is made of its impact on the growth and importance of the credit rating agencies. Rating agencies have enjoyed a dramatic expansion phase over the past decade as the debt markets deepened and broadened. Much of the growth was in the speculative-grade and bank loan markets where many credits had been unrated. Growth in the use of sophisticated fixed-income instruments and hybrids created another growth area for the agencies where investors needed more guidance to evaluate these situations.

But the bubble burst with the high-profile collapse of investment-grade and former investment-grade credits such as KMart, Enron, WorldCom.

The agencies were heavily criticized for their role around these credits. These and other incidents led to structural change at the agencies, changes to their people and processes, and systemwide reviews and numerous downgrades. Agencies were soundly criticized for their failure to identify high-profile credit meltdowns ahead of time and have been exposed to intense external scrutiny. Academic studies indicate that though agency information is helpful to and relied upon by the credit markets, it is not believed to incorporate all public information efficiently, and the probability of defaults of adjacent rating categories is not always considered to be significantly different. For example, the ratings of Creditform, in Germany, are found to improve the predictive power of default risks; however, publicly available information has additional explanatory power, and statistical testing indicates the agency is overemphasizing firm size in the construction of the rating index.[2]

Agencies have responded to market criticism with actions designed to address concerns with reviews of rating policies, scrutiny of governance and accounting practices, and enhanced communication with market participants. Moody's reorganized its corporate industrials group structure and added more analysts and specialists. S&P shifted analysts among portfolios, called fresh eye analysis. Both agencies have increased their frequency and intensity of analytics. Fitch has sought to capitalize on S&P's and Moody's vulnerability by aggressively promoting its services.

Issuers must expect more skepticism from investors and agencies around their forecasts, increased reliance on LTM versus long-term forecast numbers, reduced time allowance to achieve target ratios, more emphasis on qualitative factors and a host of other changes reflecting a more conservative analytical environment.

The agencies have added accounting and governance specialists, increased their frequency and intensity of analysis and special comments, and refined analytics:

- Higher importance of stress scenarios and contingent funding plans due to proliferation of confidence sensitive reactions
- Closer look at rating horizon which may not necessarily match the economic cycle
- More attention to debt and equity market price information
- Issuers, acquiring a credit rating for the first time (so-called first time issuers) experiencing lower ratings versus the pool of existing credits

After default rates and downgrade-to-upgrade ratios peaked at historically high levels in 2002, ratings dynamics have moderated substantially. The agencies have returned to a more sanguine outlook, with sector and systemwide reviews largely completed. Though conditions have normalized, conservatism remains strong.

EMPIRICAL EVIDENCE

Trends in distribution across industries follow broad structural shifts in the economy: The industries with highest growth in rated companies were Telecom, Media, Healthcare, and Technology. The number of rated Telecom credits jumped over 500 percent over the decade. The slowest growing pools of rated credits were Utilities, Capital Goods, and Transport. Materials and Consumer were the two largest industry groups in 1993 and had the largest number of additions over the 10 years.

Much of the growth in the pool of rated credits was among speculative credits, the final frontier of credit. Of the 794 credits in 1993, 62 percent were investment grade; by 2003, they had been diluted down to 43 percent of the total 2,246 credits. This represents a growth of the speculative grade, not a trend of increased leverage, of the 656 continuously rated credits. Leverage and ratings have been relatively stable otherwise.

LIMITATIONS OF QUANTITATIVE CREDIT ANALYSIS

Credit analysis, by definition, looks forward. All looks into the future will be subjective and involve many unique industry and issuer factors. This process cannot be reduced to a formulaic methodology or quantitative model.

Drawing from the past, credit analysts attempt to focus on a longer-term, future perspective. They must look through the cycle and through any potential accounting distortions. Finally, they must examine a variety of reasonably adverse scenarios to incorporate sensitivity to risk. Sovereign, economic, and industry factors influence risk. Soft facts, or subjective judgments, add valuable information to the credit analysis process.[3] Quantitative and qualitative pitfalls exist in the quantitative portion of any analysis.

Finally, it is also important to note the difference between *relative* and *absolute* quantitative credit analysis. Relative analysis of comparable credits allows us to understand whether, after controlling for all differences in (for example) size, financial leverage, profitability, cash flow and liquidity, the credit is rated consistently with its group of comparables. But this does *not* answer whether the entire group of comparables is rated appropriately. This question may only be answered through an absolute default and recovery analysis to gauge investor risk and reward.

Relevant Data

Quantitative analysis is subject to a high degree of judgment in developing relevant data; comparables, history, and data cleaning are key decision points. For example, pre-9/11 airline industry data tends to be less relevant today. Similarly, transformative acquisitions can make company history less relevant. In many cases, more data are better, such as all rated Capital Goods companies, all rated nonfinancials with revenue between $100 million and $1 billion, or all rated, domestic, "asset-light" service companies. Some credits are best evaluated from a wide range of recent cross sectional data; others with few economic comparables will require many years of few companies (time series data). We often exclude the data of foreign companies and American Depositary Receipts (ADRs) to avoid variation in the data from accounting conventions. Similarly, financial institutions or companies with large captive finance companies are typically treated separately. Many listed companies with captive finance businesses report an ".F" version of their financials in Compustat/FactSet that effectively excludes the financial assets net of funding liabilities and places net interest income below the line for profitability purposes, akin to the agency treatment where FinCo capitalization is evaluated separately.

Multicollinearity

Multicollinearity is a statistical term akin to double counting. When related variables (e.g., crosscorrelation of 50 percent or more) are used simultaneously, statistical significance can appear good (high R^2 and low standard error), yet stability and reliability suffer. Practically, this problem often manifests in an overweighting of the importance of some factors and insensitivity to others.

Table 6.1 provides an example from the machinery manufacturing sector of Capital Goods. Typically, market-based size and leverage measures have the strongest statistical significance but are highly correlated with income; thus, they steal sensitivity from actionable ratios like leverage and coverage which are more useful to include for financial planning purposes.

Qualitative Factors

A balance of business information and financial data is needed to evaluate a credit. Quantitative analysis may be less useful if underlying financial data are believed to be unreliable. If so, more weight could be given to qualitative information, such as size and seasoning, competitive position, brands, patents and intangibles, industry and regulatory factors, management

TABLE 6.1 Multicollinearity Matrix

	Ln (MktCap)	Ln (Sales)	Ln (Assets)	Debt/ EBITDA	FFO/ Debt	EBIT Coverage	EBITDA Coverage	Debt/ EV	Debt/Capital	EBIT/Capital	Cash ROCE	EBIT/ Sales	Cash Conv.	Current Ratio	Liquidity Ratio
Ln(MktCap)	1.00														
Ln(Sales)	0.85	1.00													
Ln(Assets)	0.88	0.98	1.00												
Debt/EBITDA	(0.67)	(0.41)	(0.44)	1.00											
FFO/Debt	0.81	0.70	0.71	(0.45)	1.00										
EBIT Cov.	0.76	0.66	0.67	(0.45)	0.90	1.00									
EBITDA Cov.	0.77	0.69	0.69	(0.46)	0.89	0.99	1.00								
Debt/EV	(0.86)	(0.52)	(0.54)	0.77	(0.72)	(0.65)	(0.66)	1.00							
Debt/Capital	(0.72)	(0.70)	(0.72)	0.49	(0.80)	(0.72)	(0.73)	0.67	1.00						
EBIT/Capital	0.79	0.54	0.54	(0.74)	0.76	0.75	0.74	(0.84)	(0.57)	1.00					
Cash ROCE	0.85	0.58	0.60	(0.57)	0.79	0.69	0.70	(0.89)	(0.60)	0.78	1.00				
EBIT/Sales	0.78	0.48	0.51	(0.70)	0.78	0.80	0.78	(0.84)	(0.60)	0.91	0.79	1.00			
Cash Conv.	0.75	0.40	0.48	(0.49)	0.72	0.63	0.64	(0.83)	(0.55)	0.61	0.93	0.75	1.00		
Current Ratio	(0.28)	(0.49)	(0.41)	0.25	(0.18)	(0.24)	(0.25)	0.08	0.19	(0.38)	(0.08)	(0.26)	0.20	1.00	
Liquidity Ratio	0.02	(0.28)	(0.17)	(0.01)	0.12	0.00	(0.01)	0.21	0.06	(0.12)	0.24	0.03	0.51	0.91	1.00

strength, business strategy, financial conservatism, and the history of the agency relationship.

Agency Relationships

The rating agencies and their relationships with issuers remain an important factor in the determination of a credit rating. Some issuers do a much better job of managing their relationships and their dialogue with the agencies.

WHAT METRICS MATTER MOST?

Investors and agencies evaluate a company's ability to withstand financial stress operating on concepts and guidelines rather than on rigid rules. Because of the importance of qualitative factors, it is difficult to reduce such a holistic view to a set of financial ratios. Quantitative analysis is an important part of the evaluation of a credit but cannot fully capture the facets of a company's financial risk.

Nonetheless, we do observe correlations between ratings and ratios with a significant and increasing degree of statistical explanatory power. Though coefficients of determination (R^2) have remained relatively stable, t-statistics for individual metrics have improved across the time period.

And agencies view ratio analysis as an important part of the rating process, especially when they believe that financial data are reliable. Furthermore, from a policy perspective, ratios rather than ratings represent more manageable targets to manage toward.

In statistical tests of correlation between credit ratios and senior issuer bond ratings, there is a general trend of increased statistical significance over the prior decade for most metrics, and across most ratings categories and industry sectors. Notwithstanding recent high-profile incidents that might seem to suggest the opposite, the data show that, on average, quantitative methods have become a more reliable tool to evaluate credit profiles. This may be due to improved financial reporting consistency and reliability. We define and discuss several measurement categories and measures within each category: definitions, trends, applicability, and limitations.

Size

Larger companies tend to have higher credit ratings. Empirically, size metrics offer the strongest statistical correlation with credit ratings, reflecting important qualitative factors such as geographic and product market diversification, competitive position, bargaining power, market share and brand stature. As this relationship diminishes with size, it is best modeled as a natural log (ln) function.

Size proxies may be revenue, net tangible assets, capital employed, or market capitalization. The more relevant unit economics for some industries will tend to be assets or capital (financial institutions), whereas others (professional services businesses) tend to be more revenue based. We employ industry judgment and empirical analysis to test for the most relevant and statistically robust metric.

For example, ln (market capitalization) often offers the most powerful predictive power due to its incorporation (capitalization) of consensus forward cash flows; however, this metric is often problematic, in practice, and can lead to inappropriate guidance for setting corporate policy around financial leverage. In multivariate regression analysis, the strong correlation of this metric often leaves little variation in the data to be explained by other factors, leading to small regression coefficients for financial leverage and other important credit considerations. Ultimately, credit models that incorporate market capitalization as a size metric can be too insensitive to marginal changes in financial leverage and other important metrics.

However, though size can be used as a helpful statistical anchor in estimating credit profiles, it falls short for financial policy purposes, hardly an actionable target to manage toward; completely removed from financial health, this metric must only be used with caution.

Financial Leverage

More highly leveraged companies tend to have lower credit ratings. Companies with a higher proportion of debt are at greater risk of being unable to make full principal and interest payments on a timely basis across a spectrum of business performance scenarios. From a corporate financial policy perspective, financial leverage is the key driver to target and manage optimal capital structure. Corporate financial policy typically attempts to optimize financial leverage at a point that provides sufficient financial flexibility to support a value maximizing strategic plan, while providing financial strength well suited to competitive dynamics and an efficient weighted average cost of capital.

Debt/EBITDA is one of the more universal leverage ratios that works reasonably well for speculative and to a lesser extent for investment grades, as well as across most nonfinancial industries. We adjust the ratio to recognize the economic obligation of operating leases—tantamount to debt—in lease-intensive industries such as transport, retail and capital goods. We present value operating lease commitments at an appropriate pretax cost of debt and add this obligation to the numerator but then increase earnings before interest, tax, depreciation, and amortization (EBITDA) by the rent expense. To adjust debt/EBIT or earnings before income and taxes (EBIT) coverage, only that portion of the rent expense representing interest (versus depreciation in an amortizing lease), say one third, should be added back to EBIT. A common shortcut employed by many Moody's analysts is to use a capitalization factor, say 8x, to approximate the off-balance sheet debt. However, this simplification can risk overstating the value of the obligation, especially for shorter life assets or shorter leases (shorter leases frequently demand higher payments as consideration for the increased financial flexibility of a short lease).

Debt/EBITDA can be a poor metric to employ where large variation across credit data might be expected (e.g., cyclical investment grade credits, especially midway through or at the top of the cycle). This metric is also problematic where taxes or depreciation are unusual, such as asset-light service industries or sectors characterized by short asset lives. EBITDA-based metrics also entirely ignore growth in working capital, quality of earnings, and liquidity.[4]

Book leverage (debt/capital, debt/equity) has been fading in popularity and statistical validity but still has currency with large investment-grade issuers. It suffers from its reliance on book equity, that is, the quality and consistency of which is skewed by goodwill, write-offs and other charges, share repurchases and asset accounting. Though many issuers do set and communicate corporate financial policy in terms of book leverage, this may constrain their ability to make shareholder distributions; therefore, equity is reduced as cash flow-based leverage targets are unaffected by dividends and share repurchases.

Market leverage (debt/enterprise value) addresses the shortfalls of book leverage by not relying on accounting artifacts of historic book capital. It offers a further advantage of incorporating the objective, forward-looking cash flow consensus of the market, which is capitalized into market value. However, it is viewed with skepticism by agencies since stock market values are prone to periods of overvaluation and undervaluation, leading to overestimates and underestimates of appropriate debt capacity. Internet valuations in 1999 and 2000 suggested tremendous debt capacity where there was none. Stock prices also are not actionable, that is, stock market volatility creates a moving goalpost, making this a poor choice for corporate financial policy.

Coverage

Coverage ratios (e.g., EBIT/interest expense and EBITDA/interest expense) are higher for stronger credits, implying less risk to the timely service of principal and interest payments across a full spectrum of performance. They are more frequently EBIT-based (versus EBITDA) to ensure credit protection measures reflect business needs for continued reinvestment. Financial institutions, where depreciation is less material, often focus on EBIT coverage.

Coverage ratios have improved over the decade, despite rising debt, due to falling interest rates and a steepening of the yield curve. Interest expense has been managed down through floating-rate funding and floating-rate swaps, and growth in the use of convertibles (where the cost of servicing is reduced by the amortization of the value of the warrant). These factors have eroded the statistical validity of coverage ratios, with the exception of financial institutions and to a lesser extent the speculative grades, where more tightly clustered data yield better reliability.

Cash Flow

Agencies focus intently on an issuer's free cash flow (FCF) generation, typically defined as cash from operations less capital expenditures and dividends. There is direct correlation between an issuer's FCF/debt ratio and its ratings profile. FFO/debt emerges as an increasingly helpful metric for stronger investment-grade credits and in periods of time closer to the middle or top of the cycle. This metric is more prevalent in the Fitch and S&P literature versus Moody's, which focuses on RCF/debt with retained cash flow (RCF), defined as funds from operations (FFO) minus dividends. Historically used for real estate investment trusts (REITs), FFO has grown in use. Empirically, it is helpful to investment grade Media, Consumer, Pharmaceuticals, and Capital Goods.

Profitability

Greater profitability tends to support higher quality long-term ratings. The higher the company's profitability, the less the risk to debt servicing and the fewer years it would take to retire debt from cash flow. Statistically, profitability is most relevant for high-quality investment grades and the turbulent Technology and Telecoms.

We typically evaluate return on capital employed (ROCE) as net operating profit after tax (NOPAT) divided by beginning period net assets) or EBITDA Margins (EBITDA/Sales), but many other industry-specific ones may be used. Profitability's importance is replaced by liquidity metrics for short-term ratings.

Liquidity and Short-Term Ratings

Stronger liquidity supports stronger ratings; while useful in determining short-term ratings, liquidity is less predictive of long-term ratings. We typically use current ratio (current assets/current liabilities), cash conversion ratio (operating cash flow/sales), or liquidity ratio (cash plus operating cash flow divided by short-term debt) as our metrics though CP reliance, looming puts and maturity towers, backup facilities, and other qualitative factors can be just as important.

Liquidity is viewed in the context of an issuer's ability to meet all possible direct and contingent claims. Short-term ratings, most commonly used for CP programs, apply to an individual issuer's capacity to repay all short-term obligations and to issuer's entire senior, unsecured obligations at maturities less than one year.

Though guidance regarding short-term ratings may seem confusing, the empirical relationship between long-term and short-term ratings is clear (Figure 6.1). There are a few cases of exceptions, and complications, such as S&P criteria dictating that BBB issuers with a negative outlook must be rated A-3 versus an A-2 rating. In a few cases, companies with large cash balances achieve an A-1 rating despite only being rated A− long term. Similarly, a few A-rated companies are held at A-2 due to the negative overhang of qualitative considerations.

Agencies critically evaluate sources for funding immediacy, quality, and diversity. For this reason, self-sufficiency from internal sources of liquidity (i.e., cash on hand, near-term liquid assets, working capital) is preferred for normal operating liquidity. Liquidity risk insurance needs may be more efficiently met through external or off-balance sheet sources, such as undrawn line and backstop, bank and other facilities, asset sales, securitizations, and contingent capital. Critical to the assessment of an issuer's liquidity is its ability to cover near-term obligations from stressed cash flow.

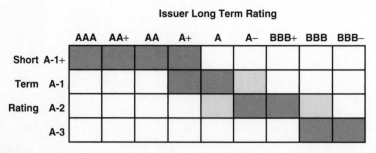

FIGURE 6.1   Short-Term versus Long-Term Ratings

CASE STUDY: TREATMENT OF PENSION
AND POSTRETIREMENT LIABILITIES

In their analysis of profitability, the agencies have long attempted to normalize or undo certain distortions or problematic accounting treatments, attempting to strike a balance between what is most economically reflective and what is practical.

In early 2003, the agencies clarified their incorporation of the economic obligation of underfunded defined benefit pension and postretirement benefits.[5] Where material, the agencies adjust capitalization and cash flow protection measures to reflect such obligations. In practice, the adjustments are neither universally nor mechanically applied and are most frequently made in the United States and for pensions (versus postretirement healthcare). Ratios are often calculated with and without the adjustments.

More recently, the Financial Accounting Standards Board (FASB) has been stirred to initiate a comprehensive review of pension and postretirement liability accounting. The first phase will involve shifting these liabilities from the footnotes to the balance sheet. The second phase, though further away from implementation, may involve greater recognition of other factors, such as variation in asset strategies and their inherent risks. Ratings agency treatments remain largely unaffected by this latter issue, with no formal recognition of the role that different asset strategies may play in credit quality.

In Figure 6.2, debt is increased by the after-tax total unfunded projected benefit obligations (PBO) for pensions, and the total accumulated postretirement benefit obligations (APBO) for other postretirement obligations (OPEB). This equals the difference between end of period PBO/APBO and the market values of the plan assets (plan assets are zero for OPEB, and in some countries, even for pension), after tax. Equity is reduced by the after-tax unfunded PBO/APBO (less any preexisting liability already recognized on the balance sheet). EBITDA is increased by the total pension expense, less economic service cost to eliminate all accounting artifacts that stem from the smoothing approach of accounting rules. Interest expense is increased by the pension interest cost, less the actual return on plan assets (up to the amount of the interest expense but not beyond). FFO is increased by the amount that benefit contributions plus actual plan asset returns exceed service and interest cost, after tax. Funds from operations is calculated as net income from continuing operations, plus depreciation, amortization, deferred income taxes, and other non-cash expenses. In some cases, plan asset returns may be normalized and certainly capped.

Financial Statement Adjustments			Credit Metrics	
Debt		3,000		
PBO	3,000			
Plan Assets	1,500			
Unfunded PBO	1,500			
Tax Rate	30%			
A/T Debt Adjustment	1,050			
Total Adjusted Debt		4,050		
Book Equity (incl. min. int.)		5,000	Debt/Capital	38%
Unfunded PBO	1,500		Adj. Debt/Capital	50%
On-balance sheet portion	100			
A/T Equity Adjustment	980			
Adjusted Equity		4,020		
EBITDA		1,000	Debt/EBITDA	3.0
Pension Expense	150		Adj. Debt/EBITDA	3.8
Service Cost	75			
Pension Expense Adjustment	75			
Adjusted EBITDA		1,075		
Interest Expense		175	EBITDA Cov.	5.7
Pension Interest Cost	200		Adj. EBITDA Cov.	5.4
Return on Plan Assets	175			
Interest Adjustment	25			
Adjusted Interest Expense		200		
Funds from Operations		2,000	FFO/Debt	67%
+ Contributions	50		Adj. FFO/Debt	49%
− Service Cost	75			
− Pension Interest Cost	200			
+ Return on Plan Assets	175			
A/T Cashflow Adjustment	(35)			
Adjusted FFO		1,965		

FIGURE 6.2   Illustration of Pension Adjustments

In our example, the pension adjustment adds a near full turn to the Debt/EBITDA ratio, more than 10 percent to the debt/capital ratio, and nearly 20 percent to the FFO/debt ratio. This likely represents a full notch overhang to the rating despite the negligible impact to coverage ratios.

MULTIVARIATE CREDIT MODELS

Credit analysts have long relied on multiple ratios for their quantitative analysis, frequently leading to questions around the relative importance of each. Regression analysis can be employed to determine an optimal basket of metrics for a given sample of historical data and assign relative weightings to each ratio. A multivariate model is effectively a weighted average approach to multiple ratios.

For example, continuing with the data from our machinery manufacturing example, we develop a model that is a weighted score of size, financial leverage and interest coverage ratios (Figure 6.3). This model explains a full 90 percent of the variation in all long-term ratings across the sector (26 rated companies with LTM cross sectional data); however, the standard error shows that predicted ratings can be of by a full notch.[6] The model works best in the middle zone of the rating range (A through B) but maintains reasonable predictive power to the extreme scores. In practice, we tailor industry-specific models with a narrow dataset and high explanatory power. Standard error can be problematic, and all scores often fall within two notches at 95 percent confidence. When we sorted the residuals to understand the model error better, we could qualitatively reconcile the bulk of the error.

The model predicts Flowserve as a stronger credit by one notch (BB− versus B+) but their acquisitive nature and aggressive financial policies are clearly an overhang on the rating. Danaher (A) is similarly acquisitive. Danaher may also suffer because of the significance of the AA threshold; Danaher is acquisitive and is not of the size or profile we expect to see among AA companies. Watts Water (BBB−) is predicted almost two notches lower; however, at the cusp of investment grade, the agencies may be reluctant to downgrade the company into junk if the company can improve its cash flow protection measures in the near term.

Our best models draw from the best data, with great care taken in selecting a relevant range of data with sufficient variation to discern relationships but not so much as to overwhelm the significance of other factors. Relevant comparables (size, rating, business model, economics, and channels), relevant data (sufficient history and credit variation, used or meaningless fields) and a systematic approach to selecting the best team of independent variables are critical.

For example, commingling speculative grade and investment grade credits may dilute the power of a model. A+ through BBB− might be most relevant to a BBB+.

SUMMARY OUTPUT

Regression Statistics

Multiple R	0.95
R Square	0.90
Adjusted R Square	0.88
Standard Error	1.23
Observations	26.00

ANOVA

	df	SS	MS	F	Significance F
Regression	4.00	290.24	72.56	47.92	0.00
Residual	21.00	31.80	1.51		
Total	25.00	322.04			

	Coefficients	Standard Error	t Stat	P-value	Lower 95%	Upper 95%
Intercept	19.67	3.21	6.13	0.00	13.00	26.34
Ln(Assets)	(0.77)	0.37	(2.10)	0.05	(1.53)	(0.01)
EBITDA Coverage	(0.11)	0.05	(2.14)	0.04	(0.21)	(0.00)
Debt/Capital	4.98	3.01	1.66	0.11	(1.27)	11.23
Cash ROCE	(28.23)	6.48	(4.36)	0.00	(41.71)	(14.76)

OUTLIER RESIDUALS

Observation	Predicted Code	Residuals	Company
8.00	11.32	(2.32)	PALL
14.00	12.74	(1.74)	WATTS WATER TECH.
20.00	15.69	(1.69)	VALMONT INDUSTRIES
6.00	10.33	(1.33)	HARSCO CORP.
3.00	9.31	(1.31)	DOVER
4.00	9.08	(1.08)	EATON
19.00	12.93	1.07	ACTUANT
2.00	5.36	1.64	DANAHER
22.00	13.01	1.99	GARDNER DENVER
21.00	12.90	2.10	FLOWSERVE

FIGURE 6.3 Regression-Based Credit Model

Quantitative models are useful for financial planning and analysis and for setting corporate financial policy. But quantitative models inherently carry standard error because, ultimately, qualitative factors play a vital role in the evaluation of any credit. These models are best used in conjunction with insightful qualitative analysis, carefully applied with an experienced understanding of the underlying company data and industry fundamentals.

INDUSTRY CONSIDERATIONS

With respect to industry considerations, leverage ratios vary widely between industries, even within the same ratings categories (similar results were obtained for FFO/debt as debt/EBITDA), due to differences in earnings quality, outlook, sustainability, and qualitative factors. But there is less dispersion among the stronger rating categories; industry factors decline in importance as credits are held to the same high standards, suggesting many participants may have more difficulty to achieve the strongest categories in some industries.

Utilities, repeat fee-based businesses such as cable TV and transaction processors, and to a lesser extent telecoms tend to carry more leveragability within the same rating versus general corporate industrials. Regulation reduces credit risk by lending more predictability and certainty to cash flows.

Technology and healthcare (excluding pharmaceuticals and biotech), exhibit the least debt capacity within each rating due to perceptions of greater technology and/or regulatory risk, cash flow volatility, shorter product lives, product liability, and less fixed asset intensity. Asset intensity generally provides support to a credit.

Consumer products credits are heavily influenced by numerous qualitative factors (franchise strength, bargaining position, brand, market share, and diversity of revenue) for which quantitative factors (ln of revenue) can serve as a proxy. Retail revenue tends to be accorded smaller size coefficients, empirically, due to thinner margins and a higher concentration of end market risk.

CASE STUDY: PROPERTY AND CASUALTY INSURANCE

Financial institutions are complicated by their many definitions of capital: statutory or regulatory capital, economic or risk capital, and accounting or book capital. In the insurance industry, considerable attention is given to financial strength ratings (FSRs). These are credit opinions on the underlying financial strength of insurers in terms of their ability to punctually repay senior policy holder obligations and claims.

FSRs differ from senior unsecured bond ratings in that they are not security-specific, and that insurance companies are often owned by holding companies, which may be the issuers of long-term debt. FSRs incorporate capitalization, profitability, liquidity, market stature, and competitive advantage (underwriting, distribution, cost control, service, innovation).[7]

Though ratings are less sensitive to financial leverage than core business risk, company size, and other factors, EBIT coverage and book leverage work better in these industries than most. In terms of the statistical power of several Property and Casualty metrics in predicting ratings, the strongest predictive power is achieved with gross underwriting leverage, financial leverage, pretax return on equity, and size.[8]

Several important factors are not in our model, due to challenges with statutory data quality and timeliness. Others received coefficients of the wrong sign, perhaps due to multicollinearity or for being too small for sufficient sensitivity, make them impractical. Finally, numerous qualitative considerations are not captured.

Gross Underwriting Leverage

Gross underwriting leverage (gross premiums written plus gross loss and loss adjustment expense reserves/book equity) alone explains more of the variation in FSRs than any other single metric: It captures the size of total policy risk supported by the capital base. More policy risk per dollar of capital weakens a credit.

Financial Leverage

Financial leverage (total debt and hybrids/average of market and book equity plus total debt and hybrids) is much less statistically significant among financial institutions though the inclusion of this metric is essential for use as a financial planning tool. More financial leverage leads to a weaker credit.

Return On Equity

Pretax return on equity (EBIT/book equity) is the second most significant ratio and acts as a performance-based modifier to the model's intercept, working much in the same way as size, i.e., greater profitability and size lend support to stronger credit scores.

Size

Size (ln of book equity) may, to some extent, serve as a proxy for relative franchise strength, market presence, and diversification, all being important factors in the evaluation of an insurance credit.

APPLICATION ISSUES

Many issues arise in the appropriate selection, application, and interpretation of numeric methods, arising from the data as well as the quantitative methods. An appropriate time period must provide sufficient data yet be relevant despite changes in interest rates, business cycle and outlook, competitive dynamics, acquisitions, and of course, force majeur. The data may require normalization for special charges, variations in accounting, off-balance sheet items, and other accounting issues.

Net Debt or Gross Debt?

The relationship between leverage and rating can be much stronger on a gross debt basis than on a net debt basis. Once an issuer has sufficient operating liquidity and strategic reserves, surplus cash is generally better directed toward debt reduction. However, operating liquidity needs do generally rise for weaker credits, where businesses are typically weaker, higher fixed charges must be covered, and income statement gearing creates income volatility. Cash levels are higher due to restricted cash and covenant requirements.

Investment Grade Versus Speculative Grade

Size tends to be a more significant factor for speculative-grade credits showing diminishing returns to scale. Again, debt/EBITDA works better below investment grade, and coverage ratios become much more meaningful. Profitability metrics emerge as more statistically helpful in the analysis of investment-grade credits (notwithstanding their general importance to Technology credits).

HOW TO MANAGE YOUR AGENCIES

The rating process, and the agency relationship that goes with it, are critical inputs into any rating outcome. Some issuers manage this process better than others and approach their agency relationships with the same thought and effort as they might put into key customer, employee, or shareholder relationships. We outline below observations of best practices, based on our own experience.

Best practice issuers understand what agencies need from them in today's difficult credit climate, and they approach their relationship as positively and proactively as they would with any other key insider:

- Explanation of business strategy, legal and management structure, parent and subsidiary structures, and management processes including total compensation
- Frank discussion of risks and weaknesses with special attention to the issuer's approach to enterprise risk management, and corporate financial policy
- Clear articulation of and adherence to acquisition philosophy and other financial policies (leverage, share repurchases, dividends) that tend to impair ratings
- Timely and granular updates on operating and financial performance, plus any material changes in the business environment, corporate performance, or potential financing or M&A transactions

The rating process balances qualitative and quantitative approaches, and because quantitative analysis requires significant discretion and judgment (e.g., ratings must capture underlying creditworthiness throughout an entire cycle), special attention needs to be paid to a plan for the agency dialogue that must support any release of material information.

The annual review is a chance for a formal comprehensive review with an issuer. Agencies usually meet after the end of the financial year though it need not be after external public filings as the agencies are insiders, bound by the responsibilities of confidentiality, and should be treated as such. The meeting ideally involves the CEO, CFO, Treasurer, and selected line management. Hosting the meeting at the issuer every few years makes it easier to include this larger group and tour operating facilities. Holding the meeting at the agency makes it easier to draw higher-ranking agency figures, with access to credit committee members and agency management. This contact is especially helpful in difficult situations.

Best practice companies tend to preface their quarterly releases with a short informal call to their agency relationships, especially in cases where expectations are not met, to avoid surprises and provide the accompanying explanation.

Similarly, announcements of material changes or events are handled proactively to avoid surprises, recognizing the insider status of the agencies, allowing them more time to ask questions, clarify issues, and prepare their position.

Proactive communication is more prevalent in the other direction for best practice relationships, where downgrades may be handled with more advanced discussion, room for input and clarification, and time to prepare and communicate positions. The issuer's response is important to market stability in the event of a downgrade or reduced outlook.

Finally, management access for the issuer and agency is a common factor among best practice relationships; the importance of qualitative factors and the appropriate interpretation of analytics necessitates a healthy, high-level dialogue.

CASE STUDY: ILLUSTRATION OF SECURED AND UNSECURED NOTCHING

Figure 6.4 illustrates a framework for notching up secured debt and notching down unsecured debt. In practice, conventions may vary. Rating agencies have differing notching criteria for investment-grade and high-yield issuers. Typically, investment-grade issuer notching of subordinated debt is limited to one notch below the issuer level, whereas it is generally two notches lower for high-yield issuers. Because investment-grade issuers typically do

Secured Debt (Notching Up)				
Net Receivables	150	85%	128	Bank Line (drawn or undrawn)	100
Net Inventory	200	65%	130	Term Loan	300
Net PP&E	1,000	50%	500	ARS	50
PV of Operating Leases	100	50%	50	Lease Financing	50
Intangibles	—	10%	—	PV of Operating Leases	100
Stressed Asset Value (SAV)			808	**Total Adj. Secured Debt**	600
SAV/TASD	1.3				
Minimum for Notch Up	1.0				
Maximum TASD			808		

Unsecured Debt (Notching Down)		
Total Assets		1,500
− Goodwill		—
− Intangibles		—
+ 10% of Assets		150
+ PV Operating Leases		100
Total Adjusted Assets (TAA)		1,750
TASD/TAA	0.34	
2-Notch Maximum	0.30	525
1-Notch Maximum	0.15	263

FIGURE 6.4 Illustration of Notching Up and Notching Down

not have secured debt in their capital structures, their senior unsecured debt is usually rated at the issuer level.

In this illustration, the issuer has secured debt of $600 million (drawn and undrawn secured lines, revolver, term loan, securitizations and leases), less than the $808 million threshold for a one-notch upgrade (from the issuer level) on secured debt. However, secured debt is higher than the two-notch threshold for notching down lower-priority ranking debt (investment grade has one threshold at 20 percent); therefore, the unsecured debt is notched down two notches. Reducing secured debt from $600 million to $525 million would improve this to only a one-notch downgrade on lower priority debt. Reducing it below $263 million would remove any notching down on the unsecured debt.

CHAPTER 7

Today's Optimal Capital Structure

With interest rates still near a 40-year low, many senior executives are asking if these times call for a way to manage differently. How does one best manage for value in a low rate time? What financial strategy is best suited to an era where U.S. Treasuries hover near 5 percent?

Along with the media, our debt and equity capital markets are signaling we have entered a lower rate period. No one can be certain how long this will last. While it is continuing, senior executives must manage accordingly. We present several practical recommendations to tailor your financial strategy to this low rate time.

VALUE-BASED FINANCIAL POLICY

A common mistake made even by large, well-known companies, is one of inconsistency. What financial policy is most consistent with the business strategy? What financial policy is most consistent with market expectations and valuation? Too often, companies rush to tactics without consideration of an overall financial strategy, and they ignore the interdependencies between strategic choices and policy elements.[1]

Optimal financial policy (capital structure, cash and liquidity, and shareholder distributions) is not so much one of finding the correct settings as one of overall alignment with each other and consistency with company strategy and market expectations. The element of surprise, when actions strike a discord with expectations, wreaks havoc on a company's share price. Witness the case of Tyco, where markets were surprised twice, with the announced breakup and the abrupt abandonment of this about-face in strategy.

	Low Growth	High Growth
Leverage	More leverage to minimize WACC Reduce agency costs Access to capital less important than its cost and capital efficiency	Higher credit quality Greater financial flexibility Access to capital through cycle

Liquidity	Less liquidity
	Minimize capital employed
	Valuation less predicated on growth,
	   access to capital than existing cashflows,
	   and maximizing their value
		Greater liquidity and self-sufficiency
		Insure equity; preserve growth options
		Cost of liquidity far below opp. cost
		   of growth

Distributions	More use of dividends and buybacks
	Reduce agency costs, minimize excess
	   capital, and provide steady yield
		Dividends and share repurchases
		   less consistent with growth image
		Preserve cash for liquidity and growth

FIGURE 7.1 Framework for Financial Policy

The elements of a financial policy must be well aligned with each other, with the management agenda, and with the expectations reflected in the company's valuation. Figure 7.1 introduces a framework for aligning the elements of financial policy: financial liquidity, financial leverage, and shareholder distributions, with the business strategy and market valuation.

Though depressed stock prices often reflect depressed operating cash flows, they can reflect reduced expectations for future cash flows, that is, reduced growth values. Any stock price mathematically implies some expectation for long-term growth that, in turn, requires an appropriate degree of financial flexibility. A higher stock price for a given baseline level of performance implies a higher expectation for positive net present value (NPV) growth, or growth in economic profit (EP). Today's low cost of capital environment leads to a larger present value to any given level of operating cash flows. This, in turn, leaves less value attributable to positive NPV growth for a given market value.

But strategic corporate finance can be used to build and support enterprise value. We draw on the well-known Black-Scholes option valuation model to illustrate value drivers in corporate financial policy, with emphasis on the strategic implications of your valuation:

- **Share Price.** Build the value of underlying assets through organic and acquisition growth and new service offerings. Leverage product and process technology into other geographic or product markets.
- **Strike Price.** Minimize the investment required to exercise growth options with contiguous growth that brings economies of scale by leveraging network assets and fixed costs or brings international partnerships and alliances that minimize initial investment and provide an affordable option to abandon.
- **Dividend.** Minimize erosion in the value of the underlying asset, such as loss of share, through continued investment in brand strength and service reliability. Provide a full gamut of services to increase customer switching costs.
- **Term.** Opportunistically raise capital for investment. Build and maintain sufficient cash and liquidity to fund organic and acquisition growth to replenish future prospects. Minimize dividends and buybacks to preserve cash for investment.
- **Volatility.** Create upside with investments that have potential for significant upside and a growth strategy that measures and manages risk rather than avoiding it outright.

LESS DEBT IS NOW "OPTIMAL"

Optimal capital structure is a topic of continued academic research and debate. Although the trade-offs between debt and equity are well documented, the over-riding needs of a company and the intangible nature of many of the costs and benefits of leverage have relegated much of the debate to academic quarters. Practitioners tend to make their decisions based on target credit ratings and other factors, albeit with modest consideration to financial theory.

The benefits of debt have been well documented. Debt is the most convenient form of financing that avoids diluting the ownership interest of equity holders while funding growth. Debt service is a tax efficient use of operating cash flows. Financial leverage can reduce your weighted average cost of capital (WACC) by substituting lower cost debt for more expensive equity. Leverage reduces agency costs through increased fiscal discipline, sending a positive signal to the investment community.

The overall WACC function is lower, flatter, and more shifted to the left (Figure 7.2). The WACC, over different target amounts of financial leverage, has changed. The optimal proportion of debt in the composition of a corporation's capital structure has been steadily reduced since 1998 through the confluence of three factors. A combination of explicit costs and intangible considerations combine to keep the cost of leverage high in a low

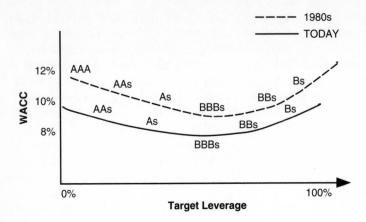

FIGURE 7.2   Value Proposition of Debt

rate era. Three factors contribute to the reduction in the optimal level of debt for today's capital structures:

1. Equity is now cheaper
2. Ratings are tougher
3. Debt carries hidden costs

Equity is Now Cheaper

The monetary policy of our low rate era contributes to a lower cost of equity. With long-term U.S. Treasuries in the 5 percent range (versus 8 to 10 percent only a few years ago), there is a much lower baseline cost for risk-free capital. And though credit spreads over Treasuries have widened for debt, the market risk premium (MRP) for equity has narrowed. A reduced cost of equity is apparent in our own expectations and current valuations, as well as analysis of historical excess returns in equities.

The dramatic market declines of recent years have had quite the dampening effect on investor expectations. At the height of the bubble, it was commonplace to witness, and expect, annual equity returns of 15 to 20 percent. With the experience of losses and low returns, irrational exuberance has been replaced with more reasonable expectations. Long-term return expectations are now more typically in the range of 7 to 9 percent per year.

A deleveraging event can, therefore, create tremendous value for a highly leveraged company in today's environment. Equity values are often constrained under severe leverage as is generally evidenced in lower trading multiples. With higher capital costs and reduced financial flexibility, equity values are lower because of the constraints imposed on the opportunity for positive NPV growth.

However, the bulk of the value will accrue to the bondholders (bonds trade up on reduced default risk) unless the benefit can be captured in a lower interest expense. A shorter duration liability structure with a variable margin (pricing grid) can increase the wealth transfer to equity holders in a deleveraging event. As a result, if deleveraging is a consideration, it should be done before, or in conjunction with, a duration extension designed to take advantage of historically low interest rates.

Ratings are Tougher

The ratings agencies (primarily Moody's, Standard & Poor's, and Fitch) have been under siege since the bankruptcy of investment-grade KMart and the sudden collapse of many high-profile credits (e.g., Enron and WorldCom). The agencies have responded with enhanced capabilities in such critical areas as corporate governance, derivatives accounting, and structured finance, and a rash of downgrades. The number of credit downgrades far exceeds the number of upgrades. Many companies sense that the ratings requirements, especially the important thresholds for investment grade (BBB−) and A1/P1 commercial paper access (roughly equivalent to the long term A rating), have been tightened.

In today's market, higher leverage and lower credit quality can impede market access. The debt and equity markets are larger and more accessible for higher quality credits. The number, size, and marketability of issues in lower credit quality markets is more restricted, and the market is more often closed altogether.

Credit quality provides availability of capital for growth and possibly ready access to the commercial paper markets. High leverage reduces financial flexibility and credit quality, which drives not only the cost and availability of credit but also serves as a signal to the markets, customers, and suppliers of overall financial viability. This becomes especially visible in difficult times when credit quality is a focus. Higher growth expectations generally imply a greater need for, and value to, financial flexibility.

Debt Carries Hidden Costs

Although Treasury rates remain near historic lows, the cost of lower credit quality debt remains high because of credit spreads. Highly levered firms experience higher funding costs and may have difficulties in raising capital. In difficult markets, access may be closed, insufficient, or prohibitively expensive. Other costs run the gamut from higher surety and insurance premiums to the inordinate toll on management time by the need to manage within the confines of high leverage.

Excessive leverage can actually increase WACC due to the combined cost impact of wider credit spreads, increased risk of financial distress, and the reduced tax shield value. Increased leverage reduces the probability for realization of tax shields as the likelihood of sufficient profits falls with rising interest expense. Loss carry forwards are not fully utilized, time value is lost, and tax shield value is diminished by the risk of financial distress.

EXTEND DURATION WHEN RATES ARE LOW

Beyond managing down the overall proportion of debt within your capital structure, a low rate era brings further opportunity to create value in optimizing the construct of your debt portfolio—liability management. We use an efficient frontier approach that draws from portfolio theory with liability management application to evaluate the cost-risk trade-offs around your decisions for fixed-floating mix and term/duration structure.

Liability management has traditionally centered decisions on vague notions of asset-liability matching (ALM). Most companies establish a stable policy to somehow reflect the asset mix in their business by implicitly matching assets and liabilities. A common policy, for example, is to maintain a fixed-floating mix of 60:40 if fixed assets tend to be 1.5×net working capital.

But these simplistic practices of ALM do not provide a natural hedge. The relative amount of net working capital is roughly constant over time, suggesting it is really a permanent asset. Nor does the rate of return generated by working capital typically reflect the cost of floating-rate debt. However, true ALM approaches do prove useful (as we will discuss in Chapters 10, 11, and 12), and it is important to view floating-rate exposure more holistically, including the impact of cash and other investments, pension assets and liabilities, and so forth.

Another common approach is to try to balance financial risk against operating risk. Businesses with stable margins and volumes can afford more low-cost short-term floating-rate debt. Interest rate–sensitive businesses might use more long-term fixed rate debt to hedge against a nexus of high interest rates in a poor operating environment.

But businesses with little debt, or more cash or other interest sensitive assets, or higher margins, can afford more floating-rate exposure in their liabilities. And our analysis of operating company interest rate sensitivity is often inconclusive. The risk of interest expense rising when operating income is falling is not constant. Interest rate sensitivity is volatile and unpredictable. Attempts to quantify the relationship run into challenges with reliability. And basing funding decisions on perceived operating risk yields an inconsistent, readily definable financial policy.

Dynamic Fixed-Floating Ratio

With interest rates low, the lure to term out with low-cost, long-dated paper is intuitive to every homeowner. However, poor operating results and low short-term rates can make the earnings benefit of short-term floating-rate debt more appealing than ever. Figure 7.3 illustrates the efficient frontier concept, by plotting funding cost against funding risk. The curved line illustrates the resulting cost-risk trade-off of various fixed-floating ratios (from 90 percent fixed/10 percent floating all the way to 10 percent fixed/90 percent floating). This is frequently modeled over the past 20 to 50 years of corporate bond yields, with results varying widely depending on the window of history selected.

In our example, the lowest cost approach is a liability portfolio with a composition that is 10 percent fixed rate debt, a cost of about 8.7 percent, and a risk (standard deviation) of about 2.6 percent. The lowest risk approach is about 80 percent fixed rate debt, a cost of about 9.8 percent, and a risk (standard deviation) of about 1.3 percent. Adding any more fixed rate debt adds more risk and cost. Thus, the efficient frontier is anywhere along this line, that is, below 80 percent fixed.

But despite the widespread belief that there is an optimal ratio, the optimal fixed-floating mix varies. Dynamic strategies that react to market information can lower funding cost and risk simultaneously. A static policy unnecessarily adds risk and cost. Our historical simulation demonstrates

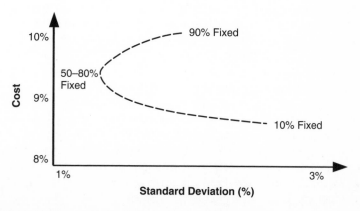

FIGURE 7.3 Dynamic Strategies Outperform Efficient Frontier

that dynamic fixed-floating strategies can outperform the efficient frontier. The dynamic strategy is cheaper than being only 10 percent fixed and is safer than being 80 percent fixed. Our algorithm reassessed fixed-floating mix on a quarterly basis and made changes according to the target mix guidelines. The mix is achieved through an efficient combination of swaps and new issuance, as needed.

In general, an optimal dynamic fixed-floating policy will term more out when rates are low and will float more when rates are high, to take advantage of the current favorable interest rate environment and improve the cost-risk profile of liability structures for any interest rate environment. This is not speculating on interest rates but is prudent interest rate management. Interestingly, Boards of Directors are more supportive of CFOs being opportunistic in issuing equity or buying back stock than they are with liability management.

Swaps and Treasury Locks

The use of swaps to manage the proportion of floating-rate debt should not be a distraction. They are the best means to affect changes in fixed-floating ratios. Negative sentiment around derivatives and speculation distracts us from what is fundamentally a superior approach to interest rate management in terms of cost and risk.

Interest rate volatility can be managed with tools such as swaps and Treasury locks. Their use seems especially appropriate with interest rates at historic lows and future moves more likely to be up than down. Beyond terming out and reducing the proportion of short-term floating-rate debt, duration can be extended by swapping floating-rate notes to fixed-rate ones, lifting fixed-to-floating swaps and shortening the terms of any fixed-to-floating rate swaps. Rolling swaps down the yield curve to shorter terms, while maintaining or even increasing the notional amount swapped to floating, and can preserve the low-cost benefits (positive carry) but reduce interest rate risk by extending duration.

Treasury locks and forward-starting swaps fix much of the cost of new issues by hedging all or a portion of the pricing (T-locks, or rate locks, secure the underlying Treasury rate; forward-starting swaps also lock in the A-rated credit spread, as this is the basis of the swap curve). Treasuries and provide another tool to extend duration and lower risk. New bond issues for refinancing or growth can be a larger source of interest rate risk than floating-rate debt because the period of exposure tends to be too short to average out sufficiently. Even intraday risk can be high as we have seen in the turbulent markets of the past few years.

Ladders, Gaps, and Towers

Avoid maturity gaps and maturity towers in the construct of your liability maturities. Staggered maturities decrease variability as the interest cost each year is a rolling average of interest rates. Thus, laddered maturities lower funding risk akin to dollar cost averaging. Cost is reduced opportunistically by increasing issuance, lengthening terms, avoiding callability, and terming out when rates are low. Ladders are built by targeting a fixed percentage of total liabilities to mature in each year (e.g., 10 percent per year for 10 years). Ten-year to 15-year ladders provide the best mix of cost and risk performance. Larger companies (total liabilities exceed $2 billion) will tend to use a 10-year to 15-year ladder, yet smaller companies will only have sufficient liabilities to construct a five-year to seven-year ladder.

MAINTAIN FINANCIAL LIQUIDITY TO "INSURE" YOUR EQUITY

We have seen analysts and agencies placing a greater emphasis on carrying a stronger cash and liquidity position, yet low interest rates have led to some large short-term floating-rate debt portfolios. A combination of the following actions enhance liquidity:

- Improve base case quarterly cash flows, or identify discretionary sources of liquidity (such as deferrable costs, capex, dividends, and working capital).
- Hold more operating cash and marketable securities.
- Maintain near-cash equivalents such as undrawn lines (beyond what is required to backstop a commercial paper program).
- Reduce commercial paper exposure.

Essentially, two types of cash draws exist: expected and unexpected. Events whose timing and amount are determined are a draw on operating cash flow and external financing. For example, repayment of a previously incurred liability or contractually obligated payments such as underfunded pensions and postdirect benefits. Events that are uncertain with respect to amount, timing, or occurrence are a draw on liquidity. Financial and operating leverage magnify their impact, but liquidity should be sufficient to absorb these events, such as volatility of interest rates, prices, costs or volumes, environmental liabilities, litigation.

Cost of Financial Liquidity

The costs of holding too much cash are more apparent in this low interest rate environment than ever, with a low rate of return earned, double taxation of interest income, and the temptation to waste cash on low return investments (agency costs). Conventional wisdom has companies going to great lengths to minimize cash balances because you cannot earn your after-tax WACC on cash balances. Most favor near-cash equivalents in the form of undrawn lines and commercial paper (CP) access. But many companies are sitting on billions of dollars in CP that must be continuously refinanced. Some companies even raise commercial paper to invest in money markets as a supplementary form of earnings accretion. But short terms bring refinancing risk. Floating rates bring interest rate risk.

In February of 2002, Qwest Communications was forced to draw down its $4 billion bank facility. It used the proceeds to pay down all of its $3.2 billion of commercial paper. Drawing on bank lines can be a negative signal to the equity markets, and in this case, Qwest was downgraded by the rating agencies following the announcement. As with other high-profile case studies of liquidity crisis (e.g., Lucent, Xerox, and Tyco), the Qwest case was a complex one that involved more than just liquidity. Many are complicated by earnings disappointments, accounting concerns, multiple credit rating downgrades, and significant challenges in refinancing maturing liabilities. However, massive losses in shareholder wealth illustrate the ultimate cost of poor liquidity. In the Qwest case, $11 billion, or 75 percent of the equity value, evaporated in the months around the liquidity crisis.

Liquidity is more important, and its cost even less significant, for those premium companies with the highest relative growth valuations. The cost of strong liquidity can be a fraction of the economic value it supports. Liquidity reduces the risks that stem from markets closing to the issuer, i.e., refinancing risk. Strong liquidity can help offset volatile operating cash flows and interest rate volatility. Liquidity is more important than ever before and its cost remains small.

Operating cash levels help minimize the transaction costs associated with raising funds and support important investment funding when it might otherwise be unavailable or would be prohibitively expensive. Liquidity can have a strategic rationale in the signaling value it offers to comfort customers, warn competitors, or provide a financial buffer to a hostile labor environment. It can preemptively signal a capacity and commitment to retaliation against hostile labor action or competitive market encroachment.

Always positioned for growth, Southwest Airlines has historically grown when times were difficult, acquiring equipment and competing aggressively on price. Southwest carries considerable cash on hand despite being the only investment-grade credit in the sector. Companies such as Microsoft or

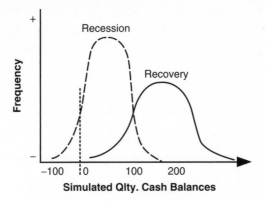

FIGURE 7.4   Volatility and Outlook Drive Liquidity

Yahoo, where most of the enterprise value must be attributed to the present value of operating cash flows above their current level, hold billions of cash and near cash on hand. The risk of foregone opportunity is greatest in the growth stages of a company life cycle when most of the enterprise value is premised on growth.

Figure 7.4 illustrates a speculative-grade industrial company's worsened liquidity outlook (due to unfavorable commodity pricing and the foreign exchange or FX) by identifying the probability of need for external sources of funding over the next four quarters. A low likelihood (less than 1 percent probability) of need for external sources of cash over the next four quarters represents strong liquidity. In our simulation, increased volatility and a reduced operating forecast increased probability of need for external sources of cash, from less than 1 percent to 10 to 15 percent, with the maximum potential draw increasing from $50 million to $75 million. As a remedy, the company increased target cash from $50 million to $100 million to maintain 99 percent confidence on liquidity, and it increased undrawn available lines from $75 million to $150 million, or twice the maximum draw, to cover any potential cash shortfall.

A NEW PERSPECTIVE ON EQUITY

Though many people might equate share price with the corporate cost of equity, equity's true cost is determined by the interest rate environment and investor expectations. Both are at historic lows. As outlined earlier, the cost of equity has fallen. There has been a significant decline in the expectations of the equity capital markets, from analysis of historical excess returns and from the implied expectations of more recent equity market valuations. Several macroeconomic forces have conspired to reduce equity returns. We have empirically measured and documented the effects of structural change and offer the following economic rationale:

- **Size.** Larger markets provide more liquidity and less volatility and risk.
- **Globalization.** Global economic growth and trade has lowered total equity risk.
- **Information and technology.** Improved financial reporting, disclosure, and information technology has reduced uncertainty and required returns.
- **Agency costs.** Investors are more active in influencing companies to maximize shareholder value, which reduces the risk of common stock.

But issuing equity at low share prices leads to significant dilution of the existing ownership interests, a practical impediment to issuance no matter how compelling the rationale. How then, can equity be most efficiently raised in this environment?

Debt-for-Equity Exchange

Many highly leveraged companies find themselves boxed in by the combination of share price and reluctance or inability to increase leverage any further. In these cases, a debt-for-equity exchange captures any discount on the bonds as an economic offset to the cost of equity dilution. Successful exchanges can be structured to share the value created through deleveraging and appeal to the concerns of bondholders and equity holders, leaving the company more appropriately capitalized after the exchange.

Forward Equity

A forward issuance of equity can raise capital today to facilitate the benefits of immediate deleveraging but defer the cost of equity dilution to the future. Unlike a rights offering, there is no option but an obligation to issue equity at a future date.

Equity Shelf

Equity shelf programs allow issuers to dribble small amounts of equity into the market over long periods of time. With all the advantages of dollar cost averaging, they are suited to today's turbulent equity markets. Typically limited in size, they do not risk the dilution of a large equity issue.

Hybrids

Recent changes in the way rating agencies accord equity treatment (50 to 100 percent) for certain hybrids (such as long-dated junior subordinated bonds that contain forced deferral provisions and restrictions around refinancing, i.e., replacement language) have made this an attractive approach to strengthening a balance sheet. Furthermore, convertibles remain a significant pool of capital. Mandatory convertibles tend to be accorded especially high equity content (50–80 percent). Convertibles are a hybrid financing vehicle, essentially a combination of a warrant (long-dated equity call option) and a bond. Convertibles have become popular in today's uncertain market, in part, because they effectively monetize the volatility of the stock.

The value of the warrant permits a lower coupon. Higher volatility brings more value to the conversion option, regardless of the low expectations that depress straight equity values. Tax enhancements are frequently employed to bring further substantial benefits. Depending on the specific type, ratings agencies can accord some equity content to the instrument, providing support to the credit profile.

Pension Funding

Poor equity markets have led to large underfunded pensions. Prefunding underfunded pension liabilities is increasingly attractive with analysts and rating agencies focused on this new liability. Hybrids and convertibles are suited to reduce these liabilities efficiently and to add equity to the balance sheet.

Distribute Less

Shareholder distributions (dividends plus buybacks) represent equity issuance in reverse. Regardless of pending changes in dividend taxation, any distribution of excess funds back to shareholders is just that: taking surplus money out of the business to give back to shareholders. Distributions should be a second-order decision in the event a better use of funds cannot be found.

However, with interest rates low, equity markets uncertain, and share prices down, it may be tempting to enhance a stock's appeal with unwarranted boosts in shareholder distributions (with dividends or buybacks). Avoiding this temptation (and distributing less rather than more) is akin to equity issuance without the fees and provides an efficient source of equity funding for the business.

CASE STUDY: DOES TECH NEED DEBT?

We highlight many of the principles of today's optimal capital structure with a case study for the technology sector. Technology faces many of the issues with which corporations are struggling but in more extreme proportions. The appeal of low interest rates raises the question of whether additional debt would be more appropriate. Large and growing cash positions raise questions of optimal cash for operating liquidity and forms of secondary liquidity. Dividends and buybacks are now a perennial Board of Directors agenda item in technology.

Though a case for a modest increase in financial leverage may exist among the larger, more mature technology companies, the case is more compelling—and the value proposition far greater—for technology companies to optimize (i.e., in most cases, reduce) their cash balances and investigate alternative means for secondary liquidity to buffer event risk (as we outline in our chapter on strategic risk management). Share repurchases and, in some cases, special dividends represent the most efficient mechanism to reallocate this capital to more productive and profitable uses. (See Chapter 8 for more on dividends and buybacks.)

WACC Minimization Does Not Equal Value Maximization

Intrinsic value purists routinely assume that the optimal capital structure puzzle is an exercise in WACC minimization. The premise is that since firm value is the present value of all future cash flows, it stands to reason that value is maximized when the discount rate is minimized. Though this logic seems correct on the surface, the requisite simplifying assumption is that future cash flows are a constant and are not affected by the financial leverage of the enterprise. As financial leverage increases, financial strength decreases, potentially impairing the company's growth in future operating cash flows, particularly in extreme cases where R&D may be reduced, capital expenditure rationed, acquisitions curtailed, and long-term sales contracts jeopardized, in the face of reduced financial strength.

In technology, this is especially true. Market values tend to be more premised on growth than on the present value of current operating cash flows, and these expectations for growth often imply substantive investment. Financial strength may have implications for bargaining power, competitive response, risk management, and funding for customer financing.

Figure 7.5 illustrates the spectrum of WACC and enterprise values for two hypothetical companies—an A-rated high-growth company and a strong B-rated, mature company—over a wide range of choices in financial leverage. In both cases, enterprise value is maximized. In the case of the

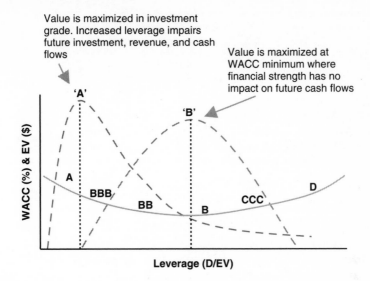

FIGURE 7.5 WACC Minimization Doesn't Equal Value Maximization

A-rated company, WACC is not minimized; in the B case, WACC is minimized. The B company valuation is predicated largely on the present value of current cash flows, so its value is maximized when the discount rate is minimized. In the A case, maximizing the value of current cash flows through WACC minimization is less important than financial strength. The A company valuation is largely predicated on positive NPV growth beyond the level of current cash flows, so financial strength, strategic liquidity, and access to capital are critical value drivers.

Optimal Capital Structure Begins with Optimal Financial Strength

Rather than beginning with WACC, our starting point for determining optimal capital structure is to determine the requisite financial strength to support the business and its strategy.

Figure 7.6 illustrates a conceptual framework that outlines the key determinants of requisite financial strength, broadly categorized according to an adapted version from the Porter framework for competitive advantage: external threats, competitive forces, and customer/supplier bargaining power.

Increased financial strength may be warranted in operating environments that involve heightened regulatory interference or constraints, threat of litigation (e.g., asbestos, product liability, environmental remediation),

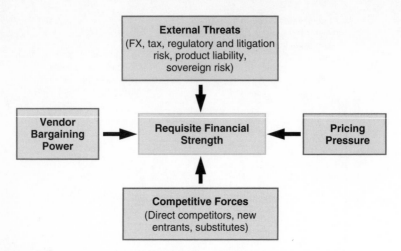

FIGURE 7.6   Framework for Optimal Financial Strength

labor hostility, or sovereign risk. Alternatively, insurance, or contingent capital, may be used to afford similar protection against event risk.

Financial strength may be advantageous in preempting or responding to competitive forces, such as direct competition, new entrants, or competitive substitutes. Financial strength may afford higher levels of investment, acquisitions, higher marketing costs, aggressive pricing, R&D, and more competitive labor rates.

Finally, greater financial strength may be advantageous in providing increased bargaining power with suppliers, or in sustaining pricing pressure in competitive markets. Businesses involving significant counterparty risk, such as financial institutions, business process outsourcing, and project engineering, can be especially sensitive to credit ratings.

Value Proposition of Debt

The value proposition of debt has shifted dramatically over the past 20 years since many of our finance textbooks were first published. The classic post-Miller and Modigliani proposition suggests that tremendous intrinsic value may be created through the substitution of debt for equity in a capital structure due to the tax shield of interest expense. The exact amount of intrinsic value created will be a function of the difference between the cost of equity and the after-tax cost of debt. This spread is, in turn, a function of the riskless rate, levered beta, the amount of debt substituted for equity and its impact on credit rating, and credit spreads.

As we had illustrated earlier in Figure 7.2, the value proposition of debt has changed in the low rate environment of this decade, versus the high rate environment of the 1980s. The overall WACC function is now lower and flatter, and its minimum has shifted to the left. Perhaps counterintuitively, the reduction in WACC achieved (and intrinsic value created) by leveraging a firm is less than what would have been achieved in a higher rate environment. The value proposition of debt in a low cost of capital environment is less compelling.

However, the value proposition of debt is less compelling in a low cost of capital environment, and there are other value drivers to consider.

Beta   Higher beta companies face a higher cost of equity, potentially increasing the spread between the cost of equity and the after-tax cost of debt and increasing the value proposition of debt. The WACC function is higher and steeper (i.e., more concave) at the equity end of the leverage spectrum. Unfortunately, in practice, high beta companies often carry less debt capacity and face lower cash tax rates, leading to higher after tax funding costs and a lower value proposition for debt.

Credit Spreads   Speculative-grade credit spreads vary widely, making it them an impractical input from which to base long-term financial policy. However, much like beta, credit spreads can affect the value proposition of debt. When spreads are tighter and funding costs lower, the value proposition of debt increases, with a lower WACC curve on the leveraged end of the spectrum. The WACC curve rises and its inflection point (i.e., minimum) moves toward equity as spreads widen and funding costs rise.

Technology Considerations

The economic advantages of debt are documented in the literature. Much of this case is premised on the intrinsic value of interest expense tax deductibility and a rather benign cost to the firm for the risk of distress under modest amounts of financial leverage. However, in the technology sector, these conditions do not hold as well as they do for many industrials.

Taxes   Many technology companies have low cash tax rates. Early stage technology companies have not become profitable. Many others carry significant loss carry forwards. The prevalence of broad-based employee stock options further reduces taxable income. Technology companies tend to go global at an earlier stage in their life, creating opportunities for efficient global tax planning.

Debt Capacity   The relative value of tax shields are further reduced by the lower degree of leveragability of technology companies. Most technology companies are accorded less debt capacity per dollar of earnings before interest, tax, depreciation, and amortization (EBITDA) than would be a credit from other sectors such as industrials or power. This is because rating agencies are less comfortable with the quality and sustainability of these cash flows. A perception of less certain market outlooks, shorter product cycles, higher risk of substitute technologies, fewer and less valuable assets to liquidate, and a generally more dynamic operating environment all give creditors greater cause for concern.

Valuation   Technology valuations tend to be more predicated on growth and future prospects than on the present value of current operating cash flows. Therefore any threat to this growth in future cash flows will have a relatively more profound impact on the overall valuation. The cost to the firm for the risk of distress, illiquidity, or constraints on growth and investment represent a much greater proportion of the total enterprise value in a more mature company.

Value Proposition of Excess Cash

The value proposition of excess cash is more significant than the value proposition of excess debt capacity. Though the value proposition of debt is scrutinized, less attention is generally paid to the value proposition of cash (notwithstanding our earlier chapter on cash). Generally speaking, the returns on cash, on an after-tax basis, are far below the WACC, a shortfall frequently on the order of 5 to 7 percent in after-tax terms. The cost to intrinsic value of this shortfall tends to be more significant in a low rate environment. And many corporations today face large and growing cash balances.

Table 7.1 illustrates the value proposition of excess cash. From the first panel, after-tax returns on cash will generally be in the range of 2 to 3 percent. Most corporations face a WACC of about 7 to 9 percent, though in practice, they may be employing a higher internal hurdle rate. In a higher rate environment, when cash returns might reach 4 to 5 percent, WACC could reach 10 to 12 percent. The second panel shows the NPV of $1, held in perpetuity, at rates below WACC. One dollar of cash earning 3 percent after tax, subject to a corporate WACC of 10 percent, is worth only $0.30. This opportunity cost far exceeds the opportunity cost of inadequate leverage.

Theoretically, one could argue that the WACC of excess cash is closer to the riskless rate than the corporate WACC, limiting the value destruction of excess cash to the bid/ask spread on cash management plus the cost of double taxation. However, for this position to hold and for the cost of

TABLE 7.1 Value Proposition of Excess Cash

NPV of $1 Cash

A/T	WACC				
Return	8%	9%	10%	11%	12%
2%	0.25	0.22	0.20	0.18	0.17
3%	0.38	0.33	0.30	0.27	0.25
4%	0.50	0.44	0.40	0.36	0.33
5%	0.63	0.56	0.50	0.45	0.42

A/T Return

Tax	Cash Return				
Rate	1%	2%	3%	4%	5%
0%	1.0%	2.0%	3.0%	4.0%	5.0%
10%	0.9%	1.8%	2.7%	3.6%	4.5%
20%	0.8%	1.6%	2.4%	3.2%	4.0%
25%	0.8%	1.5%	2.3%	3.0%	3.8%
30%	0.7%	1.4%	2.1%	2.8%	3.5%
35%	0.7%	1.3%	2.0%	2.6%	3.3%
40%	0.6%	1.2%	1.8%	2.4%	3.0%

excess cash to be the matched maturity cost of debt, the presence of excess cash should lead to greater debt capacity. If the excess cash consumes debt capacity that might otherwise be used to fund general corporate purposes, then the true cost of these funds is not the after-tax cost of matched maturity debt. Analysis of credit ratings and credit spreads indicates that the markets generally evaluate credits on a gross debt basis, indicating that empirically, the cost of excess cash is in fact the corporate WACC. (See Chapter 5 for more on cash.)

One might hope that equity markets see things in a different light, perhaps attributing some degree of cushioning to stocks with excess cash. But empirically, systematic risk is unrelated to cash levels and there is no support to show that betas are reduced by the presence of cash. Empirically, the cost of excess cash appears to be the full WACC.

In jurisdictions, such as Europe, and for a few others, where ratings are still premised on net debt ratios, excess cash does not consume corporate debt capacity and may be reasoned to have a cost equal to the after-tax cost of matched maturity debt. In these cases, the value destruction of excess cash is the difference between the pretax return and the after-tax cost of short-term funds.

CHAPTER 8

Dividends and Buybacks: Calibrating Your Shareholder Distributions

In the face of recent events, dividend and share repurchase policies are being rewritten. Dividend and buyback announcements are increasing as companies struggle to deal with languishing share prices and uncertain futures. Low interest rates, weak share prices, uncertain markets, and large and growing cash balances are putting pressure on companies to increase shareholder distributions (dividends and buybacks).

Shareholder distributions are under intense scrutiny. The first announcement by Microsoft to initiate a small dividend (and its subsequent announcements to double and double again its dividend to distribute $75 billion over three years in dividends and buybacks) contrasted with an announcement the prior year to reinvest $10 billion in additional research. Dividends and share repurchases have reached significant levels in Technology, despite the sector's tremendous growth prospects (Figure 8.1).

During 2005, most companies of the S&P 500 index repurchased their own shares and paid. Over the past 10 years, shareholder distributions have changed significantly.

- U.S. buyback volume more than tripled as a percentage of the market value of equity.
- Dividends have declined over the same period. Yields and payout ratios fell by about 25 percent.
- Share buybacks have replaced dividends as the largest volume mechanism for corporate cash disbursement.

All this buyback activity has not increased corporate leverage. In fact, overall leverage has been trending downward despite buyback activity. The valuations of the late bull markets reduced the debt-to-enterprise value ratio

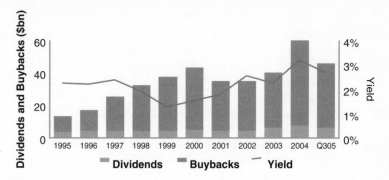

FIGURE 8.1 Technology Sector Dividends and Buybacks

for S&P 500 companies from the mid-twenties and low thirties earlier in the decade and with the sluggish market performance of the last few years now behind us, leverage ratios are again strong.

Shareholder distributions are typically lowest in industries with the most value attributable to future growth. Growth companies are most likely to need to reinvest to achieve their growth and may have the best chances of investing at returns above their cost of capital. Microsoft still pays only a notional dividend with cash primarily reserved for development, acquisitions, and its ongoing antitrust defense.

Any distribution of excess funds back to shareholders is just that: returning surplus money from the business to shareholders. Distributions should be a second-order decision in the event a better use of funds cannot be found. Companies lacking sufficient growth prospects to earn returns above their weighted average cost of capital (WACC) can best serve shareholders with cash distributions: some mix of dividends and share repurchases, after determining cash generation, investment opportunity, capital structure, and liquidity.[1]

Ideally, the distribution determination is a residual one, after determining cash generation, investment opportunity, capital structure, and liquidity needs. In practice, the decision is somewhat anchored by prior year practice, requiring a form of incrementalism to avoid unintentional signaling to the market. The implications for corporate financial policy are clear:

- Large and growing cash balances increase the urgency to distribute excess cash.
- The optimal total shareholder distribution (dividend and buyback) level remains a second-order residual policy, after determining business needs.

- The optimal mix of dividends and buybacks is another decision point for policy; dividends are best employed only for the most certain baseline excess quarterly cash flows, with buybacks and special dividends suited to less certain cash flows, or surplus amounts.

Open market repurchase programs are the best alternative to dividends and are especially appropriate for uncertain cash flows. Changes in accounting and public opinion have made conventional option-based (i.e., writing puts) repurchase programs much less attractive, but new, accounting-friendly, structures are available. Dutch auction self-tender offers (versus fixed price) remain the most effective mechanisms to create value through increased leverage, signal an undervalued stock, or manage rapid change in ownership.

THE CASH PROBLEM

The costs of holding too much cash are more apparent than ever in this low interest rate environment: a low rate of return earned, double taxation of interest income, and the temptation to waste cash on low return investments (agency costs). Conventional wisdom has companies go to great lengths to minimize cash balances because you cannot earn your after-tax WACC on cash balances. Most favor near-cash equivalents in the form of undrawn lines and commercial paper (CP) access to provide event risk liquidity. Cash balances are at historic highs and growing despite a growing wave of distributions. Figure 8.2 illustrates for the technology sector, where the cash problem has been epidemic.

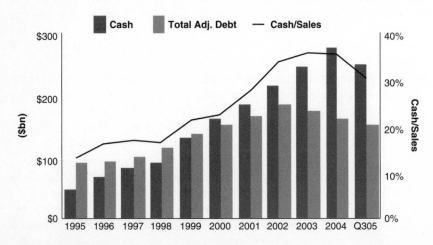

FIGURE 8.2   Technology Sector Cash and Debt

Liquidity helps offset volatile operating cash flows or interest rate volatility. It is more important than ever before and its cost remains small. The cost of strong liquidity can be a fraction of the economic value it supports. Operating cash levels help minimize the transaction costs associated with raising funds and support important investment funding when it might otherwise be unavailable or would be prohibitively expensive. Liquidity reduces the risks that stem from markets closing to the issuer: refinancing risk.

Liquidity can have a strategic rationale in the signaling value it offers to comfort customers, warn competitors, or provide a financial buffer to a hostile labor environment. It can preemptively signal a capacity and commitment to retaliation against hostile labor action or competitive market encroachment.

Liquidity is more important, and its cost is less significant, for premium companies with the highest relative growth valuations. Companies such as Microsoft or Yahoo hold large amounts of cash on hand. The risk of foregone opportunity is greatest in the early stages of a company life cycle when most of the enterprise value is premised on growth.

DIVIDENDS ARE BACK

Dividends are back in fashion. This dividend renaissance is due to the culmination of several contributing factors, including capital market conditions, the growth of governance, and changes to accounting and taxes. And Microsoft alone has had a profound impact on global dividend policy. Though its case would seem unique—with profound levels of cash, cash flow, and a seemingly unassailable market position—boardrooms around the world and across all industries benchmark themselves to this company. The adoption or increase of dividends by admired corporations, no matter how different their circumstances, has forced the dividend discussion into Board of Directors agendas where it might otherwise never have surfaced.

Capital Markets

With interest rates still low by historic standards, many investors are looking for dividend income. Generally, poor equity returns have added momentum to this trend because of a general perception that dividends provide a safe haven in turbulent markets. The tremendous growth of the income trusts market in Canada, international development of the real estate investment trust (REIT) market, resurgence in master limited partnerships (MLPs) in the United States, and the perceived success of extreme dividend policy adopters in the United States has added broad momentum to dividend discussions. Several high-profile corporations initiated dividends, including Microsoft, Federal Express, and Qualcomm. Each of these companies cited reduced capital expenditure requirements and a desire to provide more certainty to investors about future returns.

Governance

Early in the decade, the advent of numerous accounting scandals and cases of corporate fraud made investors wary, even of investment-grade companies and household names. One prominent news magazine noted that a majority of 500 institutional investors polled by Cisco would like a dividend when the tax law changed. Another magazine suggested that evidence of profitability in the form of dividend check would help many investors sleep better, as their skepticism of accounting-based earnings had grown. Another highlighted the same issue stating that, in 2002, stocks of S&P 500 companies that did not pay a dividend had performed twice as badly as those that did.

Stock Options

Dividends reduce the value of stock options. Option holders are ineligible to receive the dividend, and no matter the valuation model employed, distributions reduce the residual value of underlying assets, reducing the value of options. Though share repurchases erode the value of the underlying asset, they also reduce the shares outstanding, such that the option holder is made whole. As the popularity of stock option-based compensation programs soared over the past decade, the economic incentive to favor repurchases over dividends grew. Furthermore, share repurchases are commonly employed as a mechanism to offset the earnings dilution of stock options.

The decline in stock options removed the economic penalty of dividends and left companies with more excess cash to redeploy. Stock options fell out of favor as stock prices fell and millions of option grants became worthless. Many companies reported the uncomfortable situation of a bifurcated employee base of haves and have-nots to be untenable. Changes to accounting that required stock options to be expensed sealed their fate and many companies switched from stock options to restricted stock, again following the lead of Microsoft.

Dividend Tax Cut

Changes to the taxation of dividend income in the United States put dividends and buybacks on more equal footing. The tax cut on dividends was revealed in the 2003 State of the Union Address and made the dividend portion of the total shareholder return (dividend income plus capital appreciation) taxed at the same rate as capital appreciation. However, many shareholders are tax-exempt, or tax-deferred, and in many cases, the marginal bidder driving the price of the stock was already in a favorable tax position. There are also individual limits on the tax exemption and complications for foreign investors. However, ownership composition has changed with interest in dividend stocks and some flows out of corporate and municipal bonds.

HOW DIVIDENDS AND BUYBACKS CREATE VALUE

Beyond understanding your own capital position and future needs, you must understand how dividends and share repurchases affect value to determine if you should distribute money to shareholders and what the mix of dividends and repurchases should be.

On the face of it, the popularity of share repurchases is easy to understand. By purchasing its own stock, a company reduces the number of shares outstanding without affecting its reported earnings (ignoring foregone interest income). Generally speaking, that increases the company's earnings per share (EPS), but that is not how buybacks create value. Contrary to the conventional wisdom, buybacks do not create value by increasing earnings per share. The company has, after all, spent cash to purchase those shares, and company's intrinsic value is reduced by the amount of capital redeployed, reflected by reductions in cash and shares. Indeed, if increasing EPS were the only rationale for buybacks, there would be no impact on value, which, as we have seen, is not the case.

A similarly misguided view of value creation for dividends is frequently espoused. Dividend policy clearly affects the marketability and ownership composition of new issues and seasoned stocks alike. Therefore, conventional wisdom has it that long-term supply/demand relationships may be affected through the fine tuning of a cunning dividend policy. However, for the majority of stocks, the level of dividends has no bearing on its valuation in that there is generally no correlation between multiples and yields; where there is, it is negative. Low-growth companies with lower valuations pay out more in dividends. Whether studied across time or by sector, no positive correlation between dividend yields and trading multiples exists. In fact, valuations are negatively correlated with dividends, due to the higher dividend policies undertaken by lower growth businesses. We find no significant impact on systematic risk (beta), stock volatility, or stock liquidity. Even with dividend increases, most stock prices are not materially affected.

Though investors may do well to invest in dividend stocks (which are generally low beta) during turbulent times, it does not follow that issuers should adopt a higher dividend during turbulent times unless they believe their betas may be reduced through the act of adopting a higher dividend policy, which does not seem to be the case. Nor is there a sufficiently limited universe of investors and consequent price elasticity that price support may be achieved through this change. Empirically, the price elasticities of stocks are near zero.

In the strictest sense, shareholder distributions (i.e., dividends and buybacks) should be a zero net present value (NPV) proposition; excess capital is redeployed back to investors. But given the complications of reality, dividends and buybacks can and do create value and in three potential ways:

1. **Capital Efficiency.** Avoid destroying value by distributing excess capital that would otherwise not earn an adequate return.
2. **Signaling.** Signal enhanced prospects for future cash flows, which can be capitalized into the share price.
3. **Capital Structure.** An efficient mechanism to increase leverage, which can sometimes lower WACC and increase intrinsic value.

Capital Efficiency

Many corporations face large and growing cash balances. Shareholder distributions create value by avoiding the destruction of value, reallocating capital that, otherwise, will not earn its opportunity cost. The after-tax returns on cash are generally far below the WACC, frequently on the order of 5 to 7 percent in after-tax terms. This opportunity cost far exceeds the opportunity cost of inadequate leverage. And the cost to intrinsic value of this shortfall tends to be most significant in a low rate environment.

The after-tax returns on cash will generally be in the range of 2 to 3 percent. Most corporations today face a WACC of about 7 to 9 percent though, in practice, they may be employing a much higher internal hurdle rate. In a higher rate environment, when cash returns might reach 4 to 5 percent, WACC could reach 10 to 12 percent. The NPV of $1, held in perpetuity, earning 3 percent after tax, subject to a corporate WACC of 10 percent, is worth only $0.30 (30 cents).

Empirically, the cost of excess cash appears to be the full weighted average cost of capital. In practice, excess cash funded with debt consumes debt capacity that might be used to fund general corporate purposes. Analysis of credit ratings and spreads shows the markets generally evaluate credits on a gross debt basis, indicating that, empirically, the cost of excess cash is the corporate weighted average cost of capital. Furthermore, the equity markets do not attribute cushioning to stocks with excess cash. Empirically, betas are not reduced by the presence of cash. Now, as outlined in the prior chapter, in jurisdictions such as Europe, and for a few others, where ratings are still premised on net debt ratios, excess cash does not consume corporate debt capacity and may be reasoned to have a cost equal to the after-tax cost of matched maturity debt. In these cases, the value destruction of excess cash is the difference between the pretax return and the after-tax cost of short-term funds, which is the bid-ask spread plus the cost of double taxation.

Signaling

The signaling effect of dividends and share repurchases has been the focus of much academic research over the past 10 years.[2] According to these studies, investors and analysts use a company's financial decisions as a window into what managers really think about the company's prospects. The announcement of a share buyback, the argument goes, indicates that managers are so confident of their company's prospects that they believe the best investment it can make is in its own shares (notwithstanding that any shareholder distribution is a divestment decision and not an investment decision). In a comparison of the three forms of common share repurchases, fixed price self-tender offers were found to be the strongest signal of stock undervaluation, followed by the Dutch auction. Open market share repurchases were found to be a weak signal. The signal was found to be strongest when insider wealth was at risk, that is, where managers did not tender.[3]

For example, Symantec announced authorization for a 500,000-share open market repurchase in November 1997, and an additional 2.8 million in June 1998, to offset the dilution of equity incentive programs. This economic nonevent had no discernible impact on enterprise value. But, in March 1999, the Board of Directors authorized nearly five million more shares in a move cited as a good use of excess cash given the weak stock price. Indeed, less than a month later, fourth quarter earnings exceeded expectations due to strong top-line growth in the corporate customer segment, and the intrinsic value gap was closed by the market. Nontendering shareholders were rewarded with the appreciation in value now spread over a smaller base of shares.

The excess returns generally associated with distribution announcements are strongly dependent on the size of the distribution, as well as its form. Researchers have found about a 2 percent impact to stock prices from open market repurchase announcements.[4] One-time actions (special dividends, modified Dutch auction self-tenders, and fixed price self-tenders) lead to larger sustained stock price premiums and are associated with stronger signals because they tend to be larger, represent a greater commitment to execute (not just an authorization), and more frequently accompany structural changes to the balance sheet.[5] They also frequently accompany changes to the business strategy.

Investors interpret a company's decisions through the lens of past experience and, in its current context, taking into account a host of other indications and signals. The information conveyed by a dividend or buyback announcement is not always what managers intended to convey. In our experience, five key considerations help avoid a potentially negative signal:

1. **Market expectations.** As with earnings announcements, dividend and buyback actions are gauged not in absolute terms but in terms relative to market expectations. Direct communications, the pattern of past practice, and established industry practice play a role in shaping investor expectations. When actions are discordant, especially if they fall far short with existing expectations, market reaction can be negative.

2. **Operating results.** Share repurchases can provide price support and liquidity to the market during a short period of investor churn, but they cannot prop up a share price over the long run. Computer Data Systems faced operating performance problems in January 1997, with fourth quarter earnings below expectations due to market and operational difficulties. After witnessing a 25 percent share price decline, the company accelerated its open market share repurchase program in an apparent attempt to support its share price. But investors were not won over, and the stock continued to slip a further 15 percent over the next six months until a financial buyer acquired the company in July 1997.

3. **Mixed signals.** Other information can contradict, and sometimes swamp, an intended dividend or buyback signal. According to one company press release, a multiyear, multibillion-dollar program was undertaken with the aim of making opportunistic purchases at attractive prices, that is, at prices they felt undervalued the company. But the buyback signal was drowned out by a succession of other news, all emitting more powerful and contradictory signals about the company's future: an aborted acquisition, protracted business restructuring, slipping financial results, and a general decay in key markets.

4. **Growth profile.** In some cases, dividends and buybacks may be construed as a company admitting it has few important investment opportunities. Long-term investors could respond by selling shares. This effect is most commonly observed in investment-laden businesses, with high research, capital investment, product development, or marketing

and customer acquisition costs, that demand companies invest more to capture higher growth potential.

5. **Insider sales.** Signaling is weakened if insiders choose to participate in a share repurchase themselves (a regular or special dividend can be a safer choice in this respect). When managers elect to sell shares rather than retain them, they have not, in effect, put their own money where their mouths are. All other things being equal, if insiders do not participate, the benefits can be dramatic. One study of tender offer buybacks has shown that programs in which managers did not participate generated returns seven percentage points higher than those in which managers did.[6]

Capital Structure

Dividends and buybacks may create value through a more efficient capital structure. Indeed, many companies use them as a permanent way to increase their reliance on debt financing. For example, in 2000, Payless ShoeSource increased its long-term debt from $127 million to $384 million by repurchasing 25 percent of its outstanding shares through a tender offer. Its debt increased from 10 percent of capital employed to 33 percent. The returns to shareholders were remarkable: On the announcement, PayLess's share price rose from $40 to 52 dollars.

However, as discussed in the prior chapter, the value proposition of debt has been greatly diminished in today's low rate environment; traditional dividend and buyback leveraged recapitalizations were more popular, and more value-adding, in the higher rate environment of the 1980s. Today's low rate environment has been more characterized by dividend and buyback decapitalizations, funded from excess cash.

Leverage has traditionally conferred two great benefits:

1. **Tax shield of debt.** The after-tax cost of debt is often below the shareholders' expected return on equity (ROE). Used in moderation, debt can reduce a company's weighted average cost of capital. A rough value of this tax shield can be easily calculated by multiplying the increase in debt by the current corporate tax rate. In the case of Payless, the value of the additional tax shield came to about $103 million ($384 million less $127 million times 40 percent). In situations involving a straight substitution of debt for equity, this value, plus the enterprise's initial value before the buyback, becomes distributed across a smaller number of outstanding shares, increasing the value of each share.

   But debt finance is only appropriate if there are profits for the interest expense to shield from taxation and if this can be done without imposing a significant risk of financial distress. As discussed in Chapter 1, the value of a tax shield fades as pretax profits fade and financial leverage increases due to the risk of financial distress and the time value of money. Companies can know the answers to those questions only if they can predict their future cash flows with a reasonable degree of confidence. That is difficult when a company is in an industry where growth comes in rapid bursts. The market value of such a company depends on investors' assessment of its portfolio of future investment opportunities rather than on expectations about the future cash flow of current operations. In such risky situations, companies should rely on more equity content versus debt.

2. **Fiscal discipline.** Unlike equity, debt binds managers to pay out future cash flows. As many financial economists have argued, the need to pay cash to bondholders prevents managers from investing in projects that earn returns below the company's cost of capital. This effect is most often observed in leveraged buyout (LBO) situations, where the company's operating performance frequently improves after debt levels have risen. Debt creation, without retention of the proceeds of the issue, enables managers to bond their promise to pay out future cash flows. Thus, debt can be an effective substitute for dividends.[7]

Though financial strategy is often interpreted narrowly as an exercise in cost of capital minimization; in practice, the determinants of financial policy must support enterprise value maximization. Certainly, the firm's cost of capital and any resulting impact on firm value is one important element, but financial strategy must support the company's business strategy and consider financial flexibility, agency, and signaling and clientele issues.[8]

Earnings and Equity Dilution

Though dividends reduce the value of stock options, buybacks are most commonly employed as a mechanism to offset the dilution of stock-based compensation programs. In many parts of this book, we illustrate that EPS accretion is by no means a measure of intrinsic value creation; however the dilution of ownership wealth is a real issue.

Whether a buyback is accretive or dilutive is a function of the company's price-to-earnings ratio (P/E). If a company's $P/E < 1/[i \times (1 - T)]$, where i is the marginal borrowing rate and T is the marginal tax rate. Then it is accretive to EPS to do a buyback; conversely, if a P/E is higher it is dilutive to do a buyback. For example, for a company with a 3 percent cost of borrowing and 35 percent marginal tax rate, a stock buyback would be accretive as long as its P/E is less than $1/[3\% \times (1-35\%)]$, or 50x. In fact, it may be completely rational to undertake a buyback that is not accretive to earnings because the P/E can expand to offset the dilution.

However, equity issuance can dilute the ownership stake of existing shareholders. Given the prevalence of equity-based compensation, companies have an incentive to repurchase shares to secure shares for option grants and to manage equity dilution. This creates a need for additional shares to exchange for exercised options. According to the commonly used Treasury method of calculating EPS, outstanding options dilute EPS (in an amount equal to their intrinsic value). Thus, share buybacks support stock option programs in two ways. They provide companies with Treasury stock for warrant exercises and help manage dilution by reducing the number of shares outstanding.

SHOULD YOU INCREASE YOUR DIVIDEND?

Dividends have several positive attributes. They are a logistically simple way to distribute excess capital, provide low-cost investor monitoring, and deliver equity returns. In many industries, dividends are an important part of total shareholder return. Once the current and future capital position has been determined, we propose a holistic approach to determine the level and mix and execution of shareholder distributions. Dividend policy can be developed from three factors: capacity analysis, empirical evidence, and market expectations.

Dividends Versus Buybacks

Dividends plus share repurchases constitute the total shareholder yield of cash distributed from the company back to shareholders. The most appropriate mix of dividends versus share repurchases is a function of the quality of the cash flows, volatility, cyclicality, and the need for financial flexibility. Every company needs to strike its own optimal balance between dividends and share repurchases. The discretionary nature of share repurchases versus the fixed cost of dividends makes buybacks more appropriate for companies with more volatile, seasonal, cyclical, or uncertain cash flows. Share repurchases are less of a fixed charge commitment than dividends, which are difficult to change due to the signaling impact. A true residual shareholder distribution policy is best suited to uncertain distributions of excess cash.

For the same reason, ratings agencies should favor buybacks over dividends because they are more easily suspended. However, dividends tend to signal financial stability, that is, a strong and steady surplus cash flow. Most investment-grade credit companies (about 80 percent of investment-grade borrowers) pay dividends, yet most high-yield borrowers do not (about 30 percent of noninvestment-grade borrowers). Furthermore, the uncertainty surrounding the size, timing, and commitment of share repurchases make rating agencies uncomfortable, as do their popularity among creditors with other aggressive financial policies, such as acquisitions and the preference of debt versus stock financing.

Option holders will continue to favor buybacks over dividends. The value of an option is diminished by the dividend yield and option holders do not receive the dividend. Some traders will claim that buyback programs can increase stock volatility, thereby adding value to option holders.

Stocks with poor stock liquidity may be better advised to employ dividends rather than to risk further eroding their stock float with a large buyback program. However, a modest program of 1 to 2 percent per year may enhance stock liquidity by providing a natural market for the stock.

Dividend Capacity

For financial planning and policy purposes, we distinguish between excess capital that is on–balance sheet or anticipated in a one-time gain, excess free cash flow that is highly certain, and residual cash flow that is less certain or regular.

Dividends are suited to distribute only the most certain baseline excess quarterly cash flow. Companies with low cash flow volatility, high operating margins, low debt service requirements, and low investment needs can best afford to pay higher dividends. To a great extent, we view the capacity for debt and the capacity for dividends to be economic equivalents, so many of our analytics for liquidity and debt capacity may be adapted for dividend policy.

Excess operating cash flow may be distributed through a combined dividend plus an open market repurchase program, shown in Figure 8.3, where we bifurcate excess cash flows into two streams: a steady baseline for dividends and a less certain portion for share repurchases.

One contributing factor in sizing the dividend is to calibrate the dividend not to impair liquidity. For example, we may employ our stochastic liquidity simulation to ensure the dividend can be funded from quarterly operating cash flows, within a 99 percent confidence level, based on quarterly cash flow projections and assumed volatilities for sales growth and earnings before interest taxes depreciation and amortization (EBITDA) margins. In Figure 8.3, we illustrate the implied ceiling for regular sustainable dividends.

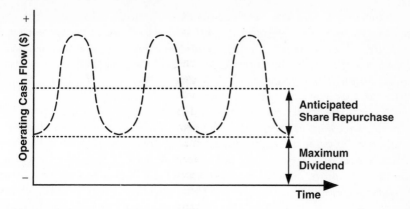

FIGURE 8.3   Dividend Capacity Analysis

Scenario stress testing may be used to provide guidance for secondary liquidity requirements to buffer event risk at various dividend levels. Finally, the dividend implications for credit quality and debt capacity can be assessed by incorporating the fixed cost of dividends into coverage and cash flow ratios. For example, Moody's employs retained cash-flow-to-debt as a measure of free cash flow after dividends to assess credits in high dividend sectors.

Ongoing share repurchase programs are suited to distribute excess cash flow with some degree of uncertainty, seasonality, cyclicality, or other irregularity. For example, in Figure 8.3, the difference between the maximum dividend (or some selected lower level) and the anticipated level of discretionary free cash flows might be allocated to a buyback program. In practice, we would budget less with the remainder going toward contingencies.

Surplus capital on-balance sheet or anticipated from a gain is best suited to a special one-time dividend or, if large enough (that is, 8 to 15 percent), a Dutch auction self-tender share repurchase.

Empirical Evidence

Our own experience, and the research of academics, shows that dividends affect ownership composition, and high dividend stocks draw more retail and income-oriented investors. And dividend policy affects stock marketability, with dividend stories making for easier going in the equity capital markets, especially new issues with less of a track record.

However, as discussed earlier, dividends generally do not affect valuations. Expectations of future (company) cash flows drive the market's valuation of a company. The dividend decision is an exercise of deciding in what form a shareholder return will be delivered to investors: capital appreciation or dividend. A higher dividend implies lower capital appreciation, all else being equal.

Accordingly, our own experience and the research of academics has found that the market's reaction to dividend increases is small, generally less than 1 percent cumulative abnormal returns. However, what these numbers fail to reflect is the wide disparity of outcomes. The law of averages obscures the more interesting question: Which stocks benefit most from dividend increases? Our own work in this area found that 8 to 10 percent excess returns are evident among a universe of companies with classic dividend characteristics:

- **Weak Valuation.** Companies with a valuation largely premised (80 percent or more) on the capitalized value of current operating cash flows tended to benefit most from dividend increases.
- **Higher Profitability.** Companies with relatively high profitability for their sector (higher EBITDA margins by 20 percent or more) tended to benefit most from dividend increases.
- **Lower Volatility.** Companies with relatively low volatility for their sector (relative stock volatility of 80 percent or less) tended to benefit most from dividend increases.
- **Uncompetitive Dividend.** Companies that benefited most from dividend increases generally had a relatively low dividend for their sector (relative payout ratio and dividend yield of 75 percent or less).
- **Large Increase.** Companies that benefited most from dividend increases generally increased their dividend by a sizeable amount (20 percent or more).

Market Expectations and Competitive Positioning

We also base dividend policy, and more importantly any changes to dividend policy, on competitive positioning and an analysis of market expectations. This is more due to the importance of signaling than on any concern about investor targeting and ownership composition.

Beyond direct communications, market expectations will be shaped by analysts, investors, and any growing consensus around what actions are necessary or pending. Market expectations are the result of established practice by the company and by others in the sector. The financial policy practices of admired companies in different sectors is generally less useful for financial policy purposes.

TABLE 8.1 Aggregate Shareholder Distribution Practices By Sector

GICS Sector Cases		1996	1997	1998	1999	2000	2001	2002	2003	2004	2005
All 1500	Dividends (%)	57%	48%	46%	45%	45%	51%	53%	54%	46%	43%
	Buybacks (%)	43%	52%	54%	55%	55%	49%	47%	46%	54%	57%
	Total ($bn)	165.9	219.0	260.6	288.3	310.6	289.9	298.2	308.8	426.2	573.6
	Yield	2.3%	2.0%	1.7%	1.4%	1.2%	1.2%	1.4%	1.9%	1.8%	2.0%
Energy 81	Dividends (%)	84%	69%	59%	91%	65%	58%	70%	65%	49%	32%
	Buybacks (%)	16%	31%	41%	9%	35%	42%	30%	35%	51%	68%
	Total ($bn)	9.1	11.8	14.4	11.7	16.7	21.8	19.1	20.8	30.4	52.5
	Yield	3.1%	2.6%	2.1%	2.7%	2.0%	1.9%	2.1%	2.4%	2.1%	1.8%
Materials 94	Dividends (%)	52%	43%	48%	58%	49%	60%	77%	73%	69%	48%
	Buybacks (%)	48%	57%	52%	42%	51%	40%	23%	27%	31%	52%
	Total ($bn)	11.1	13.9	13.1	11.4	13.1	11.4	9.0	9.6	11.5	19.4
	Yield	2.6%	2.4%	2.1%	2.6%	2.0%	2.5%	2.4%	2.6%	2.2%	2.3%
Industrials 215	Dividends (%)	58%	48%	40%	43%	45%	54%	66%	69%	53%	40%
	Buybacks (%)	42%	52%	60%	57%	55%	46%	34%	31%	47%	60%
	Total ($bn)	19.7	29.6	33.1	34.8	35.9	31.4	26.9	28.3	43.8	65.7
	Yield	2.2%	1.9%	1.5%	1.5%	1.2%	1.3%	1.5%	2.0%	1.9%	1.8%
Cons. Disc. 269	Dividends (%)	51%	41%	46%	30%	28%	38%	38%	40%	25%	19%
	Buybacks (%)	49%	59%	54%	70%	72%	62%	62%	60%	75%	81%
	Total ($bn)	19.8	26.5	37.5	36.5	40.2	27.7	24.2	26.1	54.2	59.9
	Yield	1.8%	1.7%	2.1%	1.0%	0.9%	0.9%	0.7%	1.0%	1.0%	0.7%
Cons. Staples 76	Dividends (%)	53%	44%	49%	48%	51%	49%	44%	51%	48%	46%
	Buybacks (%)	47%	56%	51%	52%	49%	51%	56%	49%	52%	54%
	Total ($bn)	23.6	30.9	29.3	34.7	32.8	37.2	42.7	39.2	48.1	52.5
	Yield	2.3%	2.0%	1.6%	1.5%	1.6%	1.6%	1.7%	1.9%	2.0%	2.0%

(continued overleaf)

TABLE 8.1 *(continued)*

GICS Sector Cases		1996	1997	1998	1999	2000	2001	2002	2003	2004	2005
Health Care 167	Dividends (%)	54%	50%	43%	39%	48%	46%	43%	39%	39%	42%
	Buybacks (%)	46%	50%	57%	61%	52%	54%	57%	61%	61%	58%
	Total ($bn)	17.5	20.8	27.5	32.8	31.6	35.6	42.2	50.4	54.4	52.4
	Yield	1.8%	1.6%	1.3%	1.0%	1.3%	1.0%	1.2%	1.6%	1.4%	1.4%
Financials 226	Dividends (%)	62%	54%	56%	60%	60%	62%	64%	71%	66%	56%
	Buybacks (%)	38%	46%	44%	40%	40%	38%	36%	29%	34%	44%
	Total ($bn)	23.5	32.0	44.3	50.8	56.8	61.5	71.6	67.4	85.7	114.4
	Yield	2.7%	2.4%	2.2%	2.0%	2.1%	1.8%	2.3%	2.7%	2.5%	2.6%
Technology 278	Dividends (%)	23%	15%	12%	12%	12%	12%	13%	14%	14%	38%
	Buybacks (%)	77%	85%	88%	88%	88%	88%	87%	86%	86%	62%
	Total ($bn)	17.2	25.0	31.9	37.9	44.3	35.0	34.9	40.8	61.8	115.4
	Yield	0.6%	0.4%	0.3%	0.3%	0.2%	0.1%	0.2%	0.4%	0.4%	2.1%
Telecom. Services 12	Dividends (%)	81%	84%	72%	62%	63%	74%	83%	89%	86%	76%
	Buybacks (%)	19%	16%	28%	38%	37%	26%	17%	11%	14%	24%
	Total ($bn)	6.6	8.5	9.9	14.1	15.9	12.9	12.3	13.1	14.5	16.8
	Yield	3.6%	4.8%	2.7%	2.3%	2.0%	2.0%	2.5%	3.9%	4.3%	3.9%
Utilities 82	Dividends (%)	75%	68%	70%	59%	58%	86%	89%	88%	68%	66%
	Buybacks (%)	25%	32%	30%	41%	42%	14%	11%	12%	32%	34%
	Total ($bn)	17.6	20.1	19.6	23.5	23.3	15.4	15.4	13.3	21.8	24.6
	Yield	5.6%	5.9%	4.7%	4.2%	5.2%	3.4%	3.9%	4.6%	4.2%	3.8%

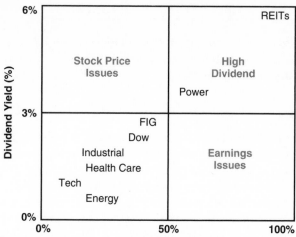

FIGURE 8.4 Dividend Policy

For competitive positioning purposes, we gauge dividend policy from the simultaneous mapping of payout ratio and dividend yield (Figure 8.4) because earnings anomalies can skew payout ratios and share price issues can skew dividend yields. In cases where depreciation is large and not representative of required maintenance capital expenditure levels, we opt to benchmark payout ratios with funds from operations (FFO) to minimize distortion.

The prevalence of dividends among the Dow 30 companies, with 2 to 3 percent dividend yields and 40 to 50 percent payout ratios, represents the center of mass for blue chip dividend policy today. Aggregate distribution practices may be viewed by industry sector in Table 8.1 on pages 175–176. Even dividend-oriented investors tend to prefer payout ratios below 50 percent to ensure sufficient reinvestment. However, different sectors exhibit different levels due to their unique profitability levels, capital needs, credit profiles, and growth prospects.

The final determination of dividend policy can be bounded by capital needs and dividend capacity, with consideration to the specific case, in the context of empirical evidence, market expectations, and competitive positioning. The residual excess capital (Figure 8.4) may then be allocated to other discretionary purposes, such as share repurchases.

HOW LARGE SHOULD YOUR BUYBACK PROGRAM BE?

The optimal size of shares repurchased in a buyback depends in part on the amount of excess capital, stock float, other company-specific factors, and in part, on the purpose of the buyback.

Capital Efficiency

In cases where a company wants a mechanism to distribute excess capital, a small, steady signal-neutral open market program may well be its most appropriate choice. The program can be turned on and turned off without the worry of sending unintended signals to the market.

Beyond simple cash management, a secondary objective common to such programs is to offset the equity dilution of equity-related compensation schemes. Therefore, these share repurchase programs are typically calibrated to maintain flat to slightly rising cash balances, with flat to slightly declining share counts. These programs typically amount to roughly 1 to 2 percent of shares outstanding annually. A quarterly budget is generally set to achieve these goals for cash and share count, but execution is often opportunistic with respect to market pricing.

In practice, so many companies announce open market share buyback authorizations that there is generally little signaling effect from authorization alone. Open market repurchases are often signal-neutral, making them more flexible than dividends for residual cash distribution.

Signaling

If the primary goal is to send a signal to investors, one yardstick for deciding the size of a signaling buyback is its materiality level, a number that measures how much impact the buyback will have on the wealth of shareholders that hold onto their shares. The materiality level for any given number of shares the company may buy back depends on the degree to which the market is believed to undervalue that company.

For example, consider the hypothetical company HypoCo Inc. Managers believe that the company's assets are worth $100, and 100 shares are outstanding. Unfortunately, the market values these shares at 80 cents each, a 20 percent discount to the insider's view of its true intrinsic value. In an attempt to rectify this, HypoCo's CEO decides to repurchase 10 percent of the shares. The total value of the discount ($20) is distributed over 90 shares rather than 100, creating a potential for a price rise of 22 cents per share, versus the original 20 cents per share, or an additional two cents.

TABLE 8.2 Materiality Levels for Share Buybacks

Share Price Discount to Intrinsic Value	Share Repurchase as % of Outstanding						
	0%	5%	10%	15%	20%	25%	30%
0%	0%	0%	0%	0%	0%	0%	0%
	0%	0%	1%	1%	1%	2%	2%
10%	0%	1%	1%	2%	3%	4%	5%
	0%	1%	2%	3%	4%	6%	8%
20%	0%	1%	3%	4%	6%	8%	11%
	0%	2%	4%	6%	8%	11%	14%
30%	0%	2%	5%	8%	11%	14%	18%
	0%	3%	6%	10%	13%	18%	23%
40%	0%	4%	7%	12%	17%	22%	29%
	0%	4%	9%	14%	20%	27%	35%
50%	0%	5%	11%	18%	25%	33%	43%

The repurchase program's materiality level is two cents, or 2.8 percent of the current share price. This indicates the size of the wealth transfer that can be realized by loyal shareholders who do not tender if all else remains constant.

Generally, a buyback needs to have a materiality level of about 5 percent to trigger any appreciable revaluation of the stock price by the market. In our experience, companies routinely underestimate what is needed to send a credible signal.

Table 8.2 shows materiality levels for a range of program sizes and value discounts. By using the table, you can estimate the number of shares your company will need to repurchase if you hope to send a convincing signal to the markets. For example, in HypoCo's case, the table reveals that a 10 percent program will have a significant materiality level if a company is undervalued by more than 20 percent. In addition to lacking a firm commitment to execution (many go unfilled), most open market repurchase programs are too small to send a signal of any consequence.

In PayLess's case, for instance, the estimated materiality level was about 8 percent of the value of its shares before it initiated the buyback program, given the 25 percent program size and a prebuyback market discount of about 20 percent. The size of the potential gain to loyal shareholders was large enough to prompt investors to look more closely at the company and consequently revalue its shares by as much as 30 percent. HypoCo's announcement, by contrast, may be a nonevent for shareholders.

Capital Structure

If the primary purpose is to reach a target credit rating or target capital structure, then the number of shares depends on the company's market value, share price, and target percentage of debt. It is a simple, if sometimes iterative, calculation (iterative because the action is likely to move the share price due to the value of a change in WACC and potentially due to market signaling).

Suppose the total market value of your company (debt and equity combined) is $1 billion, your shares are trading at $20, and you wish to shift your company's capital structure from 10 percent debt to 20 percent debt on a market-weighted basis. In principle, all you need to do is exchange $100 million in equity for debt by repurchasing five million shares. But the repurchase may, as we have seen, boost the value of the company's remaining equity because of the tax shield of debt. That would increase the number of shares you need to repurchase to reach 20 percent debt. In this example, the approximate value of tax benefits, let alone signaling, is $40 million (40 percent tax rate times $100 million increased debt), which will be reflected in a higher pro forma share price. Buying the five million shares, therefore, will not achieve the target debt level of 20 percent.

Modeling this iteratively in Table 8.3, we estimate that the company needs to repurchase 5.56 million shares at roughly $21.50, or nearly 12 percent of the shares outstanding and $120 million of new debt. This is likely to have a signaling impact, making us comfortable there is minimal risk of wealth transfer under an 8 percent premium, versus 5 percent justified by

TABLE 8.3   Sizing and Pricing a Leveraged Recapitalization

	Status Quo		Delta	Recap	
Stock Price	$	20.00		$	20.94
Premium		0%			8%
Offer Price	$	20.00		$	21.50
Initial Shares		47,500			47,500
Shares Repurchased		—			5,561
Ending Shares		47,500			41,939
Repurchase Size		0.0%			11.7%
Market Cap		950,000	71,742		878,258
Debt		100,000	119,570		219,570
EV		1,050,000	47,828		1,097,828
Leverage		10%			20%
Tax Rate		40%			40%
Value per share					**4.7%**

tax shield. Depending on the how the stock has been trading, ownership considerations, and company prospects, the 8 percent premium may be necessary to achieve 12 percent of the outstanding shares in a self-tender.

HOW TO EXECUTE YOUR SHARE REPURCHASE PROGRAM

Companies that bought back their own shares have subsequently posted returns between two and 12 percentage points above the market average, which is billions of dollars in shareholder value.[9] However, not all buybacks are created equal.

A poorly designed share repurchase can be damaging. For example, in May 1998, Samsonite announced a fixed tender offer for about one half of all outstanding shares, at a 30 percent premium over market, to increase leverage and allow a financial sponsor to exit. Investors did not believe that Samsonite's operating performance justified such a large increase in financial leverage and read the investor exit as a negative signal. The size and premium of the buyback worked against the company with the share price initially plunging 50 percent and another 50 percent over the summer. The transaction transferred $200 million of wealth from nontendering to tendering shareholders and was subsequently the target of considerable litigation.

Generally, any time a corporation transacts in its own shares there is no taxable event. Internal Revenue Service (IRS) Section 1032 exempts gains or losses from taxation. However, if an equity transaction does not benefit from Section 1032 exemptions, gains and losses may be taxable as expenses associated with executing the transaction will generally be deductible. For a traditional buyback, the accounting impact is reflected in the equity account and cash account as of the settlement date of each purchase.

Open Market Share Repurchases

Open market repurchase programs are the most common buyback mechanism and are suited to cases where the company's primary objective is to distribute residual cash flow to shareholders. Similar to normal course dividends, traditional open market share repurchase programs redeploy excess capital that would not earn its cost of capital. Open market repurchase programs are commonly employed to repurchase 1 to 2 percent annually of the shares outstanding to offset the dilution of equity linked compensation programs and to provide some degree of market liquidity in the stock.

Companies that initiate open market repurchases are required to publicly release the total number of shares or dollars authorized for potential repurchase, yet need make no commitments about price, timing, or actual execution. Thereafter, the company's treasury executes trades at its discretion.

Open market repurchases are simple and cost-effective (in fees and premiums) to execute. Managers retain control of timing, volume, pricing, block purchases, and other variables, and they are easily suspended. After a company has set target price parameters, a number of methods are typically used by companies in directing an agent to repurchase its shares through limit orders, daily volume goals, average price objectives, and/or through opportunistic buying. This transaction is governed by a number of SEC guidelines, the most important of which is Rule 10b(18):

- Although managers select one or more agents to purchase shares on its behalf, only one agent may be in the open market on any given day.
- 10b(18) limits the prices, timing and size of trading by companies in their own stock. Buying is restricted to 25 percent of the prior 60-day average daily trading volume; however, to ensure activity does not affect market pricing, buying is often kept within 15 percent of the average daily trading volume.
- Additionally, companies may not repurchase their shares when they are in a blackout with the exception of preestablished 10b(5)-1 plans.
- The Securities and Exchange Commission's (SEC) safe harbor was established to provide a guideline for stock purchases free from any claim of manipulation.

Open market repurchases are flexible and signal neutral. Though they may provide some degree of price support during periods of ownership churn or temporary price weakness, these programs are generally signal neutral because they lack the size, commitment to execution, and accompanying capital structure changes required to represent a material event. In the strictest sense, they are a zero NPV decision.

A potential disadvantage is that managers must devote time, attention, and resources to monitor market movements because the managers retain full exposure to the market while executing a large order. Open market repurchases are, therefore, inefficient for large repurchases (e.g., 10 percent), such as those required to make significant changes to the capital structure, to send a signal to the markets, or to redeploy large amounts of excess cash.

Structured and Option-Based Programs

As a variant to traditional, cash-based open market programs, many alternatives exist, including option-based programs, accelerated blocks, and structured private agreements that may be tailored to specific corporate objectives (e.g., cost objectives, risk preferences, and price targets). In some cases, opportunistic repurchases may also be undertaken by a counterparty through blackout periods unlike traditional 10(b)18 programs.

Many corporations supplement their baseline open market share repurchases with these structured programs. Changes in accounting for financial instruments (FAS 133, EITF 00-19, and the FAS 150, commonly known as liabilities versus equities) made many of the original option-based strategies (e.g., sale of put options) less accounting-friendly as they needed to be marked-to-market (MtM) for financial reporting. However, new techniques have emerged that do not involve MtM accounting treatment, are tax efficient, and enable corporations to employ options better meet their objectives for a share repurchase program.

Tender Offers

Companies usually use tender offers when they want to repurchase 10 percent or more of their outstanding shares, where great immediacy is desired to implement a change in capital structure, or due to low trading volume for the stock. Tender offers come in two varieties: fixed price tenders and Dutch auction tenders. A consideration before undertaking a tender offer is determining whether it would adversely affect the float and the trading liquidity for a company's stock. Even more importantly, they are sized and priced to minimize any risk of wealth transfer between tendering and nontendering shareholders.

Fixed Price Tender

The fixed price self-tender is a tool most commonly employed as an exit vehicle for founders and financial sponsors because a fixed price self-tender allows a much larger (usually 10 to 20 percent of outstanding) proportion of shares to be repurchased.

Fixed price self-tenders have historically been associated with the greatest premiums (frequently 10 to 15 percent) paid and, therefore, the greatest stock price impact on announcement. The signaling effect of fixed price tenders is stronger than any other form of share buyback, leading to an average immediate 12 percent appreciation in share price. Self-tenders pay a substantial premium for tendered shares.[10]

A primary consideration in a fixed price tender is that a company will have price certainty but will not have certainty as to how many shares are retired. A company can easily underprice or overprice a fixed price tender. If a buyback is undertaken for the wrong reason, or executed/communicated poorly, the share price may experience a major decline subsequent to the transaction and fall below prebuyback levels, transferring wealth from nontendering to tendering shareholders. Wealth transfer is the greatest risk in any self-tender as it rewards the wrong shareholders and weighs on the fiduciary responsibility of the Board of Directors.

The announcement and filing of a Schedule TO invites shareholders to tender their shares to the company over a 20-day to 30-day period at a preset price that reflects some premium, typically between 15 percent and 20 percent over the prevailing market price. A company must suspend its open market repurchase program during any tender and for 10 days thereafter.

Shares can be repurchased quickly, but the company can price the shares incorrectly, leading to undersubscription or oversubscription in the tender. If more shares are tendered than sought, then the company buys shares on a pro rata basis and must disclose the extent to which the tender was over-subscribed. The company may repurchase additional shares. If additional shares equal to more than 2 percent of all outstanding shares of the same class are tendered, the offer must be extended an additional 10 business days. If fewer shares are tendered than sought, then the company can decide to purchase tendered shares only, or it may increase the bid price to attract more sellers (provided the offer is extended for an additional 10 days).

With the advent of the safer modified Dutch auction, fixed price self-tenders have fallen into relative disuse. Choice of fixed price tenders over Dutch auction tends to be affected by stock trading patterns (lower price elasticity and return variance, smaller average daily trading volumes, and larger insider and fewer institutional holdings), company size (smaller market capitalization), and transaction size (larger).

Dutch Auction Tender

The Dutch auction is the most efficient means of reaching all shareholders while minimizing the risk of overpricing that may occur in a fixed price tender. Similar to Treasury auctions, or the Google IPO, the modified Dutch auction self-tender uses market forces of supply and demand to efficiently and safely price the self-tender to minimize the risk of wealth transfer.

Auction-based tenders have average returns to shareholders around the time of the announcement of about 8 percent above the market average, slightly less than the 12 percent enjoyed by companies using fixed-price tenders. But the long-run performance of auctions has fewer cases of share prices declining after the tender clears, and many cases of the share price continuing to rise in the months after the tender. In recent years, fixed price tenders have frequently been followed by a modest softening, and Dutch auctions often experience a steadily increasing stock price after announcement.

Volumes are often slightly smaller (8 to 15 percent) than fixed price tenders but with a large amount of shares repurchased quickly, most within 20 days. A Dutch tender typically gives a higher certainty of the number of shares to be purchased but introduces uncertainty in price even though it produces a fair clearing price and less risk of mispricing.

The company begins the process with an announcement that it is seeking tenders from shareholders for a specified volume of shares and is willing to pay between, say, 0 percent and 15 percent over market (the maximum permissible price range). Shareholders respond by informing the company within a specified time period (the tender must be open for a minimum of 20 business days) how many shares they are willing to sell at each given price within the range.

Once all the tenders are in, the final clearing price is set under Rule 13(e)-4 as the minimum price needed to purchase the desired number of shares (from all shareholders who agreed to sell at or below this clearing price). All shares transfer at this clearing price, the same price for all, and tendering shareholders incur no transaction costs. The appeal of the Dutch auction form is that tendering shareholders are not penalized for conveying the true price at which they would tender since they will get the market clearing price or no sale at all.

Table 8.4 illustrates the way a Dutch auction would work for a $40 company wishing to repurchase five million shares at an offered range of $40 to $46 per share. In this case, the clearing price is $43 per share, for a $215 million distribution.

If more shares are tendered than wanted (oversubscribed), the clearing price will likely be set at the bottom of the range, and the volume from each shareholder may be reduced in proportion to the amount of shares tendered. There is only an obligation to disclose the extent to which a tender was oversubscribed if all shares are tendered at the minimum price. If a

TABLE 8.4 Dutch Auction Illustration

Share Price ($)	Shares Tendered (000s)	Cumulative Shares Tendered (000s)	Cumulative Cost at Clearing Price ($000s)
40.00	500	500	21,500
41.00	1,000	1,500	64,500
42.00	1,500	3,000	129,000
43.00	2,000	5,000	215,000
44.00	3,000	8,000	344,000
45.00	4,500	12,500	537,500
46.00	7,000	19,500	838,500

tender is oversubscribed, the company may consider increasing the number of shares sought (by no more than 2 percent of outstanding shares or by a larger increase with a minimum 10-day extension of the offer), which must be announced in a press release. Alternatively, auctions are often followed by open market repurchase activity to address any remaining supply and demand imbalances.

Dutch Auction Case Study

An example of a well-executed buyback is the one launched by SPX, a diversified industrial company. In April 1997, SPX announced a Dutch auction tender offer for 2.7 million shares, or 18 percent of the total shares outstanding. The tender range was set between $48 and $56 per share, representing a 24 to 45 percent premium over the year's opening price of $38 3/4, and a 12 percent to 30 percent premium over the prior day's $43 closing price.

With its aggressive terms and size, the buyback was a clear affirmation of faith in the company, reinforced by senior managers' explicit pledge not to tender their own shares. What's more, since the buyback was financed through debt, it served to releverage the company's balance sheet.

The market approved and SPX's share price posted an extraordinary return of 20 percent over the two days following the announcement. Such was the confidence of investors in the company that SPX was unable to secure more than 80 percent of the number of shares it wanted to repurchase even at the upper price limit of $56. The company was forced to continue buying back shares in the open market. Within one month, the stock was trading over $70.

CHAPTER 9

The Stock Liquidity Handbook

S tock liquidity is an important consideration for many corporate finance decisions, including primary or secondary issuance, stock splits, share repurchases, and special dividends.

Stock illiquidity makes it difficult for investors to enter or exit a position without affecting price. It is also difficult to accumulate a sufficiently meaningful stake in an illiquid stock, which is important to investors because of the large fixed cost of maintaining research coverage for any one stock. Illiquidity creates practical limitations and inefficiencies for investors that can ultimately manifest in unusual ownership profiles and trading patterns, a higher bid-ask spread, a higher cost of equity, a lower stock price, and difficulties with market access. One study found that valuation discounts were directly attributable to the effects of liquidity: Illiquid securities exhibited greater sensitivity to market movements and exhibited higher trading costs, such that investors would expect a higher rate of return, thus raising the cost of equity.[1]

Changes to the securities industry are making stock liquidity more important. About 682 public companies have lost sell-side coverage since 2002, and 35 percent of all public companies lack research coverage.[2] More companies must now take their story to the street. One survey indicates that some CFOs spend as much as 50 percent of their time on investor relation activities.[3]

Much of the literature in this area is directed to the buy side with investor metrics of liquidity (e.g., bid-ask spreads), and lacking practical insight for issuers.[4] There is little guidance around how to measure liquidity, or corresponding benchmarks.

Illiquid stocks tend to trade at a 10 to 20 percent discount that increase with illiquidity. Stock liquidity may be impaired below $1 million average daily trading volume (ADTV) or $150 million float. Furthermore, effects of hedge fund activity can be more pronounced for illiquid stock.

Though average daily trading volume (180-day ADTV) of stocks on the New York Stock Exchange (NYSE) and the National Association of

Securities Dealers Automated Quotation (NASDAQ) averages $20 million per day, it ranges from only $10,000 at the 1st percentile (e.g., Versata), up to $272 million for the 99th percentile (e.g., Verizon). Similarly, though floats average $3.2 billion, its range is from only $3 million up to $52.6 billion.

Smaller exchanges and developing markets exhibit the greatest liquidity challenges where research coverage and trading liquidity are more problematic. ADTV on the Toronto Stock Exchange and Frankfurt Stock Exchange averages only $2 million and $3 million respectively; on the Tokyo Stock Exchange and the London Stock Exchange, it averages $5 million and $11 million.

Marketed primary and secondary issues improve stock liquidity and lead to positive excess returns among illiquid stocks. Illiquid primaries improves stock liquidity by more than 200 percent and is associated with positive excess returns 14 percent higher than those of the liquid cohort. So, liquidity is not significantly enhanced.

Illiquid secondary issues improve stock liquidity by about 175 percent and are associated with positive excess returns about 4 percent higher than those of the liquid cohort. However, most secondary issues are liquid.

Blocks are the least effective trade to improving liquidity for illiquid stocks, providing a relatively insignificant increase of 12 percent for illiquid stocks and 7 percent for liquid stocks. Excess returns for illiquid stocks are about 18 percent or 16 percent more than the 2 percent baseline for liquid blocks.

In the case of stock splits, the ADTV of illiquid stocks tends to be improved by a modest 20 percent even though the ADTV of liquid stocks is reduced by 5 percent. And for liquid and illiquid stocks, stock splits are associated with negative excess returns of −1 percent and −9 percent.

Enhanced disclosure and a comprehensive investor relations program are other useful tactics to employ to enhance stock liquidity and market access, reduce the cost of equity, and remove any potential liquidity discount on share prices.

MEASURING STOCK LIQUIDITY

There are many different alternative measures of absolute and relative stock liquidity (e.g., ADTV, float, ADTV/shares outstanding), but until recently, there were no corresponding market benchmarks to identify the approximate levels at which the effects of illiquidity generally became prevalent. Though we focus on liquidity discounts, bid-ask spreads are an indication of liquidity. Empirically, evidence shows they tend to widen as a result of underlying liquidity. However, they are more a result than a driver of liquidity, and though popular among investment finance academics, they are less intuitive, actionable, and commonly used in corporate finance. Bid-ask data have limited availability in FactSet and are not disclosed in company filings.

Benchmarks for absolute liquidity are $1 million ADTV and $150 million float. Based on our own empirical analysis, we would generally expect to see the impact of illiquidity—including a potential impairment in value, market access, and other associated trading problems—at levels below these benchmarks. However, these problems can be affected by other qualitative factors, such as disclosure and research coverage.[5]

From a statistical significance perspective (two-tailed t-test on the relative valuations in the bottom quintile of stock liquidity versus the top half of stock liquidity), ADTV and float are the most useful measures of stock liquidity. We discard the natural logarithm (ln) of market capitalization as a less practical alternative and discard the relative liquidity measures because they are insignificant (absolute t-stat greater than 1.96 is statistically meaningful at the 95 percent confidence level).

Average Daily Trading Volume ($mm and #)

Average daily trading volume is an arithmetic average of the daily volume traded. We generally use a 180-day averaging period; long periods can be better for smaller stocks and those with more volatile trading patterns. For example, stocks with strict no-guidance policies can exhibit more erratic trading volumes, with the bulk of the trading volume around the end of each quarter due to a lack of other information on which to trade. For these cases, long averaging periods may be most appropriate.

Shorter periods may be more appropriate where there has been a significant change in the ownership or trading profile of the stock to preclude the less relevant range of earlier history, for example, in cases where there has been a follow-on, stock split, or change in leverage, dividend policy, or business profile.

Though 60 percent of all companies exhibit less than $5 million ADTV, this represents only 15 percent of the market capitalization on a dollar basis because so many illiquid stocks are small companies. The ADTV benchmark is based on observed signs of illiquidity at volumes below $1 million. Though this is 1,694 of the 4,457 companies (38th percentile), it is only 4 percent of the market on a dollar basis. ADTV in terms of number of shares traded exhibits similar results though ADTV, on a dollar basis, exhibits stronger statistical significance.

Float ($mm)

A second measure of absolute liquidity is float ($ million), which is the freely traded equity stake (market capitalization, excluding the equity content of convertible bonds and employee stock options, minus restricted shares and other closely held insider holdings) averaged over a 180-day window. A large insider contingent can reduce effective liquidity due to trading restrictions (company imposed and regulatory), a longer-term investment horizon, and a typically bullish outlook on the business. A higher float is no guarantee of liquidity as other investors may also trade less.

Though 64 percent of all companies exhibit floats of less than $1 billion, this represents only 5 percent of the total market capitalization. Floats less than $150 million tend to exhibit signs of illiquidity. Though this is 1,382 of 4,457 companies (31st percentile), it is only 1 percent of the total U.S. market capitalization on a dollar basis.

ADTV/Float (%)

We also employ measures of relative liquidity. Though absolute liquidity is important, relative liquidity can help to accommodate efficient investor entry or exit from a stock (i.e., without impacting stock price). Institutional investors tend to employ many colorful, but nonetheless derogatory, terms to describe those stocks in which "you can get in, but you cannot get out." However, it can remain difficult for investors to establish a meaningful stake if absolute volumes are small, even with high relative liquidity. We divide ADTV by float to arrive at a measure of relative liquidity though it is still somewhat correlated with firm size.

ADTV/float of less than 0.10 percent can be problematic for liquidity; this is the case for 593 of 4,457 companies (13th percentile), or 27 percent of the market on a dollar basis.

ADTV/Shares Outstanding (%)

ADTV/shares outstanding is the proportion of total shares that trade on average. Stock liquidity may be impaired when trading volume relative to shares outstanding is abnormally low. A minor variant of our prior measure of relative liquidity, the enlarged divisor (i.e., total shares outstanding) is intended to reduce the risk of overstating relative liquidity in cases where there was a large insider block that reduced the size of the float. Cases of less than 0.10 percent ADTV/outstanding can be problematic for liquidity; this is 755 of 4,457 companies (17th percentile), or 27 percent of the market on a dollar basis.

Shares Outstanding (mm)

Total shares outstanding (including restricted shares but excluding the underlying shares for convertible bonds and employee stock options, again averaged over 180 days) is a measure that tends to be correlated with firm size because so many companies maintain their shares to a price point between $20 and $100 through the use of stock splits. Companies with fewer than 10 million shares outstanding tended to be associated with signs of illiquidity. Though this is 824 of 4,457 companies (19th percentile), it is only 1 percent of the market on a dollar basis. However, more shares outstanding do not ensure more trading or more float. For example, though stock splits are associated with modest increases in liquidity, they are generally not sufficient to move these stocks out of the illiquid category.

THE "LIQUIDITY DISCOUNT"

The liquidity discount may be evaluated from the relative market premiums or discounts—based on trading multiples versus the Global Industry Classification Standards (GICS) sub-industry median—with stock price premiums and discounts arrayed as a function of stock liquidity, using multiple measures of absolute and relative liquidity, including ADTV, float, ADTV/float, ADTV/outstanding, and shares outstanding. We reject price-to-earnings (P/E) multiples because they are distorted by financial leverage and more data are lost due to negative numbers. We reject EV/sales and EV/capital multiples for their higher standard error and lower predictive power.

Depending on the measure, significant valuation discounts are observable starting from about the 1st through to the 25th percentile of stock liquidity. Results are much more reliable with ADTV and less significant (statistical significance under the Wilcoxon sign-rank test at the 95 percent confidence level) for shares outstanding or for ADTV/float.

The stock price liquidity discounts range from roughly 10 percent to 20 percent and increase with illiquidity.[6] There is no premium for higher levels of liquidity though there are statistically insignificant premiums with larger floats.

The impact of liquidity goes far beyond the roughly 1,800 U.S. stocks that fall below our liquidity benchmarks. Markets outside the United States frequently exhibit considerably lower levels of stock liquidity and may face significant discounts or other abnormalities for a larger number of their listings.

IMPLICATIONS OF STOCK ILLIQUIDITY

About 1,815 U.S. public stocks have ADTV of less than $1 million or a float of less than $150 million. Stock illiquidity is found in most industries but is especially prevalent in the financial and technology sectors. Many illiquid stocks are smaller companies, but others are American Depositary Receipts (ADRs), dual-class shares, stocks with large inside ownership positions, and other stocks with unique ownership profiles.

Given the size and prevalence of a liquidity discount, the policy implications of stock liquidity are far reaching. They are equally applicable, and potentially even more compelling, for non-U.S. exchanges, where liquidity may be more problematic.

Optimal Capital Structure

Traditional capital structure considerations may need to be subordinated to the overriding concern of liquidity. Leverage policy objectives could include raising equity to enhance stock liquidity. Cash policies will be oriented toward building and maintaining large balances to counter the cost and difficulties associated with market access.

Disclosure

Illiquid companies may be able to lower their cost of equity through enhanced reporting, disclosure, and investor communications.[7]

Shareholder Distributions

Shareholder distributions (dividends and share repurchases) may represent wasted equity for the illiquid stock. However, though too large a share repurchase program risks further eroding the float; a small program (e.g., 1 percent per year) can enhance liquidity by providing a natural buyer that makes a market in the stock. A small dividend may enhance a stock's ownership profile through an increase in the number of eligible investors though this factor is often overblown.

Compensation

Employees perceive a discounted value of stock options for liquidity and lack of diversification; for employees of illiquid companies, this is even more so.[8] Cash is preferable though restricted shares can provide back-door equity issuance.

SOLUTIONS TO ILLIQUIDITY

There are many potential capital market solutions to stock liquidity problems, including primary and secondary issuance, block trades, and stock splits, but their impact on stock liquidity and excess returns are different. The impact for illiquid stocks is different than the impact for liquid stocks.[9]

Primary Issuance

Of the capital market tactics evaluated, primary issuance exhibited the greatest benefit to stock liquidity. The ADTV of illiquid stocks increases 200 percent, yet the ADTV of liquid stocks improves only about 6 percent. For 32 percent of the illiquid stocks, liquidity is sufficiently enhanced to warrant reclassification to a liquid stock. Of 1,281 non-IPO primary issues from the period 2000 to 2005, 203 were illiquid, but 65 of these were made sufficiently liquid within 45 days of offer to warrant reclassification to liquid.

Improved liquidity is associated with excess returns. For illiquid stocks, primary issuance has been associated with positive excess returns of 22 percent, or 14 percent more than the 8 percent baseline for liquid stocks (liquid and illiquid excess returns significant at 99 percent confidence level; difference significant at 80 percent). Though liquidity improved and excess returns were positive, use of proceeds is still a key factor to stock performance in primary offerings. Any uncertain or potentially unpopular use of proceeds can send a negative signal to the market and impair the stock price.

Primary Issuance and Use of Proceeds

Primary issuance has been associated with negative excess returns; however, this typically does not control for stock liquidity or the benefit of the offer period. There is a general runup in stock prices over this period. Primary issuance is beneficial to illiquid stocks, in terms of liquidity and excess returns.

Use of proceeds is a key consideration for any primary issuance. Research has shown that the market does not treat all cases equally. One published study makes an important contribution to the literature in this area, finding that the market reaction to common stock announcements is highly dependent on the use of proceeds (i.e., capital expenditures, debt reduction, and general purposes).

Capital Expenditures   Researchers found that though 2-day excess returns at announcement were −3.4 percent, returns climbed to +6.7 percent when the prior two month runup was included.[10] They also found that where proceeds were directed toward organic growth, stocks performed better if they were stocks with premium valuations and lower cash holdings. The negative excess returns associated with acquisition financing may be due to the acquisition and not the equity issuance. Issuing equity to preserve financial strength (i.e., credit rating) and maintain a target capital structure may well be the most appropriate and popular course.

Debt Reduction   Similarly, 2-day excess returns were −2.9 percent but increased to +2.3 percent when the prior two month runup was included. Where deleveraging was cited as a primary use of proceeds, the stocks that fared the best were those of more highly leveraged companies. Equity issuance for the purposes of deleveraging may involve directing proceeds to shore up liquidity, retire maturities or tender for undesired liabilities, or improve bargaining power in a refinancing context.

General Purposes   Surprisingly, 2-day excess returns were −1.8 percent and climbed to +5.3 percent when the prior two-month runup was included. Equity issued for cash and general corporate purposes was found to have the most benign impact on announcement returns although the prior 2-month runup was not as great a factor.

Secondary Issuance

Secondary issues are primarily employed by liquid stocks. Of 403 secondary issues from the period 2000 to 2005, 37 were illiquid and 366 were liquid. However, secondary issues did improve stock liquidity. The ADTV of liquid stocks increased 13 percent, and the ADTV of illiquid stocks improved 175 percent. Among secondaries, 35 percent of the illiquid stocks were enhanced to the level of a liquid stock.

In the case of secondary issues, short-term excess returns are 8 percent for illiquid stocks and 4 percent for liquid stocks. However, it is difficult to draw conclusions regarding the relative effectiveness of secondary issues because there is not sufficient data for the illiquid cases to establish statistical significance—most secondary issues are undertaken by stocks that are already reasonably liquid, by our definition. However, anecdotally, for smaller, illiquid companies, marketed secondary issuance can dramatically improve both stock liquidity and valuation. Unlike primary issuance, in the case of secondaries, establishing significance for positive excess returns associated with the marketing period is difficult.

NASDAQ Stock Market, Inc. (NDAQ) was a closely held over-the-counter (OTC) listed stock, having gone public in 2002. As an OTC (bulletin board system) traded stock, ADTV in 2004 was about 22,000 shares. In December 2004, in an effort to bolster liquidity and enhance the company profile, NASDAQ announced a secondary offering of roughly 17.25 million shares and announced a new listing on its own NASDAQ national exchange. Selling shareholders (NASD and qualified buyers of privately placed shares in 2000 and 2001) received 100 percent of the proceeds.

After closing at $6.80/share before the announcement, secondary shares were offered at $9.00/share, creating roughly $155 million of float, including the overallotment. After pricing in February 2005, single-day ADTV rose 137 percent and the stock outpaced the market by 23 percent (beta adjusted). NDAQ ADTV over the next 60 days increased roughly 780 percent to 450,000 shares or $5 million and excess returns (beta adjusted) were 58 percent.

Block Trades

Block trades are associated with a modest increase in stock liquidity; however, most blocks are liquid. Of 419 block trades from 2001 to 2005, 16 stocks were illiquid and 403 liquid. ADTV of illiquid stocks increases 12 percent, and 7 percent for liquid stocks. Excess returns for illiquid stocks are 18 percent, or 16 percent more than 2 percent baseline. (Liquid and illiquid excess returns significant at the 95 percent confidence level).

Because block trades and secondaries are not actions taken by the company per se, they carry a lower risk of adverse signaling. However, for the same reason, they are difficult actions for illiquid companies to initiate or execute and are frequently influenced by third-party tax and estate planning.

STOCK SPLITS

Stock splits are common. The widespread use of stock splits has historically kept the share price of publicly traded companies constant despite inflation and real growth. Reverse splits are used to maintain price points in much the same way.

One long-term study of stock splits for the period 1963 to 1982 showed that, on average, 6 percent of companies split their stock each year, at a median presplit price of 43.50 dollars.[11] Another study showed that the average share price on the NYSE has fluctuated between $30 and $40 since the 1930s.[12] This price range has been maintained even though consumer prices have increased by a factor of 10 and the S&P index increased by a factor of 16 since the 1930s. Of 7,726 companies, 21 percent split over the past 15 years, and 5 percent split over the past 5 years.

But since 1990, stock splits have not kept pace with the market and the average stock price has increased. Over the period 1990 to 2005, the average price of all shares outstanding rose from $18 in 1990 to $40 in 2005. Over the same period, the percentage of shares priced above $50 soared from about 3 percent to more than 9 percent.

The data do show, however, little increase in the number of companies that are willing to let their stock price go above $100, and this figure has held at about 1 percent. This seems to be primarily a marketing decision with $100 representing an important premium position price point in the psyche of investors.

The prevalence of splits has long been paradoxical because they have clear costs (e.g., listing fees, administrative costs, and brokerage commissions) yet no obvious economic benefits; the split, by itself, has no favorable impact on future cash flows.

The Cost of Stock Splits

Stock split costs include higher costs to the company for registration and administration and higher brokerage commissions borne by investors. For companies listed on the NYSE, new shares created by a split will incur an initial listing fee, up to a maximum of $250,000, and may lead to increased annual listing fees. Administrative costs include higher printing and mailing costs to service a larger shareholder population. One estimate puts the costs of a stock split for a Dow 30 company above $1 million.[13] In addition to the costs borne directly by the company, a stock split increases the costs borne by investors, and brokerage commissions typically increase with the number of shares traded even when the dollar amount of the trade is the same.

Benefit of Stock Splits

Many reasons are cited to explain the prevalence of stock splits. In terms of value creation, these arguments may be categorized along one of four rationales: ownership, stock liquidity, buy-side signaling, and sell-side promotion.

Ownership   Stock splits do typically increase the number and diversification of shareholders, ostensibly by making it easier for retail investors to purchase round lots of shares and perhaps through the irrational appeal of a lower price point. This could lead to a more liquid and efficient market in that security, with value created through lower bid-ask spreads, less risk, and a lower cost of capital.

One survey found that 98 percent of managers cited lower round lot costs and 94 percent cited an increase in the number of shareholders as benefits of stock splits.[14] A stock split reduces the cost of a round lot. A stock split also appears to increase the number of shareholders. A lower stock price is associated with a substantial increase in the number of shareholders when we compare different companies at the same point in time. We found that a higher split factor (i.e., the ratio of post-split to presplit shares outstanding) is associated with a substantial increase in the number of shareholders. One study found that company size (total market value of equity), stock volatility, and stock price explained 32 percent of the variation in the number of shareholders of Compustat companies. Holding size and volatility constant, each $1 reduction in stock price increased the number of shareholders by 1.4 percent. This model implies that a two for one split that reduced a stock price by $25 would increase the number of shareholders by 42 percent. Similar results were achieved with a time series model across 5 years, with split factor, beginning equity market value, change in volatility, and 5-year price explaining 7 percent of the change in the number of shareholders.[15]

The greatest benefit to stock splits may be a broadened and potentially more sympathetic shareholder base. Individual shareholders tend to be more likely to support incumbent management (e.g., option reserves and director elections) than institutional shareholders. Stock splits can reduce the threat of hostile takeovers and help gain access to a more sympathetic shareholder base for proxy votes.

Stock Liquidity   Prior research shows that stock splits can reduce trading volume.[16] One study found that a two for one split reduced trading volume over a 5-year time series by 2 percent of shares outstanding of more than 20 percent of the ADTV.[17]

Of all the capital market tactics to increase stock liquidity that we evaluated, stock splits exhibited the smallest benefit. In fact, as the ADTV of illiquid stocks improves by a modest 20 percent, the ADTV of liquid stocks decreases by 5 percent. Only for 4 percent of the illiquid stocks is liquidity enhanced enough to warrant reclassification to a liquid stock. Stock splits do not generally improve liquidity in a meaningful way, most likely because stock splits do not address underlying root cause issues of float and volume. Furthermore, illiquid companies undergoing stock splits continue to be illiquid post stock split.

Evidence also exists that stock volatility increases with stock splits though the long-term increase is modest.[18] This model estimates that a two for one split increases stock volatility by 0.005, less than 2 percent of the average sock volatility. This gives rise to another manager benefit to stock splits: A higher stock volatility makes existing stock options more valuable; however, future option grants may be revised downward over time to offset this effect. Nor is there evidence to support a lower beta (cost of equity) due to splitting or among splitting companies. A lower beta is required to support the liquidity argument or the tax option argument; increased volatility adds a tax option value and, thus, lowers the stocks expected or required rate of return.[19]

Signaling   Stock splits can provide a way for managers to signal more positive future prospects, increasing the stock price through a higher attribution of growth value.

However, for liquid and illiquid stocks, signaling seems poor; stock splits are associated with negative excess returns, −1 percent and −9 percent, respectively.[20] Furthermore, studies have shown the long-term excess returns are negative. One long-term study found 5-year post-split excess returns to be significantly negative.[21] Though abnormal stock returns were positive for the first year after the ex-date of a split, they were negative for the second through fifth years after a split, with a mean 5-year matched buy-and-hold cumulative abnormal return of −16.2 percent.

Splits are often associated with other changes (e.g., profits and dividends), making it difficult to establish cause, versus mere association. Bid-ask spreads, as a percent of stock price, increase after a stock split proportionally to the decrease in stock price due to the split. Companies may use splits as a favorable signal effect.[22] The signaling argument is only justification for a stock split if the split causes the market reaction and not other concurrent or expected events. But one study found that companies maintained their excess return only if the split was employed to affect a dividend increase.[23] Companies that failed to increase their dividend lost part or all of their excess return. If the split, rather than the prospect of an increase, caused the excess return then a failure to increase would not erode the return. Research shows that the market reaction to a second stock split is reduced if the earnings improvement following the first split was below average.[24] A share repurchase likely provides a better signaling mechanism than a stock split.[25]

Promotion   Some have proposed that because stock splits increase brokerage commissions and generate transaction fees, they may lead to increased research and sales coverage. Brokerage commissions are higher for smaller investors and smaller trades, and bid-ask spreads are larger for lower priced stocks. Some believe that these incentives improve the supply and demand situation and increase share price.

However, our own analysis as well as published research suggests that splits do not benefit trading volume or stock prices, making the sell-side promotion rationale a weak argument to justify a stock split.

For companies that do choose to split their stock, we recommend they revisit dividend policy and consider maintaining the same dividend per share, an effective dividend increase, particularly if signaling is the rationale for the split.[26] We propose that stock options be adjusted for the split, and that grant targets be adjusted for the split by multiplying target grants by the split factor. The objective of fixed share grant guidelines is to align manager and owner interests, and the fixed percentage ownership interest can only be maintained with this adjustment.

Managing the Enterprise

Strategic Risk Management: Where ERM Meets Optimal Capital Structure

A large energy company sells future oil production today, locking in price and interest rates, with proceeds used for share repurchases. A well-known technology hardware company increases the size of its bank line and foreign exchange (FX) hedging program to feel more comfortable with its decision to reduce the size of its large and growing cash balance. An international retailer de-risks the investment portfolio of its pension plan to accommodate increased financial leverage. The lines between enterprise risk management (ERM) and optimal capital structure have been blurred.

Many companies have undertaken broad risk management initiatives not necessarily to reduce risk, but to more actively manage it, and analysts have taken note:

> *Increasing numbers of companies are undertaking enterprise-level approaches to risk, a more encompassing and systematic review of potential risks and ways to mitigate them. These assessments typically are rolled up to a corporate level, sometimes with direct input from the Board or Audit Committee. These assessments have often been relatively broad, focusing on reputation, litigation, product development, and health and safety risks, rather than focusing solely on financial risks. Where we have seen these assessments implemented we have commented favorably, particularly when the Board or Audit Committee is actively involved.*[1]

ERM has grown to occupy a significant portion of most Board of Directors agendas, yet interpretations of the domain and objectives of ERM vary. Further, there is little quantification of the value of risk management, use of empirical data, or connection with the existing literature in corporate finance. The ERM literature remains largely predicated on conceptual frameworks and qualitative discussion.

The key questions for Boards of Directors are the same across industries and regions: What are our principle types of risk and what are their key drivers? What are our best measures of risk and what are their benchmarks? How does risk management create value? How do the markets and ratings agencies view risk management? What are the best practices in risk management?

Risk management is a strategic issue for most large companies today, which face a wide and complex range of responses to risk. Though perhaps not obvious substitutes, potentially appropriate alternatives may range from avoiding and laying off risks, to hedging risks and capital structure solutions for coping with residual risk.

For example, Sarbanes-Oxley Act of 2002 (SOX) and other post-Enron governance reforms have placed an added emphasis on identifying and managing sources of operational risk. And more companies have modified sourcing and pricing patterns, or made other operational changes to more closely match their revenue and cost footprints. Yet, operational constraints, competitive response, and strategic flexibility may require financial hedging where naturally hedging economic exposures is suboptimal.

Risk management also involves active choices around managing positions of risk, hedging tools, horizons and amounts. This can enhance transparency, liquidity, the cost of capital, and the capacity to execute on strategic priorities.

Finally, with financial sponsors and hedge funds putting more pressure on balance sheet efficiency, we have witnessed a resurgence of interest in the economic substitution of risk management for equity, such as de-risking business assets and cash flows to create more debt capacity to repurchase equity or having access to contingent capital rather than carrying excessive cash reserves to manage event risk.

THE VALUE OF RISK MANAGEMENT

Enterprise risk management can enhance firm value in many ways. ERM can reduce the volatility of assets and cash flows, leading to enhanced strategic liquidity, a lower cost of debt, increased debt capacity, and improved transparency.[2]

Strategic Liquidity

Cash flow volatility can lead to delays or even cancellation of strategic investments to help bridge cash shortfalls. This will impair growth prospects and future cash flows, reducing intrinsic value. Through risk management, a firm can reduce, or even eliminate, the probability of a cash shortfall that defers or reduces strategic investment. This enhances forward visibility and liquidity, improving managers' ability to plan for the level of investment required (through a business cycle) to execute their strategy and build shareholder value.

For example, Merck has been a popular risk management case study where successful management of FX and interest rate risk helps to ensure strategic liquidity for the continuation of their multibillion dollar R&D investment program. The net economic exposure that gets hedged is based on an evaluation of natural offsetting exposures, volatilities and correlations, and the cost of hedging.

The Cost of Debt

Risk management can reduce cash flow volatility and the unsystematic portion of total risk, enhancing credit profile, debt capacity, and cost of debt. Unlike beta and the cost of equity, these elements of weighted average cost of capital (WACC) are influenced by diversifiable risk, a reduction in cash flow volatility reduces unsystematic risk and the cost of debt. Empirically, the rating agencies look more favorably on firms with less volatile cash flow and earnings metrics (Figure 10.1). These stronger credits are, in turn, associated with lower credit spreads and a lower cost of funds.

Horizontal bars represent the interdecile range for roughly 1,900 rated companies in the industrials Global Industry Classification Standards (GICS) sector 20. Cash From Operations (CFO) volatility defined as the 5-year standard deviation of quarterly cash flow from operations as a percentage of income volatility is a 5-year standard deviation of quarterly net income as a percentage of sales. Earnings before interest taxes depreciation and amortization (EBITDA) margin volatility is the 5-year standard deviation of quarterly EBITDA as a percentage of sales.

Our own univariate regressions of cash flow and earnings volatility metrics provided further empirical support. We find correlation between volatility and credit quality. To the extent that cash flow volatility can be managed down through risk management, we would expect credit to manifest in the form of stronger ratings; this may take some time once the improvement is evident.

Risk management also lowers the after-tax cost of debt through lower taxes. Lower earnings volatility can increase the utilization of the tax shield

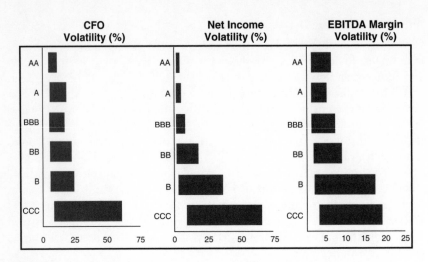

FIGURE 10.1 Lower Volatility Associated With Higher Credit Quality

of debt. Although many tax codes have a mechanism for offsetting net operating losses (NOLs), the inherent convexity of a progressive tax rate (earnings in peak years tend to be taxed at higher tax rates and NOLs are consumed in low-income post-trough years that otherwise would have been subject to lower tax rates), the loss of NOL time value, and the asymmetrical alternative minimum tax (AMT) reduce the value of taxes paid by companies with less volatile pretax earnings. Risk management can also lower the risk of financial distress and increase the expected value of debt's tax shield.

Debt Capacity

Empirically, lower volatility is also associated with greater debt capacity. Volatility is a significant contributor to credit risk. Firms with greater cash flow certainty and stability appear generally able to borrow greater amounts than firms with less certain and more volatile cash flow while maintaining similar or better credit ratings. Reducing risk increases the capacity for risk bearing, leading to more debt capacity, higher quality debt, lower WACC, and higher intrinsic value.

We introduced an independent variable that controlled for volatility into our credit model for the mining industry. Our multivariate regression analysis of 1,908 rated industrials in GICS sector 20 led to a more predictive and reliable regression model, based on an extra-sum-of squares F-test. The EBITDA margin volatility significantly improved our ability to predict credit ratings quantitatively (at the 99 percent confidence level). EBITDA margin volatility was based on 3-year trailing quarterly standard deviation. Estimated credit score $= 21.5 - 1.5$ Ln(revenue) $- 3.5$ FFO/debt $+ 16.6$ FFO/sales volatility, based on 10 years of data for 35 comparable companies. Our model predicts that reduced volatility will lead to increased debt capacity. In practice, we expect that a change in risk management policy may need to demonstrate a record of lower volatility before manifesting in additional debt capacity.

We estimated a reduction in earnings before interest taxes depreciation amortization and rent (EBITDAR) margin volatility (through risk management) could lead to capacity for $200 million more debt and a 3 percent share repurchase within the existing rating, reducing WACC by 5 to 10 bps, implying $400 million to $600 million of intrinsic value ($1 to $1.50/share). Near-term earnings accretion ($2 EPS) was to be achieved at only a slight cost to VaR ($8.65+/−1).

In the case of a large, investment-grade technology company, we estimated a reallocation of its own pension assets from 75 percent equity/25 percent fixed income to a more conservative 30 percent/70 percent mix could create roughly one half of a notch of debt capacity, enabling the company to execute a modest increase in leverage with proceeds directed toward share repurchases within a similar credit profile.

One energy company hedged proven developed producing reserves (crude) as a tax efficient substitution for equity, enabling higher leverage and a lower cost of capital. They also implemented a value-based management system that included mark-to-market changes in their estimated value of proven and probable developed and undeveloped reserves, and centrally hedged price exposures for internal SBU performance measurement and management purposes.

Transparency and Governance

Hedging exposures can isolate operating performance, eliminating the noise caused by price or rate fluctuations. This allows investors and managers to more clearly assess and better respond to the underlying business fundamentals. One large industrial company engages in commodity, interest rate, and currency risk management to reduce the sensitivity of its own cash flows to market fluctuations. With respect to its aluminum contract hedging program, the company uses futures contracts (typically within 3 years) to hedge purchases.

Sensitivity Analysis of ERM Intrinsic Value

In net present value (NPV) terms, the value proposition of risk management is dependent on several factors (Figure 10.2). Since risk management is

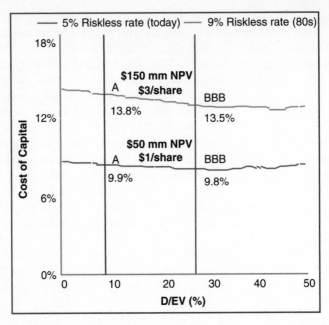

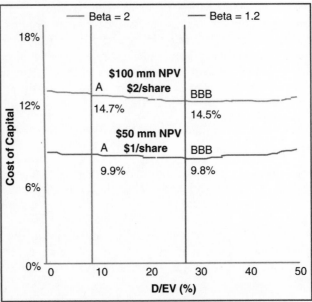

FIGURE 10.2 The Value of Risk Management Varies

effectively a (tax efficient) substitute for equity, the value proposition of risk management increases with the cost of equity. Therefore, its intrinsic value increases with stock beta and the riskless rate.

Lower interest rates serve to lower and flatten the WACC curve. Not only is the cost of equity reduced overall, but the relative advantage, in WACC terms (and ultimately to NPV), of being able to increase leverage is also reduced. This reduces the value proposition of risk management. However, this effect is partially mitigated by today's attractive credit spreads, which increase the value proposition. Similarly, lower betas reduce the level of the WACC function and make it flatter. Again, as the curve flattens, the value proposition is reduced.

MAPPING AND MODELING RISK

The Six Sigma literature provides a framework (Define, Measure, Analyze, Improve, and Control) suited to implementing a holistic ERM control process. In this section, we will outline the first steps: defining, measuring, and analyzing the risks and their drivers that the enterprise faces. The remainder of this chapter, as well as the next chapter, will address the final management portion (i.e., improve and control) of the process.

Though definitions in the literature vary widely, we will define enterprise risk to include the operational and financial risks (Figure 10.3). Operational risks are generally a product of the operating environment (e.g., location), internal processes (e.g., policies and procedures), and the organization (e.g., its people and organizational structure). These risks may include political, economic, labor, regulatory, product liability and litigation, and execution risks.

We define financial risk (also known as market risk) to include liquidity, interest rate, credit, currency, and commodity price risk. Financial risks tend to be the domain of corporate treasury and are subject to considerable scrutiny and quantitative analysis.

However, some asset classes such as pensions and real estate contribute considerable financial risk to the enterprise and are frequently outside the domain of corporate treasury, making much of this analysis incomplete. Furthermore, the lines between operational and financial risk are often blurred.

For example, Treasury operational risk may manifest in financial risk. Manufacturing and sourcing patterns can be modified to match cost footprints more closely with revenue footprints and to minimize logistics and currency risks. Operational constraints may require financial hedging where natural matching is suboptimal. Where financial markets are illiquid or uneconomic, physical hedging and pass-through pricing might be employed.

Enterprise Risk	
Operational Risk	**Financial Risk**
political risk	currency risk
environmental risk	commodity risk
litigation risk	interest rate risk
labor risk	credit risk
supplier/customer counterparty risk	liquidity risk
execution risk	
reputational risk	
regulatory risk	
financial reporting risk	

FIGURE 10.3 Components of Enterprise Risk

There is even blurring within financial risks, where multiple currency, interest rate, and commodity risks can be netted to manage economic exposures more efficiently.[3]

Measuring and Analyzing Operational Risk

In a risk management context, Six Sigma's goal of variation reduction translates to an economic one of reducing cash flow uncertainty and volatility, that is, an enterprise-wide process control to mitigate risk and enhance the quality of cash flows.

Process Flow Diagrams

- Risk mapping begins with process flow diagrams to help identify all potential risks, their root cause and risk drivers, and their economic consequences. In conjunction with root cause analysis, process flow charts drive the fundamental improvement and control processes. Existing and redesigned processes are checked, analyzed, and improved until each risk measure falls within acceptable tolerances from their benchmarks.

Pareto Analysis

- Prioritization of efforts, for analysis and management, is essential to making progress with an ERM effort. Pareto analysis, ideally in terms of approximate potential economic impact (qualitative or quantitative), provides an effective mechanism to help rank and prioritize risk mitigation efforts. This helps to allocate scarce resources to their most promising and productive uses by focusing on the greatest risks.

Fishbone Charts

- Root cause analysis on potential sources of risk is the key to process improvements and risk avoidance or mitigation. Working from undesirable outcomes such as actual or potential economic loss, the tool helps identify all potential causes. Process redesign efforts stem from this exercise, aided by process flow diagrams, such that processes are changed to incorporate enhanced prevention measures and checks and balances. Key risk drivers will be constrained to the level necessary for operations to be maintained within acceptable tolerances of established benchmark outcomes.

Measuring and Analyzing Financial Risk

Measuring and analyzing financial risks requires an understanding of the risk drivers, their spot and forward rates, distribution, volatility, and correlations. Then, they can be modeled stochastically to capture the economics of the risk dynamic.

For example, we mapped and analyzed the financial risk drivers of a forest products company to evaluate their net economic exposure from multiple input and output factor risks (i.e., commodity, currency, interest rate), with correlation between factor prices. Though we did find crosscorrelations, they were generally lower and less stable than expected. Furthermore, though the executives had been operating under the assumption of strong correlations between their operations and financial market factor inputs, we found these correlations to be weak and unstable, similar to the problems we experience with country equity risk betas.

As is often the case, business correlations tend to be much weaker and less stable than those that we find with the major currency and interest rate financial markets. Therefore, though large complex financial models (complete with stochastic analysis) may be developed to include business volatility drivers, they often lend an air of false precision as their underlying volatility and correlations are not constant.

Limitations to stochastic models, such as constant volatility (i.e., a single volatility for each factor that does not vary over the simulated period) and no drift or mean reversion property, are most simply addressed through stress testing for reasonableness under deterministic rate scenarios.

Interest Rate and Credit Risk   Treasury rates, term structure, and corporate credit spreads affect the value and cash flows related to financial obligations, such as debt and leases, and affect cash and investments, pension assets and liabilities (and other post retirement benefits), and certain economic provisions and reserves.

Most companies test rate risk with a simple what if analysis of the impact of a 1 percent change in rates, a parallel shift in the yield curve. Though appealing in its intuitive simplicity, testing the impact of a 1 percent increase or decrease in rates overlooks that rate changes are typically different across the term structure of the yield curve. Therefore, cash holdings may not provide a natural hedge for floating rate liabilities since long rates (and interest expense) may well rise even as short rates (and interest income) remain low.

Stochastic models can more realistically simulate net exposures. We draw independent shocks from a lognormal distribution to derive expected future short rates with a range that widens with time. We draw term spread shocks from a normal distribution and apply them to term spreads such that the range of potential spreads is constant through time. Monte Carlo simulation of a two-factor variant of the Rendelman and Bartter model generates multiple independent cases of the complete term structure in a stochastic framework. The risk-neutral process for short rates in the one-factor Rendelman and Bartter model is $dr = \mathrm{pr}dt + \mathrm{O}rdz$ where p and O are constants. Credit spread risk can be modeled as an independent addition in an interest rate model. A simple model of future credit spreads can be constructed and calibrated to historical data.

These types of models may be fit to any forward curve, bootstrapped from spot rates, with simulated rates bounded at zero. We often test against the market implied yield curve, a bias-adjusted yield curve, and a user-defined interest rate forecast. Yield curve adjustments based on historical analysis or mean reversion assumptions are increasingly common departures from market expectations for base case modeling purposes. However, the relevant range of history to serve as the basis for any adjustment suffers the same challenges as establishing the ideal historical period for estimating equity betas and market risk premiums. Uncertainty around interest rates and long-term equilibrium exchange rates has made user forecasts more prevalent.

Currency and Commodity Risk   Currencies and commodities are often a *more* significant economic factor in revenues and costs but tend to receive *less* attention among corporate finance practitioners. This may be partly due to the perceived complexity of the risk, as well as a historical preoccupation with interest rates in corporate treasuries. In the technology and healthcare sectors, where little debt and few cash flows exist, tend to be more global, the vast majority of *financial* risk stems from currency and commodity exposures.

Though there is a large and growing number of countries to keep track of, the number of currencies that most companies deal with is less; this is especially true if we borrow from the Pareto principle or essentially the 80/20 rule. Furthermore, many are correlated with each other. The bulk of the risk will be captured by modeling a few major groups of exposures, in terms of currencies and commodities. Despite the allure of false precision, stochastic models are most effective when the number of live drivers is kept small.

Finally, we avoid complexity with our focus on (net) economic exposures; balance sheet exposures tend to be less important (e.g., translation risk) from an economic perspective unless they may be factored into future cash flows.

MANAGING TO A BENCHMARK

Benchmarks must be set once risks have been mapped, measured, and modeled. Managers analyze these risks and set risk mitigating benchmark targets to track deviations from benchmarks. From a policy perspective, this is where the real difficulties begin.

In practice, we find considerable variation and uncertainty with respect to benchmarks, a practice unlikely to continue to be tolerated in today's post-SOX environment. Key questions, not being answered by the experts, remain:

- Should we measure the risk drivers or the impact of these exposures?
- What are the best measures?
- What are the right benchmarks?
- Where do others fall on these benchmarks?

Though the answers to these fundamental questions vary on a case-by-case basis, there are a few common themes to keep in mind. But first, we outline the most common metrics and benchmarks in use today.

- Annual hedge ratio and size of commodity or currency hedge each year. Generally lacking any optimal benchmark or economic rationale, this measure describes the size of a financial or physical hedge transaction. This also ignores correlations and natural hedges.
- Fixed–floating (%) mix dominates interest rate management discussions even though it does not capture the impact of duration, asset and other natural interest rate exposures, or currency issues. Anecdotal

benchmarks prevail (e.g., 30 percent) but lack any economic rationale, are insensitive to changes in rate conditions, and are never updated to accommodate dynamic strategies.

- Debt duration and currency mix is another common descriptor but again lacking any accompanying optimal benchmark and rationale. The impact of correlation's and natural exposures is overlooked, with financial liabilities considered in a relative vacuum.
- Value@Risk has emerged as a Holy Grail, though it generally lacks a benchmark and corresponding rationale (i.e., How Much Is Too Much? and What Is The Right VaR?). The definition of Value at Risk (VaR) varies, in some cases overlooking important sources of risk, such as cash, other assets, currency, leases, pensions, and other liabilities. Finally, not all risk is bad risk. An overreliance on this static metric overlooks the importance of evaluating the tails of alternatives in any risk analysis.

"The Goal"

We employ value-based objectives to manage risk. Such objectives however, are typically constrained by ratings, accounting, and other considerations. With these limitations in mind, we often target intrinsic value maximization within a target credit rating, subject to accounting-friendly treatment and practices that fall within the industry norms. Our intrinsic value perspective is typically at the consolidated cash flows (or core earnings as a proxy) and net economic exposures (to facilitate a netting of risks and simplification of the analytical process).

One company considered the following factors in their benchmark: Manage interest income and expense on a net basis, such that net interest income is optimized from a risk-return perspective. Now, its cash and investments far exceed liabilities, making the asset side of the equation most critical. But a simple netting overlooks mismatches in duration, thereby requiring simulation analysis and stress testing to model the risk and return from a near-term and longer-term perspective for funding alternatives. Finally, planned deleveraging was likely to reduce floating rate exposure, moving the company in the wrong direction.

The best goal is to maximize intrinsic value within the constraints of appropriate levels of risk for the business. And a focus on the tails of such simulations can be more important than the expected values of a simulation. For example, if two expected values are reasonably similar, but the one alternative faces a greater dispersion in outcomes, the optimal choice will depend on the tails. If most of the risk is downside risk, then the alternative with greater certainty surrounding its expected value will be the better choice.

But not all risk is bad; some risk is good risk, and this is a point frequently overlooked by today's VaR analysis. If most or all of the uncertainty is upside uncertainty, then the alternative with less certainty around its expected value may be the better choice, especially if the downside risk is within tolerable limits or predetermined constraints.

Any risk that materially reduces liquidity or financial strength (e.g., estimated credit profile, or long-term and short-term target credit ratings serve as a reasonable proxy) to the point of impairing capital access, business plan execution, or WACC, will diminish intrinsic value.

Constraints

Though our objective is to manage net economic exposures within an intrinsic value maximization framework, there are practical considerations and constraints that must be incorporated to operationalize enterprise risk management. The most important of these are investor positioning and credit rating treatment considerations. Potential near-term financial impact, though not the objective, must be understood and within the bounds of a message that can be articulated to the financial markets or risk diminishing market values.

Ranges

Financial policy benchmarks specify a permissible range or tolerance around a target to accommodate reasonable fluctuations, as well as opportunistic movement away from the target and perhaps to take advantage of a view on markets (in the short term or generally). Any benefit of moving away from a target is measured by comparing the actual (*ex post*) or expected (*ex ante*) costs with the costs that would have been achieved if the company maintained a benchmark portfolio. *Ex post* monitoring of the impact of deviations from the benchmark may take some time to become observable with any degree of statistical reliability. Stochastic modeling enables informed policy choices to be made on an *ex ante* basis, from an estimate of alternative NPVs and the near-term fiscal impact.

One A-rated company evaluated the strategy of de-risking pension assets to enable a higher degree of financial leverage and share repurchases. A move from 75 percent equity to 30 percent equity for this company represents a shift of nearly $500 million of corporate pension assets, with the 5-year present value (PV) of earnings per share, or EPS, (notionally a VaR approach) falling 7 percent from $9.00 +/− 1.39 to $8.35 +/− 1.02 and 6 percent near-term EPS dilution (from $2.00 to $1.88).[4] But the cost to VaR and EPS can be offset by the increased leverage and a share repurchase; theoretically, the company can add almost $400 million of new debt and repurchase 6 percent of its own stock (boosting EPS to $2.20 and the 5-year PV of EPS to $8.49 +/− 1.16), though ratings treatment may constrain this size.

EXTERNAL CONSIDERATIONS AND CONSTRAINTS

Near-term financial impact, though not an objective, must be understood and within the bounds of a message that can be articulated to the financial markets or run the risk of market values that do not fully capitalize intrinsic value creation. We consider the impact with specific consideration given to accounting treatment, industry practice, rating agency treatment, and investor perspectives:

- **Accounting Treatment.** Changes in the accounting for financial assets and liabilities (e.g., FAS133) has greatly increased the degree of mark-to-market accounting and means that certain risk management strategies display greater earnings volatility. However, in many cases, it has been balance sheet and noncash earnings hedges that have been made less accounting friendly. Cash-oriented economic hedges generally receive more favorable treatment though there is some work required to get these hedges to qualify.
- **Industry Practice.** At the least, a significant deviation from past practice, or the conventions of established industry practice, is likely to demand greater communication, education, and justification to make analysts, agencies, and investors comfortable with the departure and to avoid a negative impact on external perceptions. Unfortunately, limited public disclosure makes peer comparisons on meaningful VaR metrics is almost impossible. Comparisons are more often made on hedge ratios, currency mix, fixed-floating percentages, duration, financial ratios, and qualitative policy descriptions.
- **Agencies and Investors.** Rating agency treatment directly affects the practical viability of the value proposition for risk management. Intrinsic value creation is frequently predicated on being able to exploit the debt capacity created. Investor reaction is similarly important if any intrinsic value creation is to be incorporated into the actual market values achieved.

Rating Agency Considerations

Target ratings and their associated qualitative and quantitative profile will generally constrain the value maximization objective. However, such targets provide the appropriate financial strength for the competitive dynamics and financial requirements of a business plan.

Generally speaking, comprehensive risk management programs are viewed positively by the rating agencies, assuming the program objective is to stabilize cash flows and enhance the predictability of results. Debt capacity can be created where improved credit metric stability is demonstrated though the agency may take a wait and see approach.

Standard & Poor's (S&P) comments specifically on hedging programs and benefits, "From a ratings standpoint, a key motivation for hedging is to provide a certainty of cash flows for associated debt issuance. Entering hedging agreements for some portion of production creates stable and secure cash flow coverage for interest and principal payments."[5]

However, agencies tend to give no credit and may react negatively to cases where companies employ opportunistic hedging programs as these strategies are generally viewed to be more as sources of risk (i.e., speculative) rather than a way to mitigate risk.

Interestingly, S&P believes that the value of a risk management program is, in part, a function of company size, "For larger, higher-rated companies, a lack of hedging is not considered a weakness from a ratings perspective because their strength, size, and diversity are incorporated in the assessment . . . treatment of hedging is indicative of S&P's commitment not to rate to the pricing cycle, but rather on the strength of the company's asset base and overall business profile as indicators of its ability to service debt."[6]

And risk management alone cannot offset an otherwise weak business position (e.g., a high-cost position in a commodity industry). Agencies believe the most important factor for a commodity producer facing volatile prices is a low-cost position and limited debt. Therefore, introducing a comprehensive risk management program may not alter a credit profile though increased debt capacity or a change in rating.

There are cases where risk management can support (versus boost) ratings for a short to intermediate period of time. Hedging for discrete project financing or other debt-financed expenditures is likely to receive favorable consideration in the ratings process.

For example, companies considering a large debt-financed acquisition can ease rating agency concerns by hedging a large amount of the company's commodity-sensitive operations for a 1- to 3-year period to enhance the stability of cash flows (i.e., providing a transparent path to consistent debt reduction). This is common in the energy and petroleum (E&P) sector, particularly in environments where oil and gas prices are at high levels. In such situations, implementing a short-term hedging strategy may allow a company to stretch its debt burden beyond levels that would otherwise be consistent with its rating, given the higher degree of certainty to getting back to the target capital structure. This must be complemented by appropriate positioning from the company to show commitment to achieving ratios more consistent with the rating. In project finance, the management of currency, commodity, and interest rate risk allow considerably larger debt burdens than would otherwise be accommodated within a given credit rating.

Lender covenants and rating agencies will generally provide hard stop constraints, including target leverage ratios, such as debt/EBITDA, interest coverage, FFO/debt, and debt/capital and including volatility metrics, such as EBITDA margin volatility or FFO volatility.

Analyst and Investor Perspectives

Though risk management practices are most sophisticated among resource companies, their use in this sector is the most controversial among equity analysts and investors. Though many support the intrinsic value argument for risk management, others are not interested in intrinsic value. Many commodity producer shareholders opt to play commodity pricing cycles by rotating in and out of the stocks of commodity producers. Though exchange-traded options (e.g., the London Metal Exchange or LME) provide a cleaner exposure to these economics, many investors seem reluctant or are unable (e.g., prohibited from trading in derivatives and other asset classes by charter) to do so.

For example, Rio Tinto is one of the world's leading mining groups with a diversified mining portfolio, by mineral and geographically. The company believes commodity price hedging would not provide long-term benefit to shareholders. The company is also exposed to fluctuations in U.S. dollar (USD) exchange rates between the Australian dollar and the South African rand. According to company statements, a 10 percent change in the average annual market prices of copper, aluminum, and gold will impact the company's net earnings by +/− $160 million, $110 million and $40 million respectively.

Company managers and their Boards of Directors must decide for whom they are managing the company: investors or traders. The opposing views are outlined by a Moody's analyst: "Investors are essentially seeking strong returns in a rising commodity price environment while maintaining the option to sell if prices fall. Companies that layer significant hedges reduce price risk and may not be as attractive to some shareholders. At the same time, the ability of hedge positions to protect capital expenditure programs or lock in acquisition economics creates shareholder value."[8]

The investor communications task in ERM is not a small one, involving a disclosure role and education and justification for the program. Though an annual communication is typically made to shareholders with respect to risk management, shareholders generally receive too little information too infrequently. One survey found that CEOs were not communicating issues of corporate risk management to investors as frequently as discussions were being had with senior management and the Board of Directors.

ERM CASE STUDY: METALLGESELLSCHAFT AG

In 1992, the U.S. subsidiary of Germany's 14th largest industrial company, Metallgesellschaft (MG), implemented a risk management strategy. With a natural long position in petroleum products, the company hoped to insulate itself from oil price risk. The company agreed to sell specified amounts of petroleum products every month, forward up to 10 years at fixed prices that were higher than current market prices, and then purchased short-term futures to hedge the long-term commitments, otherwise known as a stacked hedging strategy.

Their objective was that if oil prices fell, the hedge would lose money as the fixed-rate position would increase in value; if oil prices rose, the hedge gains would offset the losses on the fixed rate position.

However, a problem with this strategy became evident as oil prices tumbled throughout 1993 in the aftermath of the war in Kuwait. The short-dated stack hedging strategy exposed the company to two significant risks: liquidity risk and credit risk.

Liquidity risk arose because, as oil prices fell and markets were in cantango (spot prices below future prices), losses on the hedges were realized immediately, the offsetting gain was longer dated, and cash flows for margin calls became extraordinarily burdensome. Though the company had unrealized gains on long-term contracts, this hedge tenor mismatch created negative cash flow and a funding crisis emerged in late 1993.

Credit risk arose when the cost of rolling over the short-dated futures contracts rose significantly as cantango persisted. The company represented such a large percentage of the total open interest on the New York Mercantile Exchange (NYMEX) that liquidation of its position was problematic. In late 1993, MG reported staggering losses on its futures positions. Only a massive $1.9 billion rescue by 150 banks kept the parent company from bankruptcy.

This failure is not an indication that hedging is problematic; rather, the demise of MG provides a reminder of the risks of misunderstanding natural risk exposures and hedge positions. Liquidity risk, rollover, funding, basis risk, credit risk, and counterparty risk are important factors to be considered in developing any risk management strategy. In this particular case, the use of options, versus forwards and futures, must be considered more seriously despite their explicit cost, especially where long-dated disaster insurance is a primary objective for a risk management program.

CAPITAL STRUCTURE SOLUTIONS

Companies face a wide spectrum of potential responses to risk (Figure 10.4), all of which have capital structure implications due to the interchangeability of these alternatives. They range from avoiding and laying off risks, to hedging risks or capital structure solutions to cope with residual risk. Capital structure solutions might involve simply holding more (excessive cash/equity reserves) capital, using more cost-effective hybrid capital, or creating options on contingent capital, to manage event risk.

With advances in capital markets technologies, we have witnessed a resurgence of interest in the economic substitution of risk management for equity, which de-risks business assets and cash flows to create more debt capacity to repurchase equity, described in more detail for the case of corporate pensions in the final chapter of this book.

Control (Avoid/Mitigate)

Controlling risk by avoiding or mitigating exposures is the first choice to consider though the needs of the business will often make this alternative impractical. Many operational risks can be avoided or mitigated through the Six Sigma process control initiatives briefly outlined earlier. Business reasons make financial risks generally more difficult to avoid, and exposure to business markets will create natural exposures to currencies, commodities, and rates. However, business opportunities may pass these risks through.

Re-Insure (Lay-Off/Pass Through)

Risk may be re-insured with operational choices that naturally and cost-effectively lay this risk off to a counterparty or pass the exposure through

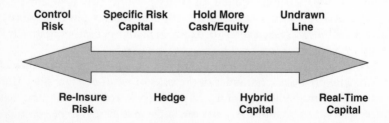

FIGURE 10.4   Strategic Risk Management Spectrum

to a counterparty upstream or downstream in the value chain. For example, cost-plus pricing quoted as a spread is frequently used to pass commodity exposure through to a downstream customer. Explicit USD pricing is frequently employed in commodity and shipping sectors, yet implicit USD pricing is common in Latin American markets, shifting currency exposures between sellers and buyers. Similarly, operational decisions may provide natural hedges to manage risk better.

Hedge (Physical and Financial)

The most common hedge is the natural hedge, which is borrowing in a local currency to provide a liability to match an asset, and more importantly, a local use of funds to match the operating cash flows to leave a nearly zero net economic exposure. But operational decisions may provide natural hedges to offset risk exposures.

For example, foreign direct investment and local sourcing provide a cost footprint that may better match the revenue available in an overseas market. Multinational corporations (MNCs) may go further than natural hedges by opportunistically shifting production volumes to take advantage of anomalous pricing in currencies, labor markets, or other input factors.

Financial hedging the net exposures of revenues and costs is most commonly employed for currency exposures though commodity exposure hedges are another common tactic in risk management. Financial hedging is prevalent in global industrial and technology companies and the commodity sectors. However, interest rate management is more frequently driven by the opportunistic market views of managers than anything to do with risk management.

Hold More Cash/Equity

The natural default for most companies, holding more equity capital—often in the form of excess cash and liquid assets—is one way to deal with all the residual risks a business faces.

For example, many technology companies retain the active involvement of their founders who remember earlier days when they faced unreceptive capital markets, greater uncertainty, and capital shortages. These companies today, awash in cash, are understandably reluctant to manage their balance sheets more efficiently, given their high opportunity cost to any capital shortages and the undiversified nature of their founders' holdings.

U.S. auto assemblers Ford and GM have tended to hold large excess cash positions in part to fund their underfunded pensions and unfunded postretirement health care benefits and in part to buffer the volatile economics of uncertain revenues coupled with a high fixed cost structure.

However, in cases where unmanaged residual risk is to be countered by more capital, alternative sources of capital may be more attractive than straight equity.

Hybrid Capital

Hybrid capital is a generic term that encompasses many products structured with characteristics of debt and equity. These products are designed to behave and appear as much like equity as possible while still receiving the tax benefits of debt. Although once constrained to financial institutions where hybrid instruments have long been a part of the capital structure, corporate hybrids have become an increasingly popular capital choice. Hybrid capital can be much less expensive than straight equity, while still affording some benefit to credit ratings. Hybrid products offer companies with limited access to the equity markets an opportunity to raise nonequity capital that has more flexibility than debt.

Traditional hybrid instruments generally consist of deeply subordinated long-dated debt with deferrable coupons. Though the instrument is issued at the cost of debt, its long-dated maturity and deferrable coupons lend elements of preferred equity (akin to a trust preferred). Like preferred equity, coupon payments take precedence over stock dividends but can be deferred on a cumulative or noncumulative basis at the discretion of the issuer. Covenants generally contain triggers that, when tripped, initiate mandatory coupon deferral. Ratings agencies assign partial equity credit that depends on the final features incorporated into the covenants.

Specific Risk Capital

There are small and specialized markets available for issuers to reinsure risk by passing exposures through to the capital markets. The insurance sector's catastrophe bonds are one example of laying off specific event risk to investors. Similarly, commodity-linked notes have been used by commodity producers to pass price risk through to their investors, like pricing practices designed to move price risk to their customers. On the equity side, commodity-denominated dividends have been used for similar risk management purposes.

Undrawn Line

The simplest capital structure solution to ERM is the bank line. Undrawn lines have long been used to provide secondary liquidity directly or as a backstop to a corporate CP program. Often underpriced, this form of contingent capital is a large, cost-effective market that remains easy to implement.

Real-Time Capital (Capital On Demand)

Innovations in capital products have extended beyond traditional hybrids to option-based capital arrangements. Real-time capital (i.e., contingent capital, capital on demand, and off-balance sheet capital) is access to capital that is created today that remains off-balance sheet but may be brought on balance sheet when needed. Rating agencies give high equity credit to real-time capital since there is a ready source of capital for a firm. Though insurance and reinsurance companies have been the first to use real-time capital, it may also fit well with the needs of technology companies and others who could lean out their balance sheet.

The product works as follows: An entity (i.e., a special purpose trust or partnership) is established for the sole purpose of raising capital that can be used by another company at a later date. The company pays for the right to use capital when and if it is needed. Capital is returned via call options in the case of preferred stock or share repurchases in the case of straight equity.

For example, a special purpose trust raises $500 million by issuing trust certificates to institutional investors with the return to investors will be determined at the outset of the transaction. The special purpose trust will pay a stated yield to investors. The special purpose trust invests the proceeds in a cash-equivalent short-term Al/P-1 CP portfolio generating income at a 30-day CP rate.

The company enters into a put option agreement with the special purpose trust to enable the company to draw on the cash held by the special purpose trust any time and unconditionally in exchange for the delivery of preagreed securities. The yield on the securities will be identical to the yield on the trust certificates. The company will pay a monthly put premium to the special purpose trust, which will be the difference between the income on the CP portfolio and the monthly coupon payable to investors.

When the put option is exercised, the company issues the preagreed securities to the special purpose trust. The special purpose trust uses the proceeds of the CP portfolio redemptions to purchase the preagreed securities issued by the company. Going forward, the company will pay the stated coupon on the company securities issued to the special purpose trust, which will then distribute payments on the trust certificates to investors.

Real-time capital is a valuable risk management tool that resides within the capital structure. A firm that uses real-time capital can more closely match actual capital-to-capital needs more closely and efficiently. Real-time capital can be a less expensive solution than the opportunity cost of holding excess capital. Surplus capital need not be held, but within reach. As a firm anticipates a new risk, or expects to change its risk profile, additional capital can be tapped real time at a price that reflects the current risk position.

CHAPTER 11

Best Practices In Hedging

The high cost of fuel has helped drive airlines into bankruptcy. Sharp currency movements have had a dramatic impact on corporate results. For example, DaimlerChrysler reported that a favorable currency environment generated half of its second quarter 2003 earnings. U.S. dollar (USD) movement against the Euro, Yen, and Canadian dollar (CAD) have forced CEOs and CFOs to think more strategically about and to revisit antiquated risk management policies and practices. Increasingly, companies are examining exposures from multiple sources: mergers and acquisitions (M&A), foreign assets and liabilities, foreign sourced costs and profits, and existing hedge contracts.

Regardless of the details regarding how we define and quantify exposures, they are a large and growing factor in business models today. For example, global growth, global sourcing, and foreign direct investment often represent valuable opportunities. But they bring additional sovereign, currency, and interest rate risks. Though many companies attempt to modify sourcing or other operational changes to match their revenue and cost footprints more closely, operational constraints, competitive response, and strategic flexibility may require financial hedging where natural hedging is suboptimal.

As discussed in the prior chapter, mismatches in future sources and uses of cash represent true economic exposure. Hedging can reduce the responsiveness of cash flows to risk drivers such as rate fluctuations. This can enhance transparency, weighted average cost of capital (WACC), liquidity, and the firm's capacity to execute on strategic objectives. A policy to hedge a portion of near-term to mid-term net economic exposures can reduce cash flow volatility and enhance firm value.

A hedging program involves choices around objectives, exposures, benchmarks and constraints, amounts, horizons, tools, execution, and control process. Program design begins with objectives, such as reducing cash flow volatility, increasing debt capacity, lowering funding cost, or mitigating against disastrous outcomes. The program objectives might include constraints, such as it must serve a business purpose and not create any new exposures, as well as outline tolerance ranges and the opportunity for discretion. Hedging policy specifies five main attributes of hedging, such as what to hedge, the hedge horizon, hedge ratios and discretion, forwards versus options and other structures, and execution.

Finally, best practice includes a robust reporting and control process. A hedging program may be monitored regarding its impact versus the benchmark to the three main elements of corporate cash flows: operating, investing, and financing. Fluctuations in risk drivers will create volatility in each one of these building blocks of a company's cash flow.

WHICH "EXPOSURE" TO HEDGE

Many companies have responded to increased exposures and risk with more resources (i.e., people and capital) devoted to risk management. But to develop an effective risk management strategy, there must first be agreement in the definition and determination of the exposures. And yet, there is a major discrepancy between accounting practice and economic reality in terms of what constitutes an exposure. In practice, the term *exposure* remains open to wide variation in interpretation, frequently leading to differences in opinion at the Board of Directors level around appropriate policy and action. We outline the most frequent types of exposure (i.e., transaction, translation, and economic) below (Figure 11.1).

Transaction Hedging

Transaction exposure most frequently arises from revenues and costs in nonlocal currencies. Anticipated transaction currency exposure hedging is common and, if properly structured, is allowed and treated favorably by Financial Accounting Standards (FAS) 133. However, recent volatility of the USD against other major currencies may have driven some hedges deep into or out of the money—rendering them less effective. Companies may consider restructuring hedge books to avoid unwanted cash flow and earnings events.

Most companies start out with simple transaction exposures, stemming from the possibility of future exchange gains or losses on transactions entered into (booked) and denominated in a foreign currency. Transaction exposure is measured currency by currency and equals the difference between contractually fixed future cash inflows and outflows in each currency. These

	Transaction Hedge	Translation Hedge	Economic Exposure
Accounting Friendly	√√	X	√
Improve Transparency	√	X	√
Debt Capacity	√	X	√√
Credit Quality	√	X	√√
Intrinsic Value	√	X	√√√

FIGURE 11.1   Hedging Alternative Exposures

exposures are often decentrally hedged on a transaction-by-transaction basis throughout the company.

This approach ignores tremendous opportunity to gain efficiencies through the economies of scale in hedging, as well as that offsetting exposures would likely become evident from an aggregate view. In a transaction approach, cost-based risks may be obscured by the complications of cost accounting and functional currency practices, concealing true net exposures. Transaction exposures deal only with firm commitments, but considerable exposure may arise from unbooked transactions that are expected; variability in rates, thus, affects the value of the firm through expected future transactions, that is, contingent exposure. Furthermore, competitive exposures arise from induced changes in sales, market share, and net cash flows. Transactions are only one element of total exposure.

Nor does transaction exposure make the accountants happy. Though some unsettled transactions are on—balance sheet (foreign currency denominated debt, and accounts receivable), other obligations (future sales and operating leases) are not. Transaction exposure neither captures all accounting exposure nor economic risk.

Accounting Perspective

The accounting perspective looks to mitigate the impact of risk on reported earnings, and to a lesser extent, balance sheet ratios. Accounting hedges are intended to manage noncash charges, such as translation gains or losses.

Balance sheet translation exposure arises from net investments in foreign operations. A hedged balance sheet attempts to avoid unexpected changes in balance sheet ratios. With the USD weak by historic standards, many companies may look to secure the USD value of foreign assets and/or create new foreign currency debt positions.

Unhedged foreign earnings are subject to change in value, putting future reported earnings at risk. Securing current rates for future foreign net income removes this uncertainty and avoids analyst surprises. Profit hedging frequently requires special structures to gain accounting effectiveness. These are generally only successful in the near term.

Many companies hope to generate a steady pattern of growing earnings, which helps explain the prevalent historical relationship between accounting translation methods and corporate hedging practices.[1] Accounting measures, such as translation, focus on the impact of risk on the book values of assets and liabilities. However, book values reflect historical costs, and economic value reflects future cash flows. The risk to a firm's future cash flows and operating results may have no relation to retrospective accounting techniques. Decisions and hedges based on accounting information may adversely impact the real economic performance and value of a business.

For example, the problem of acting on the basis of balance sheet exposure rather than economic exposure was illustrated by a French subsidiary of an American company that should have expanded sales under a declining French franc but is asked to scale back on sales to reduce the accounting exposure to devaluation.[2]

One of the unintended benefits of FAS133 has been to reduce the prevalence of accounting hedging. Balance sheet and other noncash hedges often do not qualify for hedge accounting, requiring them to flow through the income statement when marked-to-market.

Economic Exposure

Economic exposure is the extent to which the value of the firm, as measured by the present value of expected future cash flows, can change when a risk driver fluctuates. Hedging economic risk, risk to sources and uses (expected, rather than booked) of future cash flows, can substantially mitigate cash flow volatility and enhance firm value.[3]

As an example, one industrial company had over 85 percent of its revenues in USD and sold products with prices set in USD as is customary in many commodity industries. Only 25 percent (USD200 million) of cash operating expenses (labor, raw materials and other manufacturing expenses) were USD based; however, an additional natural hedge was derived from largely USD-denominated debt and, hence, the interest expense. The company faced a USD1 billion net USD/CAD economic exposure, extending

HEDGING M&A

Best practice companies give specific consideration to currency issues; currency movement can have a significant impact on transaction net present value (NPV), cost of funds, and the level of volatility of future financial performance. Bidders will consider hedging a transaction, and transaction risk arises from the conversion of funds not raised in the target currency, as well as the ongoing exposure from foreign earnings and cash flow exposure on the merged entities. Hedging tactics are reviewed within a broader hedging policy as exchange rates and outlooks change.

In our experience, the risk management approach to exposures that arise out of M&A is largely determined by company attitudes toward transaction exposure and risk. Any incremental interest rate exposure is typically not managed within a risk management framework but managed to improve the accounting impact, i.e., earnings per share (EPS) accretion, or as an extension of current interest rate policy that is largely premised on the company's views on interest rates. This pervasive practice may well be due to managers' greater familiarity with interest rate conditions and outlooks due to their own exposures that stem from personal mortgages, etc. We see three general approaches for the management of rate risk in cross-border mergers and acquisitions.

The first involves early action by the treasurer to guarantee a fixed exchange rate during the negotiation of the deal. The second entails the treasurer hedging the when the deal is finalized. A third approach is to spread the risk out over a longer period of time after the deal is finalized. As negotiations may routinely vary between one month and one year, the instruments used for the first approach are more complex than for the latter two.

For example, a weakening target currency lowers the present value (PV) of all future cash flows when translated into bidder currency, and the economic value of the target to the bidder falls. Hedging 100 percent of the net economic exposure created by a transaction would limit an acquirer's downside to a weakening currency. In a case where Euro/USD is initially 1.28 but weakens to 1.40, it can lead to EPS dilution of 8.6 percent in an all-cash deal or 4.3 percent in an all-stock deal. Conversely, the Euro bidder's return on a USD purchase will increase if the USD strengthens and exchange rates return toward 1.20, a longer-term equilibrium.

Assuming bidder and target (with premium) are at price-to-earnings ratio (P/E) parity, that is, at current exchange rates, an all-share or all-cash deal should be earnings neutral for the bidder. If the target currency appreciates following deal completion, this will have a positive effect on the bidder's earnings, in bidder currency terms.

In a cash deal and assuming the transaction is financed in bidder currency, the change in accretion and dilution is proportionate to the movement in the exchange rate. Thus, a significant part of any debt raised in the context of an into-Euro transaction will be raised locally to provide a natural hedge against currency movements as Euro operating cash flows are used to service Euro debt. To the extent a bidder borrows in local currency, this will offset the effect caused by converting the target's earnings at different exchange rates.

But to exploit USD weakness, a U.S. buyer might consider swapping near-term servicing to USD. Such a decision should be evaluated as part of the deal dynamics within the context of the bidder's tolerance and capacity for risk, time horizon, capital markets conditions, longer-term equilibrium exchange rates, and a comprehensive risk analysis of the pro forma assets, liabilities, and cash flows.

In a share deal, the EPS impact is partly hedged by the issuance of bidder shares. For example, if both parties are of identical market value at offer, the EPS impact of currency changes is halved.

Though the choice of hedging instrument (e.g., forward contracts, options, or plain spot transactions) will not have any effect on the exchange rate, the announcement of an M&A deal can result in movement of the exchange rate even if it is not accompanied by large transactions at the time (as might be expected in a forward-looking market). But the cash flow effect of an M&A transaction is often overestimated. Only very large transactions or transactions in illiquid currency markets could have an impact on exchange rates.[4]

Any large cross-border M&A transaction is likely to change the nature of the company's overall exposure profile substantially, necessitating a review of the entire program. A recentralization of the exposure measurement and management will indicate whether risk has increased or decreased (and where), how preexisting positions might be netted against newly acquired ones, and what changes are required to positions, policies, and procedures.

far into the future, that far exceeded their USD600 million profit. (At that time, we assumed 0.73 CAD/USD exchange rate; CAD revenues C$275 million, CAD costs C$825 million, CAD net loss C$550 million; U.S. revenues $1,200 million, U.S. costs 200 million, U.S. net profit $1,000 million;

USD revenues/Total revenues = $1,200/($1,200 + C$275*0.73) = 86 percent; USD costs/Total costs = $200/($200 + C$825*0.73) = 25 percent; Net profit = $1,000 − C$550*0.73 = $600). With a high degree of financial leverage and operating leverage, the company could ill afford this exposure and cash flow volatility, which impaired liquidity and debt capacity, raised capital costs, constrained investment, and created considerable distraction and monitoring costs for managers and the Board of Directors.

A large Australian mining concern employs a comprehensive strategic risk management program to monitor and manage its net exposure to fluctuations in commodity pricing and exchange rates. This company's commodity business provides a natural diversification that dampens the effects of fluctuations in production inputs and outputs. The company uses a Cash-Flow-at-Risk (CFaR) methodology to support its broader strategic objectives, where CFaR represents the worst expected loss relative to projected business plan cash flows over a 1-year horizon at 95 percent confidence under normal conditions. Though this horizon is most common, many company's manage out 3 years albeit at lower hedge ratios on the longer end of their horizon.

HEDGE HORIZON

Best practice risk management programs that involve a spectrum of exposures provide guidance around hedge horizons. Depending on the nature of the exposures and their hedge markets, many companies hedge between 1 and 3 years of exposure, with a declining proportion of net exposure hedged further out in time. There are three reasons for this approach:

1. There is less certainty around the size of the exposure further into the future. Though most forecasts anticipate top-line growth and declining costs, treasurers show a pragmatic reluctance to rush out and hedge the exposures implied by these financial plans.
2. There is less certainty around expectations for hedge markets and the prices of their underlying assets further into the future. Greater consensus around nearer term rates makes nearer-term hedges seem safer and less controversial than long-dated ones, where there is a greater risk of a hedge going underwater.
3. The bid-ask spread and cost of hedge, increases with the hedge horizon. Long-dated markets are less liquid and more expensive.

In many cases, uncertainty about the future composition of cost and revenue streams, exchange rates, and thinner markets for longer-dated contracts, constrain companies' ability to hedge far into the future.

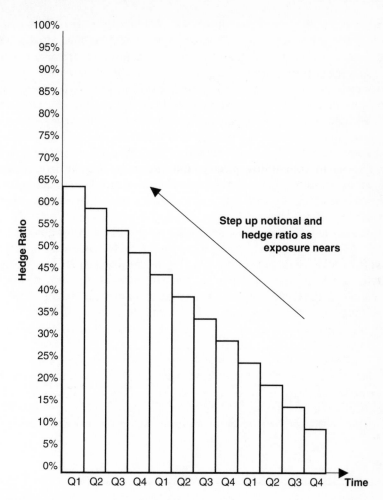

FIGURE 11.2 Illustration of Layered Hedges

Figure 11.2 illustrates the commonly employed laddered hedge tactic. Akin to a dollar cost averaging approach, laddering affords a practical method to reduce hedging cost and the volatility of the achieved effective rate. The company achieves a higher hedge ratio as the exposure nears in time by layering on new tranches of hedge each month or quarter. Layering hedges a higher proportion of the near-term exposures than of the long-term exposures by increasing the hedge ratio of distant results as they move closer in time.

For example, a company with USD/CAD net exposure of USD1 billion could ladder its hedges over a 12-quarter horizon by adding a hedge with a USD50 million hedge each quarter, starting from 12 quarters out, to achieve a 65 percent hedge ratio on next quarter's results, starting from a 10 percent hedge ratio on their estimated exposure 12 quarters forward. Assuming the third-year hedges are executed as out-of-the-money options, rather than as forwards, then the layering process will involve rolling the options into forwards as they approach years one and two.

To prevent the chance of notional amounts hedged exceeding the exposure, notional amount hedged should decline as hedging horizon increases. Longer horizons magnify volatility and introduce increased uncertainty into the forecast exposure. The slope of the ladder should be steeper for more volatile exposures.

The notional amount hedged should be realigned every quarter based on a new forecast. Though the hedging level could remain the same (e.g., 70, 60, or 50 percent), the implied hedge amount will change as the forecast fluctuates. The notional amount of forward hedges should only be adjusted for significant changes in the implied hedge amount (e.g., 10 to 15 percent of net exposure), which may include increasing the notional amount through entering into a greater number of contracts or decreasing it via curbing the existing positions.

One gold company actively hedges its output with the forward sale of production of existing gold reserves in layers up to 3 years out, with relatively high hedge ratios, though these levels do tend to vary somewhat opportunistically with the pricing environment. Similarly, one case study outlines how this approach has been employed to raise off-balance sheet debt.[5]

HEDGE RATIO

Reducing exposure mitigates volatility but only to a certain level. We have found that hedging an exposure exhibits a characteristic of diminished marginal returns, implying that full hedging is neither beneficial nor economic. Again, this depends on the company, its exposures, and its markets, but most hedges do not exceed 80 percent (i.e., 80 percent hedge ratio) of near-term exposure, about 50 percent 1 year forward and about 30 percent 2 years forward. Longer-term hedges (e.g., 3 years) tend to be small (e.g., 10 percent hedge ratio), out-of-the-money (i.e., option-based): positions that provide a form of disaster insurance and a toehold on a larger hedge as the exposure gets closer in time.

Just as companies are opportunistic in issuing or buying back stock, so will they be with risk management. Unfortunately, as is often the case with interest rate management, this can lead to practice that is too ad hoc and unsystematic to be able to be documented or articulated as any form of financial policy. From a corporate governance perspective, Boards of Directors will recognize this is a process in need of objectives, constraints, and tolerance ranges for better control.

As outlined for the case of interest rate management in an earlier chapter, a dynamic hedging strategy that incorporates market information can significantly reduce cost and risk. Hedge ratios may be managed to preset guidelines but not constant ones; they must be managed dynamically in accordance with market conditions (e.g., level, volatility, and outlook). Many companies alter the timing and notional amount of their hedge positions in light of their views.

Hedges may be layered with hedge ratio bands that afford some manager discretion within the band of tolerance (e.g., 70 to 80 percent today, 40 to 55 percent 1 year out, 20 to 40 percent 2 years out, and 0 to 25 percent 3 years out). Regular reporting helps ensure effective control.

For example, one large company hedges 70 to 100 percent of the corn and soybean inventory value that the company purchases from growers, depending on the crop and grower pricing.

OPTIONS VERSUS FORWARDS

Best practice companies incorporate a combination of operational process controls, natural hedges, and capital structure solutions within their enterprise risk management (ERM) programs, and they employ a combination of financial hedging tools (e.g., options, swaps, and forwards) to match their objectives, constraints, views, exposures, and risk preferences.

The pros and cons of each tool include its cost and degree of downside protection and its potential for upside, risk profile and behavior in extreme outcomes, accounting treatment, counterparty risk, ease of execution, and compatibility with control processes.

Best practice hedging programs combine symmetric and asymmetric strategies to enhance overall effectiveness. Hedging exposures using futures or forward contracts are examples of symmetric hedging, where outcomes are locked in and downside protection is purchased at the implicit cost of upside exposure (i.e., eliminating exposure to the upside and the downside). Asymmetric hedging is achieved through the use of options, where downside protection is purchased at an explicit cash cost and upside exposure is retained.

For example, a large diversified industrial is a well-known, conservative, commodity-driven business with exposure to emerging markets through diverse geographic location of assets and end markets. Most of their commodity hedging is performed with respect to gold prices. The company largely hedges its interest rate and currency exposure using derivative instruments to protect against movements in the South African rand, Australian dollar, Euro, and British sterling against the U.S. dollar. The company engages in hedging from time to time of its commodity, interest rate, and exchange rate price fluctuations using forwards, spot deferred contracts, futures, swaps, and options.

Symmetric Hedging

In practice, the explicit cost of options makes them far less popular. Many companies do not use financial hedges at all or they only use forward contracts to avoid any explicit cash costs for risk management as they insulate themselves from price volatility. The cost of such hedging is relatively nominal (e.g., margin and cost of carry) as there is no premium to be paid for a contract. Instead, these companies face other costs (opportunity costs); symmetric hedging eliminates the downside risk at the cost of foregone upside. But this is problematic.

The first problem with forwards is that of a foregone upside. Many companies are reluctant to hedge (e.g., long commodity positions) because they do wish to retain upside exposure to the underlying asset price. However, to avoid hedging altogether can needlessly expose the company to considerable downside risk and miss the benefits of strategic risk management we outlined in the prior chapter. These companies could use options to guard against extreme downside while retaining considerable upside opportunity.

Forwards also create management problems. When the risk being hedged does not occur and the risk driver moves favorably in the other direction, the offsetting hedge can move into a large loss position that must be marked-to-market (MtM), reported, and disclosed. Effectively a contingent liability, these items are invariably not viewed on a net basis against the offsetting gain. This creates immeasurable internal anxiety. These underwater hedges are frequently unwound at this point, the wrong time to do so, because of the intense scrutiny and controversy involved. Option hedges, on the other hand, quietly go out-of-the-money but never create the stir of an underwater forward.

Asymmetric Hedging

The amount and profile of a hedge may be more precisely managed with options. Options provide a practical way to manage the trade-offs among cost, risk, and any potential view. Even a forward may be simulated with puts paid for by calls, effectively a zero width collar.

Asymmetric hedging is consistent with the fundamental goals of corporate risk management. Eliminating extreme left-tail outcomes can be achieved with the purchase of out-of-the-money put options (i.e., assuming we hedge a long position) that eliminate the worst downside cases but preserve as much upside as the company can appropriately assume.

Going long, a put option can provide similar payoff to an insurance contract, where the insurance premium is the put option premium, the insurance deductible is the put option exercise price, and downside protection exists without impairing upside. Though the expected values of most insurance contracts may be negative, they protect the insured from a catastrophic event at an affordable cost and no impairment to the upside.

For example, though many airlines were pushed into, or remained in, bankruptcy by high fuel prices, the widely acknowledged leader of this industry continued to employ successful hedging strategies for its second largest factor input, fuel. The airline disclosed that it had a mixture of purchased call options, collar structures, and fixed price swap agreements in place to hedge approximately 83 percent of its next year's total anticipated jet fuel requirements.

ACCOUNTING CONSIDERATIONS

Global accounting standards for financial assets and liabilities now generally require derivative positions to be MtM, with resulting gains and losses forced through the income statement. However, hedge accounting allows deferring MtM flows until the hedged item hits the accounts. For example, FAS 133 hedge accounting rules define three types of hedges:

1. Fair value: recognized assets or liabilities, and unrecognized firm commitments
2. Cash flow: forecast unrecognized transactions
3. Net investment: foreign net assets.

Exposures that qualify for hedge accounting treatment include foreign currency assets and liabilities, forecast sales or costs, cash profits, including intercompany transactions, and other exposures that could affect the company's income statement. Yet a broad range of other types of exposures do not qualify, such as undeclared dividends, foreign accounting earnings, and future M&A transactions. The following parameters have generally been deemed consistent with hedge accounting treatment:

- **Amount.** At the start, the company must be able to specify the amount being hedged and the worst-case rate. Contingent instruments, such as knockout options and accrual forwards are not permitted.
- **Options.** The hedge cannot be subsidized with a net sold option. The amount of options sold must be equal to or less than the amount bought. And the maturity of the short position should be shorter than the maturity of the corresponding long position.
- **Effectiveness.** The hedge must be expected to be highly effective, defined as a requirement that the MtM on the hedging instrument should be in the 80 to 125 percent range of the hedged item MtM.
- **Documentation.** The transaction must be documented at the inception describing what is being hedged and how it is measured and monitored.

There are ways to achieve FAS 133 compliance by supplementing hedging strategies with cheap, deep-out-of-the-money options, or by potentially splitting a structure into multiple parts, some of which may qualify for hedge accounting treatment.

IMPLEMENTATION

From the foundation of a strategy, each company must develop a tactical action plan to execute its strategy. As a best practice, we see companies broadly follow these steps:

1. **Determine objectives, priorities, and constraints.** Common examples are to enhance liquidity and debt capacity by reducing the volatility of funds from operations, improve transparency of operating performance, or to reduce the chance of an adverse event.
2. **Establish relevant risk guidelines.** Identify maximum tolerable amount of positioning (e.g., all hedges serve a business purpose, no new risks or exposures will be created, hedge ratio tolerance ranges). Centralize decision making to avoid double hedging, facilitate risk netting, and improve bank bids. Evaluate potential conflicts with all incentive compensation programs.
3. **Assess net exposure to be hedged.** Define, measure and analyze all exposures to be managed, paying particular attention to any correlations and natural hedges. Determine the extent to which each exposure needs to be hedged and can reasonably be hedged, as well as the main attributes of the hedging program (e.g., hedged exposures, hedge horizon, hedge amounts, and hedge ratios).

4. **Compare suitability of various hedging tools.** Determine how various hedging tools (i.e., options, swaps, and forwards) are to be incorporated into the program to meet stated goals, views, and risk preferences for each exposure. Assess the pros and cons of hedging instruments, beyond simple cost, such as risk profile, upside exposure, and so forth.
5. **Execute trades timely and efficiently.** Identify a trading platform that answers the organizational needs and provides the necessary analytical support. Keep the group of counterparties to a manageable number.
6. **Control.** Streamline your approval and control process while ensuring timely and accurate reporting.

CHAPTER 12

ERM Case Study: Reengineering The Corporate Pension

Increasingly, capital structure optimization involves issues beyond simple choices in ratings and leverage. Corporate finance's elusive optimal capital structure puzzle has grown into an exercise in asset-liability management (ALM), with cash, investments, corporate pensions, and other (e.g., medical, environmental, litigation) assets and liabilities complicating the picture.

According to the Compustat database, corporate pension assets of New York Stock Exchange (NYSE) and National Association of Securities Dealers Automated Quotation (NASDAQ) listed firms reached $1.8 trillion (7 percent of economic value or EV) in 2005, up from just $900 billion in 1995. Moreover, cash and marketable securities have grown from $1.2 trillion to $12 trillion (12 percent to 44 percent of EV) over the same period. And though corporate pension underfunding is now largely on the mend, that the net position swung from a $250 billion surplus to a $500 billion deficit from 1999 to 2002 illustrates that optimal capital structure solutions are no longer just about how much debt or what kinds of debt.

Optimization must go beyond leverage ratios to prescribe optimal liquidity, pension funding and investment, and more from a holistic, ALM perspective. Despite their prevalence, prescriptive solutions do not readily emerge from efficient frontier analysis or from Value at Risk (VaR) analysis.

For example, the equity market recovery and rising interest rates have created a healthier pension funding position and a compelling opportunity to create value through a large and immediate shift in the asset allocations of defined benefit pension assets. In many companies, the fixed-income allocation of corporate pension assets should be increased to capture the economic benefit of earning after-tax interest on bonds in the pension at a pretax rate. Matching pension obligations with fixed-income assets allows the company to isolate the pension fund from the economic performance of the company. Further advantages include improved transparency, focus, and a reduction in pension-related costs and fees.

- Fixed-income returns can be better matched to meet projected benefit obligations and insulate company shareholders from corporate pensions.
- Reducing volatility from corporate pensions will improve financial transparency and earnings quality, increase debt capacity, and lower weighted average cost of capital (WACC).
- Financial leverage is more tax efficient when located on the right-hand side of the balance sheet, and fixed-income securities benefit more from a tax-deferred account than equities; offsetting any earnings per share (EPS) impact of a switch.
- Evidence clearly suggests a greater percentage of assets should be invested in fixed-income securities. However, until the rating agencies grow more comfortable with the benefits, our efficient frontier analysis suggests some allocation of equity to avoid adding cost and risk.
- We propose numerous capital market solutions to reduce equity exposure, optimize the risk-return trade-offs, and create shareholder value.

WHY NOW?

The equity market recovery and higher interest rates create a healthier corporate pension funding position; higher asset values and lower actuarial projected benefit obligations put adequate funding within reach for most companies for the first time this decade. This environment creates a window of opportunity to isolate shareholders from corporate pensions and create intrinsic value through large and immediate increases in the fixed-income allocation of pension assets.

A perfect storm of low equity returns and interest rates created today's underfunded position. The volatility of the net pension funding position and the severity of recent underfunding are problematic for capital planning.

As pledges of future cash flows, the ratings and investor analyst community increasingly view the net unfunded position as debt.[1] The optimal prefunding level of a pension is a function of the company's tax and legal jurisdiction, as well as ratings considerations.

Standard & Poor's (S&P) reported that by 2002, the aggregate underfunding position of the S&P 500 companies alone (with defined benefit plans) was $219 billion but is expected to have improved to a $112 billion shortfall by 2004.

The U.S. Pension Benefit Guaranty Corporation (PBGC) insures the defined benefit pensions of 44 million Americans against employer bankruptcy and other plan failures. Nearly one million individuals receive (or are owed) benefits under plans that have been taken over by the PBGC. At the end of 2004, PBGC liabilities exceeded PBGC assets by more than $23 billion and may continue to worsen.[2] Total underfunding in single-employer plans exceeded $450 billion at September 2004.[3]

In response to this situation, the U.S. Department of Labor 2006 budget proposes comprehensive reform designed to protect workers' pensions and stabilize the defined benefit pension system, with enhanced employer funding, simplified liability estimates, insurance premiums based on risk and cost, curtailed unfunded benefits deemed at risk, greatly improved plan status, and performance transparency.

THE PROBLEMS WITH EQUITY

The 25-year-old case against equity remains controversial and largely ignored in practice.[4] It is diminished by the practical limitations of the rating agencies and obfuscation created by generally accepted pension accounting methods; admittedly, this complex issue holds limited appeal for many equity investors. Nonetheless, the weight of evidence suggests that equity allocations should be reduced.

Pension Cost

Many practitioners believe they serve shareholder interests with equity-oriented investment strategies that earn higher returns, thus saving on the cost of pension benefits. But there is no free lunch: The higher return is the corollary to higher risk, leading to higher capital costs, and lower multiples. And equities face an opportunity cost in failing to make use of the favorable tax status of many pensions. Furthermore, though the higher risk may reduce the cost of the benefits, the risk also reduces the value of the benefits. Finally, equity returns are more likely to introduce pressure for increased benefits in times when equity returns are good.

A switch from equity to debt can be done without affecting EPS. The sale of equities and purchase of bonds in the fund can be accompanied by an offsetting increase in financial leverage in the company and share repurchases (issuance of debt and purchase of stock) to maintain EPS and create value through significant tax benefits.[5]

Equity Risk

If a large part of the pension portfolio is invested in equities, then the sponsoring company and, consequently, the equity investors in that company, suffer higher risk from the uncertainty of future pension assets.[6] Highly equity-oriented pensions produce a more highly leveraged exposure to equity returns. This pension risk contributes to higher equity betas, higher costs of equity, and higher weighted average costs of capital.[7]

Managers often claim the longer horizon of a pension fund diversifies away equity volatility. But if so, this benefit would be priced into the equity risk premium like the term structure of fixed-income securities (which really are less volatile over longer horizons). It is not. In fact, the risk of equities increases with time (under mean reverting and random walk assumptions).[8] Finally, companies cannot ignore shorter-term volatility if rating agencies, investors, and minimum funding needs do not.

Credit Quality

Investors are affected by the returns of underlying operating assets, and they suffer risk to their returns from the pension performance. Pension trustees and sponsoring companies now question if the risk associated with a pension fund largely (often 75 percent) devoted to equities is worthwhile.[9]

Pension liabilities represent additional interest rate risk and are recognized by rating agencies as well as analysts as economically equivalent to financial debt.[10] Furthermore, accounting changes are underway that are likely to lead to the Financial Accounting Standards Board (FASB) moving these economic liabilities from the footnotes to the balance sheet. Recent market events have led to many high-profile cases of credit rating impairment due to large and sudden underfunding situations. In practice, the adjustments to the corporate financial statements to derive more reflective credit metrics are neither universally nor mechanically applied and are most frequently made for pensions in the United States.[11]

As outlined in Chapter 6, total corporate debt is increased by the total unfunded projected benefit obligations (PBO) for pensions, and the total accumulated postretirement benefit obligations (APBO) for other postretirement obligations (OPEB). The net total unfunded is tax effected in countries where contributions are tax deductible (though often up to a full funding limitation) and for companies which are able to reap the benefit of this tax shield. Equity is reduced by the tax-effected unfunded PBO/APBO (less any recognized preexisting liability). Earnings before interest, tax, depreciation, and amortization (EBITDA) is increased by the total pension expense, less economic service cost to eliminate all accounting artifacts that stem from the smoothing approach of accounting rules. Interest expense is increased by the pension interest cost, less the actual return on plan assets (up to the amount of the interest cost but not beyond). Funds from operations (FFO) is increased by the amount that benefit contributions plus actual plan asset returns exceed service and interest cost, after tax. In some cases, plan asset returns may be normalized, and are certainly capped.

In addition to lower asset values, a fall in long-term interest rates increases the pension liability because under generally accepted accounting principles (GAAP), they are determined as the present value (PV) of future benefits, with the discount factor typically a long-term corporate yield.

For example, we illustrate the impact of a 1 percent decrease in long-term interest rates, such that the economic liability (PBO) increases by $750 million. We estimate the accounting liability will increase only about $75 million, due to the smoothing techniques. On the income statement, service cost is likely to increase about $15 million and the amortization of the underfunded amount will increase by about $75 million. However, the pension expense will only increase by about $80 million because the interest cost will be reduced by about $10 million.

Though short-term volatility is prevented, these smoothing mechanisms are criticized for obscuring the plan sponsor's true assets, liabilities, costs, and cash flows related to its defined benefit pension plans. Though accounting treatments often obscure this correlation, in the United States, these smoothing techniques and other degrees of freedom for actuarial assumptions allowed by Statement of Financial Accounting Standards (SFAS) No. 87 are under review.

Beyond mere underfunding, the leverage created by corporate pension equity assets is similar to corporate financial leverage and has a similar impact on credit risk. Equity-oriented pension assets reduce the ability of a company to employ more value-creating leverage within its own liabilities.[12] During an economic downturn an equity-oriented pension decreases in value and its cost burden increases, leading to less debt capacity, a higher cost of debt, and a higher cost of capital (WACC).[13]

Hedge

Equities may reduce company contributions but can only make the pension beneficiaries less secure since they reduce the PV of a defined benefit. Trustees should note that this holds true whether funded or not, and an increase in asset risk not accompanied by an increase in benefits makes beneficiaries less secure.

Many managers, pension consultants, and trustees continue to believe that equities provide a natural hedge against salary-related liabilities despite the proof to the contrary.[14] But equities do not grow in proportion to salaries or pension liabilities.[15] The best hedge would be an immunization strategy involving inflation-linked bonds.

Efficiency

The equity investments of shareholders are diluted by the act of corporate pension investment in equities where shareholders have no line of sight. And the company brings no comparative advantage to this activity, lacking core competencies in security selection and oversight. Furthermore, the duplicity of efforts adds intermediary costs and frictions to the investment process. The cost to manage fixed-income securities is substantially cheaper; upon switching to a portfolio of bonds, one company estimated an annual savings in fees and costs of nearly £10 million, equivalent to 67 bp of investment return, in switching into bonds.

THE CASE FOR MORE BONDS

Just as many arguments against equity exist, many corollary reasons argue for increased fixed-income allocations in corporate pension assets, such as reduced risk, improved liability matching, transparency, cost, and tax efficiency.

Volatility

Although pension fund assets and liabilities are legally separate and unconsolidated, pension assets affect the company because pension (defined) benefits are independent of fund performance. Portfolio gains and losses impact funding costs and the financial position of the company. Thus, pension fund performance affects credit quality, cash flows, earnings, and stock price.[16] Though most risk is borne by the investors, pension members benefit from reduced risk; member legal protection is weaker in many jurisdictions where there is no equivalent to the PBGC.

Increased fixed-income allocation can reduce earnings volatility from corporate pensions and improve earnings quality and liquidity for strategic investments in growth. Reducing volatility in pension asset returns increases the capacity for risk bearing of the sponsoring company leading to more debt capacity, higher quality debt, lower WACC, and higher multiples.

Natural Hedge

Fixed-income returns can be better matched to meet projected benefit obligations and insulate company shareholders from corporate pensions.

Equity returns are neither stationary nor predictable and, therefore, cannot be matched to meet pension obligations. In the absence of credit risk, the return of fixed income over the full period to repayment is fixed and can be matched to meet the benefit obligations of a pension fund and reduce the risk of having an insufficient fund.

This immunization strategy allows the company to isolate itself from the pension, exit the security selection business, and focus on core operations.

Cost and Transparency

Fixed-income investment reduces the need for the opaque smoothing entries that cushion equity return volatility and undermine confidence in earnings quality. This improves financial transparency and management efficiency. A reduction in the size of equity assets under management with a corresponding increase in fixed income reduces management fees, creating considerable value on a PV basis.

Tax Arbitrage

The Fischer Black tax arbitrage was first proposed in a seminal paper by Fischer Black.[17] The basic premise is that companies with defined benefit corporate pensions should exchange equities for fixed-income securities while simultaneously issuing debt to repurchase equity at the company level. Leverage is more tax efficient when carried as a liability where the cost of debt is tax deductible. And fixed-income securities benefit more from the tax-deferred status enjoyed by pensions than do equities. A plan sponsor can offset the EPS impact of a reduction in equities with improved tax efficiency and the repurchase of corporate equity.

Though pension assets and liabilities are legally distinct from corporate assets and liabilities, they do have a direct effect on the company cash flows, share price, and debt capacity. A company can reduce the volatility of its future cash flows by investing in less risky pension assets, thereby reducing company risk and increasing its capacity for financial leverage.

Table 12.1 illustrates this argument for the case where a company sells $1 of equity in its pension fund and uses the proceeds to buy $1 of debt. From an economically consolidated perspective, assuming 30 percent marginal corporate taxes, it should be able to add $0.70 of new debt to the corporate balance sheet with no impairment to its debt capacity (and no need for further contributions to the fund) with proceeds to repurchase $0.70 of its own equity.

The source of value is that the company earns a spread between the pretax cost of debt on the bonds invested in its pension assets, while costing

TABLE 12.1 Tax Arbitrage Illustration

Pension tax rate	0%	Corporate tax rate (Tc)	30%
Return on bonds	Rb	Personal tax rate on bonds (Tb)	40%
Return on equities	Re	Personal tax rate on stocks (Ts)	15%

Tepper Arbitrage		Black Arbitrage	
Plan shifts $1 from equities into bonds (after tax)	$(Rb - Re)*(1 - Tc)$	Plan shifts $1 from equities into bonds (after tax)	
Shareholders shift $1*(1 - Tc)$ from bonds to equities	$Re*(1-Tc)*(1-Ts)$	Company issues $1*(1-Tc)$ bonds to repurchase stock	$Rb*(1-Tc)*Tc$
Net shareholder gain	$Rb*(1-Tc)*(Tb-Ts)$	Net shareholder gain	$Rb*(1-Tc)*Tc*(1-Ts)$
NPV in perpetuity is which simplifies to	$(1-Tc)*(Tb-Ts)/(1-Tb)$ 29%	NPV in perpetuity is which simplifies to	$(1-Tc)*Tc*(1-Ts)/(1-Tb)$ 30%

only its own after-tax cost of debt. Fixed-income securities are earning after-tax interest on bonds in the pension at a pretax rate. Assuming the company invests in credits of comparable credit to itself, the intrinsic value is large. The total benefit amounts to a reduction in taxes of 21 percent of the corporate borrowing rate, or roughly $0.30 of intrinsic value for every pension dollar that is reallocated from equity to debt.

We often assume equity portfolio returns are comparable to the company equity returns. The plan swaps a diversified equity portfolio with the company's own shares, reducing the dilution to the company's true beta. In cases where the company stock is expected to outperform the market temporarily, the total benefit would amount to a larger reduction in taxes and a larger amount of intrinsic value for every reallocated pension dollar.

In cases where the company stock is expected to underperform, the total tax benefit and intrinsic value per reallocated pension dollar is reduced. The inflection point, in our example, is company stock overvalued by more than the 30 percent of intrinsic value.

Admittedly, the tax arbitrage spread can be eroded by its own credit spread if investment is restricted to Treasuries or corporates of higher credit quality than itself. Similarly, we do not recommend this plan for nontax payers, such as many technology companies where losses, stock options, and global tax planning shield the company from taxes. There is no source of intrinsic value for companies not paying taxes, or expecting to pay taxes in the future. Practical limitations, such as rating agency treatment (whether full debt capacity will be accorded) and investor communications, are important challenges that merit consideration.

Alternatively, value may be created without the company altering its own corporate balance sheet. A straight swap of equities for bonds may add value if shareholders adjust their own portfolios to exploit the change in risk.[18]

OPTIMAL CAPITAL STRUCTURE REPRISE

The elusive optimal capital structure puzzle has grown into an exercise in asset-liability management. Cash, investments, corporate pensions, litigation, and other reserves complicate the picture. The size and variability of corporate pensions show that optimal capital structure solutions must go beyond leverage ratios to prescribe optimal liquidity, pension investment and funding, and strategies for other assets and liabilities from a holistic, ALM perspective.

Though we do measure financial leverage, floating rate exposure, weighted average coupon, and duration, these metrics are static values bearing limited insight and providing unclear direction for managers. And despite the proliferation of efficient frontier and Value at Risk (VaR) analytics, these analysis are often confusing and lack prescriptive guidance for executives. Many managers have been left wondering: Where should we be on this efficient frontier? and How much VaR is the right amount? We too employ these analytics but draw upon clear goals and constraints with actionable guidance for value maximization.

ALM Perspective

Our framework for optimal capital structure employs an ALM perspective to determine guidance and direct implementation, with a focus on intrinsic value maximization within the constraints of appropriate levels of risk for the business.

Intrinsic value is typically at the perspective of consolidated cash flows (or core earnings as proxy) and net economic exposures to facilitate a netting of risks and simplification of the analytical process. Potential near-term financial impact, though not the objective, must be understood and within the bounds of a message that can be articulated to the financial markets, or it will risk diminishing market values. We view unacceptable risk as that which materially impairs liquidity or financial strength (e.g., estimated credit profile or long-term and short-term target credit ratings may serve as a reasonable proxy) to the point of impairing capital access, business plan execution, or WACC, thereby diminishing intrinsic value.

Efficient Frontier

We propose an equity allocation of about 30 percent: Our efficient frontier analysis shows that, barring the tax arbitrage, anything less than 20 to 30 percent equity is inefficient. Based on the historical market portfolio, we found that risk was minimized at about 25 percent equity, and that anything less than about 20 percent equity was inefficient, adding cost (opportunity cost) and risk. Based on our current market portfolio, we found that risk was minimized at about 35 percent equity and that anything less than about 30 percent equity was inefficient, adding forgone opportunity and risk.

Ultimately, most risk is borne by the shareholders. Although the pension fund assets and liabilities are not included on the corporate balance sheet, gains and losses on the portfolio flow through to the corporation because of its responsibility to any residual value that must be satisfied to meet the pension fund obligations. There is substantial empirical evidence showing that equity market values reflect pension positions.[19] Debt market values and credit ratings also capture this information.[20] In debt and equity markets, the funding impact is asymmetrical (since overfunding is an encumbered asset). Every dollar of increased underfunding lowers the market value of the company by about one dollar; an increase in overfunding increases the company market value by less than one dollar.[21]

Most importantly, corporate pension plan (systematic) risk is reflected in company equity risk.[22] Therefore, there is no free lunch: The higher returns of equity are paid for with commensurately higher risk. Absent tax advantages, any position along the efficient frontier, depending on the benchmark, is a rational choice as long as financial strength (optimal credit rating) is not impaired. To identify the efficient range in terms of risk and return, we constructed efficient frontiers, one from 50-year historical returns and another from current market expectations.

Our efficient frontiers were constructed using a portfolio of two mutual funds: A-rated bonds and an S&P 500 stock fund. A statistical analysis was conducted to find the mean, variance, standard deviation, covariance, and correlation of the return of the two funds. The first curve was constructed using the 50-year historical returns of the S&P returns and A-rated fixed securities, and the second uses current market expectations for the S&P and A-rated securities. The points along the efficient frontier were formulated by varying the weight of equity between 0 to 100 percent in 5 percent increments. The minimum variance portfolio formula was used to find the allocation that achieves the best expected return for the lowest possible risk; however, we do not propose that risk minimization should be the goal.

For all of the reasons cited, we propose a greater percentage of corporate pension assets be allocated toward fixed-income securities. Roughly speaking, for every 10 percent of equities exchanged for fixed-income, risk is reduced by 60 bps. However, until the rating agencies grow more comfortable with the benefits, allowing companies to exploit the tax arbitrage fully (and for nontax payers), many companies may wish to keep some equity. Depending on the benchmark, eliminating equity can be inefficient, adding considerable cost and some risk.

Value at Risk (VaR)

We employ dynamic simulation modeling to evaluate these alternative capital structures on a test case A-rated company under a net present value (NPV) basis (i.e., notionally, a VaR approach), with an understanding of near-term fiscal impact.

We generated 3,000 independent cases of the complete term structure using a Monte Carlo simulation and created a probability distribution of EPS and PV of 5-year EPS projections using stochastic interest rate models with volatilities for daily short-term rates (18 percent) and term spread (31 percent) where the mean EPS is equivalent to the consensus outlook under a bias adjusted forward curve and expected equity returns of 14 percent with a volatility of 17 percent.

A move from 75 percent equity to 30 percent equity for our test company represents a $450 million shift of corporate pension assets, with VaR falling 7 percent from $9.00 +/− 1.39 to $8.35 +/− 1.02 and near-term EPS diluted from $2.00 to $1.88. The cost to VaR and EPS can be offset in the third case, depending on the size of the buyback, where the switch is accompanied by increased leverage and a share repurchase. Theoretically, the company can add almost $400 million of new debt (0 percent equity and assumed tax rate of 49 percent) and repurchase 6 percent of its own stock (increasing VaR to $8.49 +/− 1.16 and EPS to $2.20) but we believe ratings agency treatment may constrain this size.

Our own credit analytic model suggests the company has room for $200 million of debt and 3 percent share repurchase within the existing rating before risking impairment to its own credit profile.[23] This compares favorably to the conservative Boots case (see below), where only 5 percent of the theoretical amount was implemented. Our buyback case achieves a similar estimated credit profile, at a slight cost to VaR ($8.65 +/− 1.09), and near term earnings accretion ($2.08 EPS).

CAPITAL MARKETS SOLUTIONS

The evidence suggests a greater percentage of assets be invested in fixed-income securities. However, for non-taxpaying cases, as well as until the rating agencies get up to speed,, efficient frontier analysis suggests maintaining *some* equities to avoid adding cost and risk.

Yet for some corporate plans, de-risking at current market levels may still be unattractive as this would crystallize any remaining deficit. So, these funds have established a roadmap, where equity weightings will be reduced over time as funding levels are restored. We propose numerous capital market solutions to increase fixed-income exposure, optimize the risk-return trade-offs, and create shareholder value, including the following: sell equity/buy fixed income, buy-write options programs, collar strategies, relative performance options, and swap overlays.

Sell Equity, Buy Fixed Income

The simplest strategy is to sell equities and buy fixed-income securities, or possibly entering into an equity swap, to lock in equity values and receive fixed-income returns. A swap strategy may be less attractive because transaction costs of the swap will likely exceed those of buying and selling stocks and bonds.

Leveraged Fixed Income

A more muted approach is to borrow at the parent company level to invest in fixed-income securities. This assumes that there is debt capacity within the rating for increased borrowings, and capacity within the pension for increased funding without risking an overfunded position (investing outside the pension is less tax efficient). The equity proportion and the volatility of expected returns will be averaged down, with less impact to the income statement by lowering the net pension cost.

Buy-Write Program

Another alternative is to sell away some of the upside of pension equities through a buy-write program. A buy-write covered call position is created by buying the underlying asset while selling/writing a call. Although income is boosted by the premiums collected, the cost is that entitlement to future capital gains is forfeited should the stock price rise above the exercise price.

Collar Strategy

Another equity portfolio risk mitigation strategy is to target a specified return but retain risk losses to a palatable level with a collar strategy. A collar provides a floor on equity returns (downside protection) by buying a protective put at a cost of forgone upside beyond the exercise price of a call written on the underlying asset.

Relative Performance Options

The fund may also sell outperformance calls, based on the relative performance of equities to bonds, to match the liabilities more closely. The fund surrenders any upside in equity markets above the level at which de-risking is attractive under the roadmap in return for an upfront premium. If the de-risking level is reached, then the fund receives a cost efficient reallocation into bonds. If it is not reached, then the premium received will boost solvency.

Swap Overlays

Fixed-floating swap overlays can be used to hedge against the impact to pension liabilities of any rise in interest rates. They may be used in a liability immunized active management strategy to manage the risks between a portfolio of liabilities and a market benchmark. Finally, credit default swaps can be used to enhance portfolio optimization of credit and sovereign risk independently from tenor.

Fixed-Floating Swaps   For example, Company A pays $350 million per annum to retirees for 30 years, assuming a discount factor of 5 percent. The company enters into a swap agreement under the terms that the company receives $350 million over 30 years and pays 6-month LIBOR plus 80 bps.

The company achieves two advantages: The first benefit is a substantial cash cost savings of $84 million assuming 6-month LIBOR of 3 percent. The second benefit is that volatility is reduced because the aggregate value of pension liability plus interest rate swap maintains a value that is nearly independent of interest rate movement. As standard fixed-floating swaps are designed to swap bonds—that is, with redemption at the end—the actual immunizing swaps would consist of an amortizing portfolio of interest rate swaps.

Active Liability Immunizing   Active liability immunizing is a strategy of using swaps to manage the risks between a portfolio of liabilities and a benchmark used in the market place. This allows the company to invest in a diversified portfolio managed by internal or external managers according to transparent benchmarks.

The swap overlay can be separated from the portfolio and matches the asset benchmark return to the cost of the liability. As the liabilities change over time, the swap overlay has to be adjusted for these movements; however, these adjustments are small compared to the value changes of the liability from interest rate movement.

Credit Default Swaps   Credit default swaps enable portfolio credit optimization by freeing the selection of credits from the constraints of liability matching (tenor). In particular, the credit portfolio selected can have a shorter duration than long-dated pension liabilities.

Credit risk has three key components: credit spread volatility, ratings migration and default risk, and issuer diversification. Shortening credit duration reduces credit spread volatility. Credit default risk is rating dependent and time dependent. Diversification amongst issuers is most feasible within the highly liquid 5-year to 10-year part of the credit curve. Even in a flat/inverted credit curve environment, this leads to an optimized risk-return ratio. Swaps provide access to non–U.S. denominated credit, with currency and interest rate risks fully hedged, to enable further optimizing portfolio selection.

THE BOOTS CASE

In October 2001, Boots Co. Plc announced that it had sold its entire equity holdings of £1.7 billion (75 percent of total pension assets) and invested in long-dated AAA sterling bonds with a weighted average maturity of 30 years. Initially 25 percent inflation linked, in 2002 this amount was swapped up to 50 percent. The pension fund measured £2.3 billion in assets, or roughly 45 percent as large as the company's total asset base and was not considered to be a mature pension, as half of its members were active employees.

The stock price was unaffected by the initial announcement (but weakened by half-year results) but appears to have reacted favorably to the corresponding announcement of share repurchases.

The agencies noted that though not the impetus for the change, with the recent introduction of Financial Reporting Standard (FRS) 17, by switching to 100 percent fixed income, there would be less of an accounting shock. The rating agencies made no change to the credit rating (A+/A1), but unfortunately, the share repurchase and subsequent leverage profile seem to have been significantly undersized. Initially, £300 million, the program was later upsized to £700 million.

Though application of the Fischer Black plan (Table 12.2) would suggest £1.7 billion of new debt capacity after tax and suggest increasing leverage from about 10 percent to 30 percent of enterprise value, the buyback program was funded from operating cash flow and leverage did not change appreciably. Thus, though the theoretical tax arbitrage could have created £500 million (£0.72/share or nearly 10 percent), practical ratings constraints seems to have limited value creation to about £100 million (£0.12/share).

TABLE 12.2 Boots Case Intrinsic Value

Pension tax rate	0%	Corporate tax rate (Tc)	29%
Return on bonds	Rb	Personal tax rate on bonds (Tb)	40%
Return on equities	Re	Personal tax rate on stocks (Ts)	15%

Boots Case		Black Arbitrage	
Plan shifts $1 from equities into bonds (after tax)	$(Rb-Re)*(1-Tc)$	Equity Sold	1,725
		Implied NPV	503
		Fees in perpetuity	130
Company issues $\$1*(1-Tc)$ bonds to repurchase stock	$Rb*(1-Tc)*Tc$	Potential Intrinsic Value	633
		Value of new leverage	100
Net shareholder gain	$Rb*(1-Tc)*Tc*(1-Ts)$	Fees in perpetuity	130
		Intrinsic value realized	230
NPV in perpetuity is which simplifies to	$(1-Tc)*Tc*(1-Ts)/(1-Tb)$ 29%		

Additionally, the company reduced management fees by nearly £10 million annually, or about £130 million in perpetuity (£0.15/share). Therefore, total intrinsic value created was only about £230 million (£0.26/share) or about 4 percent, explaining the market's underwhelming response to this widely cited case study.[24]

In May 2004, the company announced additional share repurchases from cash flow that would maintain leverage at about 10 percent debt/enterprise value, plus refinements to its asset strategy. About 15 percent (about £420 million) of fund assets were to be swapped back into asset classes other than bonds, including but not limited to, equities and real estate holdings.

WHY IT STILL HASN'T HAPPENED

Despite overwhelming economic evidence to the contrary, corporate pensions continue to be largely invested in equities. We identify six factors that contribute to the ongoing preference among corporate pensions to allocate the bulk of their assets to equities despite the weak economic rationale:

1. **Bull Market.** The experience of multiple consecutive years of large excess returns in the equity market made the lure of equity risk difficult to resist.[25] Many companies were able to significantly boost their reported earnings in a period when underlying operating performance

was showing signs of weakness. The market correction and its aftermath have helped bring a more realistic perspective. Recent interest rate movements make any switch to bonds cheaper.

2. **Rating Agencies.** Though change is underway at the agencies, historically the credit ratings process has not explicitly incorporated asset allocation or its financial consequences in the determination of credit quality. Though the Boots case has raised the practical issues, many more cases will be required to effect the change required.

3. **GAAP.** A biased and opaque method of accounting for pensions that highlights the rewards of equity while hiding its risks (and provides opportunity for gaming) remains a critical element of support for equity investment despite the economics.[26] The globalization of accounting standards and momentum for other politically charged changes suggests that change may be on the way.

4. **Actuarial.** Current actuarial models do not incorporate asset allocation, when determining insurance payments (the PBGC in the United States), and enable companies to cut transfer values in half relative to the economic cost of providing deferred annuities.[27] If employees can be paid a benefit but then persuaded to accept transfer values well below its economic value, then shareholders will reap a sizable gain.

5. **Fees.** Equity investment and mismatched pensions generate significant intermediary fees and help support a symbiotic relationship with outside advisors that serves to entrench the status quo. Intermediary fees might be viewed as a real option on indemnity cover, a form of litigation insurance for pension trustees.

6. **Education.** Despite the magnitude and importance of this issue, investor awareness of, and appetite for, pension accounting and economics remains poor. A growing body of topical research remains largely untapped. Education and awareness of pension economics among managers, analysts, and investors must grow considerably so they fully appreciate the risks and returns of asset allocation.

Resources

TOOLS AND PORTALS

http://pages.stern.nyu.edu/~adamodar/
http://www.statsoft.com/textbook/stathome.html
http://web.utk.edu/~jwachowi/part3.html
http://www.sternstewart.com/

NEW RESEARCH AND LITERATURE SEARCH

http://papers.ssrn.com/sol3/DisplayAbstractSearch.cfm
http://www.research-finance.com/
http://econpapers.repec.org/

ECONOMIC RESEARCH AND DATA

http://www.research.stlouisfed.org/fred2/
http://www.federalreserve.gov/rnd.htm
http://www.nber.org/
http://www.bis.org/index.htm

NEWS AND MARKET DATA

http://finance.yahoo.com/
http://online.barrons.com/public/main
http://news.ft.com/home/us
http://online.wsj.com/public/us
http://www.nytimes.com/
http://www.ifrmarkets.com/protected/ifr_main.html (subscription)

CORPORATE GOVERNANCE AND COMPENSATION

http://www.valueadvisors.com/index.html
http://www.issproxy.com/index.jsp
http://www.bloomberg.com/news/commentary/crystal.html

OTHER AGENCIES

http://www.fei.org/eweb
http://www.efmaefm.org/index.shtml
http://www2.standardandpoors.com/servlet/Satellite?pagename=sp/Page/
    HomePg&r=1&l=EN
http://www.moodys.com/cust/default.asp
http://www.moodyskmv.com/
https://www.creditsights.com/default/?select=CS_subscriber&DisplayName
    =Home (subscription)

CHAPTER 1

1. Justin Pettit, "Corporate Capital Costs: A Practitioner's Guide," *The Journal of Applied Corporate Finance* 12:1 (Spring 1999). Justin Pettit, Mack Ferguson and Robert Gluck, "A Method for Estimating Global Corporate Capital Costs: The Case of Bestfoods," *Journal of Applied Corporate Finance* 12:3 (Fall 1999). Justin Pettit *et al*, "The WACC User's Guide" available at SSRN: http://ssrn.com/abstract=683313.
2. In "The Shrinking Equity Premium," Financial Analysts Journal, 61:3, pp. 61–71 (November/December 2005). Jeremy Siegel estimates the equity premium over U.S. government bonds for the period from 1802 to 1998 to be between 3.5 percent and 4.7 percent (using geometric and arithmetic means, respectively).
3. Steve Weber "The End of the Business Cycle," *Foreign Affairs* 76:4 (July/August 1997). Steven Weber of University of California at Berkeley makes a strong case for fundamental structural economic and capital market changes making observations of events in U.S. history less representative of responses in the future.
4. Roger Ibbotson and Peng Chen, "Long-Run Stock Returns: Participating in the Real Economy," *Financial Analysts Journal* 59:1, pp. 88–98 (February 2003). The market risk premium is estimated at about 5 percent in other studies also. Scott Mayfield, "Estimating the Market Risk Premium," *Journal of Financial Economics* 73:3 (September 2004).
5. Aswath Damodaran, *Investment Valuation* (New York: John Wiley & Sons, Inc., 1993).
6. Rene Stulz, "Globalization, Corporate Finance, and the Cost of Capital," *Journal of Applied Corporate Finance* 12:3 (Fall 1999). The article discusses the impact of globalism on integrated and integrating capital markets leading both to falling risk premiums and risk premium convergence.
7. Elroy Dimson, Paul Marsh and Mike Staunton, "Global Evidence on the Equity Risk Premium," *Journal of Applied Corporate Finance* 15:4 (Fall 2003).
8. Bruner, Eades, Harris and Higgins, "Best Practices in Estimating the Cost of Capital: Survey and Synthesis," *Financial Practice and Education* (Spring/Summer 1998).
9. *Moody's Rating Methodology Handbook* (April 2003). S&P's Corporate Ratings Criteria, 2003. Fitch's *Corporate Ratings Methodology* (June 2003).
10. Tom Copeland and Fred Weston, *Financial Theory and Corporate Policy, 3rd Edition* (New York: Addison Wesley, 1992) pp. 473–478.
11. Ian Cooper and Evi Kaplanis, "Home Bias in Equity Portfolios and the Cost of Capital for Multinational Firms," *Journal of Applied Corporate Finance* 8:3 (Fall 1995). Dennis E. Logue, "When Theory Fails: Globalization as a Response to the (Hostile) Market for Foreign Exchange," *Journal of Applied Corporate Finance* 8:3 (Fall 1995).

12. Rene M. Stulz, "Globalization of Capital Markets and the Cost of Capital: The Case of Nestle," *Journal of Applied Corporate Finance* 8:3 (Fall 1995).
13. Alan C. Shapiro, *Modern Corporate Finance* (New York: Macmillan Publishing, 1990) pp. 239–268.

CHAPTER 2

1. Economic profit (EP), Economic Value Added (EVA), and so on, are effectively all measures of residual income. The framework is presented in detail in Bennet Stewart, *The Quest for Value* (New York: HarperCollins, 1991). See also S. David Young and Stephen F. O'Byrne, *EVA and Value-Based Management* (New York: McGraw-Hill, 2001). Justin Pettit *et al*, "How To Find Your Economic Profits." Available at SSRN: http://ssrn.com/abstract=505222
2. Adapted from Jerold L. Zimmerman, *Accounting for Decision Making and Control* (New York: McGraw-Hill, 1997).

CHAPTER 3

1. Dranikoff, Koller, and Schneider, "Divestiture: Strategy's Missing Link," *Harvard Business Review* (May 2002). Justin Pettit *et al*, "Positioning for Growth: Carve-Outs & Spin-Offs" (April 2004). Available at SSRN: http://ssrn.com/abstract=546622.
2. Brandimarte, Fallon, and McNish, "Trading the Corporate Portfolio: A Systematic Approach to Buying & Selling Assets Can Deliver Superior Shareholder Returns," *McKinsey on Finance* No. 2 (Autumn 2001).
3. Ibid.
4. Hemang Desai and Prem Jain, "Long-Run Common Stock Returns Following Stock Split and Reverse Split," *Journal of Business* Vol. 70, No. 3 (July 1997).
5. Maxwell and Rao, "Do Spin-offs Expropriate Wealth from Bondholders?" *Journal of Finance* 58 (Oct 2003).
6. Burch and Nanda, "Divisional Diversity and the Conglomerate Discount: Evidence from Spin-Offs," *Journal of Financial Economics* 70:1 (October 2003).
7. Ibid.
8. Brandimarte, Fallon, and McNish, "Trading the Corporate Portfolio: A Systematic Approach to Buying & Selling Assets Can Deliver Superior Shareholder Returns," *McKinsey on Finance* No. 2 (Autumn 2001).
9. McConnell, *et al*, "Can Takeover Losses Explain Spin-off Gains?" *Journal of Financial and Quantitative Analysis* 30:4 (December 1995).
10. Chemmanur and Paeglis, "Why Issue Tracking Stock? Insights From a Comparison with Spin-Offs and Carve-Outs," *Journal of Applied Corporate Finance* 14:2 (2001).
11. Michael E. Raynor, "Tracking Stocks and the Acquisition of Real Options," *Journal of Applied Corporate Finance* 13:2 (2000). Author provides an interesting argument in support of tracking stocks based on the real option framework.

12. Myron B. Slovin, Marie E. and Steven R. Sushka. "A Comparison of the Information Conveyed by Equity Carve-outs, Spin-offs, and Asset Sell-offs," *Journal of Financial Economics* 37 (1995).

13. Jeremy C. Stein, "Internal Capital Markets and the Competition for Corporate Resources," *Journal of Finance* 52:1 (March 1997). Oliver E. Williamson, *Markets and Hierarchies: Analysis and Antitrust Implications* (New York: The Free Press, 1975).

14. Timothy R. Burch and Vikram K. Nanda, "Divisional Diversity and the Conglomerate Discount: Evidence from Spin-Offs," *Journal of Financial Economics* 70:1 (October 2003).

15. Jay P. Brandimarte, William C. Fallon, and Robert S. McNish. "Trading the Corporate Portfolio: A Systematic Approach to Buying & Selling Assets Can Deliver Superior Shareholder Returns," *McKinsey on Finance* No. 2 (Autumn 2001).

16. For example, Michael C. Jensen, "The Takeover Controversy: Analysis and Evidence," *Midland Corporate Finance Journal* 4:2 (1991) pp. 6–32. See also Gary C. Biddle and Frederick W. Lindahl, "Stock Price Reactions to LIFO Adoptions: The Association Between Excess Returns and LIFO Tax Savings," *Journal of Accounting Research* Part II (Autumn 1982): 551–588.

17. Cai von Rumohr of SG Cowen Securities Equity Research, "Strategic Initiatives a Positive Step for 'Show-Me' Stock" (September 28, 1999).

CHAPTER 4

1. Sara B. Moeller, Frederik P. Schlingemann, and Rene M. Stulz, "Firm Size and the Gains from Acquisitions." *Journal of Financial Economics*, 73: 2, (August 2004). Justin Pettit *et al*, "Where M&A Pays: Who Wins & How?" Available at SSRN: http://ssrn.com/abstract=641621. Justin Pettit *et al*, "Renewing Growth: M&A Fact & Fallacy" (June 2003). Available at SSRN: http://ssrn.com/abstract=463102

2. E.F. Fama, "Market Efficiency, Long-Term Returns, and Behavioral Finance," *Journal of Finance* 1998. S. Moeller, P. Schingemann, and R. Stulz, "Firm Size and the Gains From Acquisitions," *Journal of Financial Economics* Vol. 73, No. 2, August 2004. This 2004 article proposes that the short-term return is an unbiased estimate of the impact of the acquisition to the acquiring shareholders.

3. Steven Kaplan and Michael Weisback, "The Success of Acquisitions: Evidence from Divestitures," Working Paper (October 1990). This article concludes that unrelated acquisitions are almost four times more likely to be divested than related acquisitions.

4. John A. Doukas and Ozgur B. Kan, "Excess Cash Flows and Diversification Discount," *Financial Management*, 33:2 (Summer 2004).

5. Bernard T. Ferrari, *et al*, "More Restructuring Ahead for Media and Entertainment," *McKinsey on Finance*, No. 8 (Summer 2003).

6. Sara B. Moeller, F.P. Schlingermann, and R.M. Stulz, "Firm Size and the Gains from Acquisitions," *Journal of Financial Economics* 73:2 (August 2004).

7. Michael Bradley and Anant Sundaram, "Do Acquisitions Drive Performance or Does Performance Drive Acquisitions?" (August 2004) Available at SSRN: http://ssrn.com/abstract=592761.

8. K. Fuller, J. Netter, and M. Stegemoller, "What do Returns to Acquiring Firms Tell Us? Evidence from Firms that Make Many Acquisitions," *Journal of Finance* 57 (2002).

9. Sara B. Moeller, F. P. Schlingermann, and R.M. Stulz, "Firm Size and the Gains from Acquisitions," *Journal of Financial Economics* 73:2 (August 2004).

10. Scott Christofferson, Robert McNish, and Diane Sias, "Where Mergers Go Wrong," *McKinsey on Finance* No. 10 (Winter 2004).

11. Lee Dranikoff, Tim Koller, and Antoon Schneider, "Divestiture: Strategy's Missing Link." *Harvard Business Review* (May 2002). This study covers the 1990 to 1999 time period and is based on a 200-company universe.

12. For example, Eric Lindenberg and Michael Ross of Salomon Smith Barney, "To Purchase or To Pool: Does it Matter?" *Journal of Applied Corporate Finance* 12:2 (Summer 1999). See also Trevor S. Harris of Morgan Stanley, "Overcoming Accounting Differences: A Stockpicker's Guide to the Numbers That Count" *Apples-to-Apples* (February 6, 1998).

13. G. Bennett Stewart, *The Quest for Value* (New York: HarperCollins, 1991). Tom Copeland, Tim Koller and Jack Murrin, *Valuation: Measuring and Managing the Value of Companies, First Edition* (New York: John Wiley & Sons, 1993).

14. Bain and Company, "Discipline and the Dilutive Deal," *Harvard Business Review* (2002).

15. L. Lang and R.M. Stulz, "Contagion and Competitive Intra-industry Effects of Bankruptcy Announcements," *Journal of Financial Economics* Vol. 61, No. 2 (August 1992) pp. 45–60. Philip Berger and Eli Ofek, "Causes and Effects of Corporate Refocusing," *Review of Financial Studies*, 12:2 (Summer 1999).

16. Belen Villalonga, "Does Diversification Cause the 'Diversification Discount'?" *Financial Management* 33:2 (Summer 2004). Belen Villalonga, "Diversification Discount or Premium? New Evidence from the Business Information Tracking Series," *Journal of Finance* 59:2 (April 2004).

17. Timothy R. Burch, and Vikram Nanda, "Divisional Diversity and the Conglomerate Discount: Evidence from Spin-Offs," *Journal of Financial Economics* 70:1 (October 2003).

18. John A. Doukas and Ozgur B. Kan, "Excess Cash Flows and Diversification," *Financial Management* 33:2 (Summer 2004).

19. Seoungpil Ahn and David J. Denis, "Internal Capital Markets and Investment Policy: Evidence from Corporate Spin-Offs," *Journal of Financial Economics* 71:3 (March 2004).

20. Patrick Cusatis, James A. Miles, and J. Randall Woolridge, "Some New Evidence that Spin-offs Create Value," *Journal of Applied Corporate Finance* 7:2 (Summer 1994).

21. David J. Denis, Diane K. Denis, and Kevin Yost, "Global Diversification, Industrial Diversification, and Firm Value," *Journal of Finance* 57:5 (October 2002).
22. M. Habib, D. Johnsen, and N. Naik, "Spin-off and Information," *Journal of Financial Intermediation* (1997).
23. Vikram Nanda and M.P. Narayanan, "Disentangling Value: Financing Needs, Firm Scope and Divestitures," *Journal of Financial Intermediation* 8:3 (1999). This article shows that market undervalued firms where the divisional cash flows were not observable and tended to reacted positively to divestiture announcements that created greater transparency and information flow.
24. G. Bennett Stewart, *The Quest for Value* (New York: HarperCollins, 1991).
25. This conceptual framework first appears in an article by Mark Sirower and Stephen O'Byrne, "The Measurement of Post-Acquisition Performance: Towards a Value-Based Benchmarking Methodology," *Journal of Applied Corporate Finance* 11:2 (Summer 1998). See also S. David Young and Stephen F. O'Byrne, *EVA and Value-Based Management: A Practical Guide to Implementation* (New York: McGraw-Hill, 2001).
26. Kathleen Fuller, Jeffrey Netter, and Mike Stegemoller, "What Do Returns to Acquiring Firms Tell Us? Evidence From Firms that Make Many Acquisitions," *Journal of Finance* 57:4 (August 2002).
27. Hubert Ooghe, Tine De Langhe, and Jan Camerlynck, "Profile of Multiple Versus Single Acquirers and Their Targets: A Research Note," Working Paper (2003).
28. The BUD business strategy is outlined in more detail in a case study, *Journal of Applied Corporate Finance* 14:2 (Summer 2001).
29. Sattar A. Mansi and David M. Reeb, "Corporate Diversification: What Gets Discounted?" *Journal of Finance* 57:5 (October 2002).
30. N. G. Travlos, "Corporate Takeover Bids, Method of Payment, and Bidding Firm's Stock Returns," *Journal of Finance* 52 (1987).
31. Anu Bharadwaj and Anil Shivdasani, "Valuation Effects of Bank Financing in Acquisitions," *Journal of Financial Economics* 67:1 (January 2003).

CHAPTER 5

1. David Blitzer, Howard Sliverblatt, and Dave Guarino, "Pension Status of S&P 500 Member Companies" *Standard and Poor's* (August 2004).
2. Tim Opler, Lee Pinkowitz, Rene Stulz, and Rohan Williamson, "The Determinants and Implications of Corporate Cash Holdings," *National Bureau of Economic Research*, Working Paper 6234 (October 1997). Justin Pettit *et al*, "Strategic Decapitalization: Does Excess Cash Matter?" (January 2005). Available at SSRN: http://ssrn.com/abstract=644362.
3. Mike Rowan and John Lentz, "Speculative Grade Liquidity Ratings," *Moody's Investor Service* (September 2004).
4. Paul Hsi, Mitchell Jakubovic, Richard Lane, and Brian Oak, "Balancing Growth and Excess Cash in the North American Technology Sector, or Dude, Where's My Cash?" *Moody's Investors Service Credit Research* (October 2004).

5. Rowan, Mike and John Lentz, "Speculative Grade Liquidity Ratings," *Moody's Investor Service* (September 2004).

6. Bernhard Schwetzler and Carsten Reimund, "Valuation Effects of Corporate Cash Holdings: Evidence from Germany," *HHL* Leipzig Graduate School of Management, Working Paper (2004).

7. Michael Jensen, "Agency Costs of Free Cash Flow, Corporate Finance, and Takeovers," *American Economic Review* 76:2 (May 1986).

8. Stewart Myers and Raghuram Rajan, "The Paradox of Liquidity," *Quarterly Journal of Economics* 113: 3 (August 1998).

9. Bernhard Schwetzler and Carsten Reimund, "Valuation Effects of Corporate Cash Holdings: Evidence from Germany," HHL Leipzig Graduate School of Management, Working Paper (2004). Schwetzler and Carsten define excess enterprise value as the logarithm of the ratio of actual enterprise value and an imputed enterprise value of each firm in a given industry, with imputed value determined from industry samples, assuming that industry medians are a reasonable proxy for the optimal cash holdings of all firms in this industry.

CHAPTER 6

1. Koresh Gagil in "The Quality of Corporate Credit Rating: An Empirical Investigation," Berglas School of Economics, Tel-Aviv University Center for Financial Studies, Goethe University of Frankfurt Working Paper (June 2003). Pettit, Justin, "The New World of Credit Ratings" (September 2004). Available at SSRN: http://ssrn.com/abstract=593522. Ludovic Breger, Lisa Goldberg, and Oren Cheyette, "Market Implied Ratings," *Barra Research* (July 2003).

2. According to the research of Dirk Czarnitzki and Kornelius Kraft, "Are Credit Ratings Valuable Information?" *ZEW Discussion Paper* No. 04-07 (May 2004).

3. Bina Lehmann, "Is it Worth the While?" University of Konstanz, Centre of Finance and Econometrics, Working Paper (April 2003).

4. See Pamela Stump's, "Putting EBITDA In Perspective: Ten Critical Failings of EBITDA as the Principal Determinant of Cash Flow," *Moody's Research* (June 2000).

5. Scott Sprinzen, "Adjusting Financials for Postretirement Liabilities" *Standard & Poor's Ratings Services* (March 2003). Scott Sprinzen, "Pitfalls of U.S. Pension Accounting and Disclosure" *Standard & Poor's Ratings Services* (March 2003). Scott Sprinzen, "Standard & Poor's Criteria for Assessing Postretirement Obligations" *Standard & Poor's Ratings Services* (March 2003). Gregory Clifton, *et al.* "Analytical Observations Related to U.S. Pension Obligations," *Moody's Investor Service Global Credit Research* (January 2003).

6. Estimated Credit Score $= 19.67 - 0.77 \times \text{Ln(Assets)} - 0.11 \times (\text{EBITDA/Interest Expense}) + 4.98 \times (\text{Debt/Capital})$; $R^2 = 90\%$, Standard Error $= 1.23$, Observations $= 26$.

7. Marc Serafin, Ted Collins, and Thomas Barker, "Property and Casualty Insurance Top Ten Ratios 2001 Update: Relationships Hold as Cycle Bottoms," *Moody's Investors Service, Global Credit Research* (December 2002).

8. Estimated Credit Score = $13.6 - 0.6 \times$ Ln(Book Equity) + $0.6 \times$ [(Gross Premiums Written + Gross Loss and Loss Adjustment Expense Reserves) ÷ Book Equity] + $3.1 \times$ [Total Debt and Hybrids ÷ (Average of Market and Book Equity + Total Debt and Hybrids)] $- 6.5 \times$ (Pretax Income ÷ Book Value of Equity); $R^2 = 74\%$, Standard Error $= 0.85$, Observations $= 109$.

CHAPTER 7

1. Justin Pettit, *et al*, "Financial Strategy for a Deflationary Era." Available at SSRN: http://ssrn.com/abstract=463004.

CHAPTER 8

1. See, for example, Laurie Simon Bagwell and John B. Shoven, "Cash Distribution to Shareholders" *Journal of Economic Perspectives* 3:3 (Summer 1989). This discusses the reasons for dividends. Justin Pettit, *et al*, "The Shareholder Distributions Handbook" (May 1, 2003). Available at SSRN: http://ssrn.com/abstract=463104. Justin Pettit, "Is a Share Buyback Right for Your Company?" *Harvard Business Review* (April 2001).
2. See, for example, Theo Vermaelen, "Common Stock Repurchases and Market Signaling: an Empirical Study," *Journal of Financial Economics* 9:2 (June 1981).
3. Robert Comment and Gregg A. Jarrell, "The Relative Signaling Power of Dutch Auction and Fixed Price Self-Tender Offers and Open-Market Share Repurchases." *Journal of Finance* 46:4 (September 1991).
4. Robert Comment and Gregg Jarrell, "The Relative Signaling Power of Dutch-Auction and Fixed-Price Tenders Offers and Open Market Repurchases" *Journal of Finance* 46:4 (September 1991). Kail Li and William McNally, "Open Market versus Tender Offer Share Repurchases: A Conditional Event," Case Study, University of British Columbia, Working Paper (Spring 1999).
5. Erik Lie and John J. McConnell, "Earnings Signals in Fixed-Price and Dutch Auction Self-Tender Offers," *Journal of Financial Economics* 49 (December 1998) pp. 161–186. This study concluded that earnings improvements follow both types of tenders, with no significant difference between the Dutch and fixed price tenders.
6. See, for example, Josef Lakonishok and Theo Vermaelen "Anomalous Price Behavior Around Repurchase Tender Offers," *Journal of Finance*, 45:2 (June 1990), pp. 455–477.
7. Michael Jensen, "Agency Costs of Free Cash Flow, Corporate Finance, and Takeovers," *The American Economic Review* 76:2 pp. 323–329 (May 1986).
8. See for example, Dennis Soter, Eugene Brigham, and Paul Evanson, "The Dividend Cut Heard Round The World: The Case Of FPL," *Journal of Applied Corporate Finance* 9:1 (Spring 1996). This discusses the case of the first self-inflicted dividend cut by a healthy, major U.S. utility.
9. Robert Comment and Gregg A. Jarrell, "The Relative Signaling Power of Dutch Auction and Fixed Price Self-Tender Offers and Open-Market Share Repurchases." *Journal of Finance* 46:4 (September 1991).

10. David R. Peterson and Pamela P. Peterson, "Dutch Auction Versus Fixed-Price Self-Tender Offers: Do Firms Overpay in Fixed Price Offers?" *Journal of Financial Research* 16:1 (Spring 1993).

CHAPTER 9

1. Yakov Amihud and Haim Mendelson, "The Effects of Beta, Bid-Ask Spread, Residual Risk, and Size on Stock Returns," *Journal of Finance* 44:2 (June 1989). Yakov Amihud and Haim Mendelson, "The Liquidity Route to a Lower Cost of Capital," *Journal of Applied Corporate Finance* 12:4 (Winter 2000). Justin Pettit *et al*, "Rx for Stock Liquidity" (November 2005). Available at SSRN: http://ssrn.com/abstract=845544

2. Kate O'Sullivan, "Hey! Look at Me," *CFO Magazine* (October 2005).

3. An informal poll of equity analysts indicates that CEOs (companies with $1.5 billion market cap and under) spend 20 to 25 percent of their time on investor relations, and CFOs spend an even higher proportion of their time. Harrison Hong and Ming Huang, "Talking up Liquidity: Insider Trading and Investor Relations," *Journal of Financial Intermediation* 14 (2005).

4. Richard Roll, "A Simple Implicit Measure of the Effective Bid-Ask Spread in an Efficient Market," *Journal of Finance* 39:4 (September 1984). This article showed that bid-ask spreads widen inversely to firm size. Najah Attig *et al*, "Effects of Large Shareholding on Information Asymmetry and Stock Liquidity," *SSRN* Working Paper Series (August 2004). This article showed that stocks with a greater separation between control and ownership had wider bid-ask spreads.

5. Christine A. Botosan, "Evidence That Greater Disclosure Lowers the Cost of Equity Capital," *Journal of Applied Corporate Finance* 12:4 (Winter 2000).

6. Clauido Loderer and Lukas Roth, "The Pricing Discount for Limited Liquidity: Evidence from the SWX Swiss Exchange and the NASDAQ" (September 2003). Available at SSRN: http://ssrn.com/abstract=288965 found least liquid stocks suffered discounts of up to 30%. Aswath Damodaran, in *The Dark Side of Valuation* (New York: Prentice Hall, 2001) pp. 245–249. This article indicates that liquidity discounts fall in a continuum, with private companies typically valued at a 25 to 30 percent discount.

7. Douglas Diamond and Robert Verrecchia disclosure, "Liquidity, and the Cost of Capital" *The Journal of Finance* 46:4 (September 1991). This article shows that increased disclosure can improve liquidity and reduce the cost of capital.

8. Michael Brennan and Claudia Tamarowski, "Relations, Liquidity, and Stock Prices" *Journal of Applied Corporate Finance* 12:4 (Winter 2000). The authors found that more disclosure of forward-looking and key nonfinancial information led to a lower cost of equity and higher stock prices in seasoned equity offerings with greater benefits for companies with less research coverage.

9. Lisa K Meulbroek, "The Efficiency of Equity-Linked Compensation: Understanding the Full Cost of Awarding Executive Stock Options" *Financial Management* 30 (2001). Lisa Meulbroek developed a model to estimate employee discounts based on share price volatility, which ranges for most cases from 30 to 50 percent.

10. Excess return equals aggregate movement in market capitalization, in excess of the movement in the S&P 500, over the same 45-day time period, starting with each respective date of file. Time from file is typically 20 days.

11. Marlin R.H. Jensen, Claire E. Crutchley, and Carl D. Hudson, "Market Reaction to Equity Offer Reasons: What Information Do Managers Reveal?" *Journal of Economics and Finance* 18:3 (Fall 1994), pp. 313–329. The authors employ a piecewise linear model to provide evidence that managers signal the quality of the new investment when issuing equity. File to offer period not examined.

12. Josef Lakonishok and Baruch Lev, "Stock Splits and Stock Dividends: Why, Who, and When," *Journal of Finance* 42:4 (1987).

13. James J. Angel, "Picking Your Tick: Toward A New Theory of Stock Splits," *Journal of Applied Corporate Finance* (Fall 1997).

14. Ibid.

15. Baker and Gallagher, "Management's View of Stock Splits," *Financial Management* 9 (Summer 1980).

16. Justin Pettit and Stephen F. O'Byrne, "Stock Splits: What Good Are They?" *Shareholder Value* (May/June 2002).

17. Thomas E. Copeland "Liquidity Changes Following Stock Splits," *Journal of Finance* 34:1 (March 1979). The author found that trading volume declined after a split. Josef Lakonishok and Baruch Lev, "Stock Splits and Stock Dividends: Why, Who, and When," *Journal of Finance* 42:4 (September 1987). Lakonishok and Lev concluded that trading volumes are abnormally high before a split announcement and then return to a normal level after the announcement.

18. Justin Pettit and Stephen F. O'Byrne, "Stock Splits: What Good Are They?" *Shareholder Value* (May/June 2002).

19. Ibid.

20. Christopher G. Lamoureux and Percy Poon, "The Market Reaction to Stock Splits" *Journal of Finance*, 42:5 (1987).

21. The difference between the means of liquid and illiquid returns is significant at a 95 percent confidence level.

22. Craig Dunbar, Chuan-Yang Hwang, and Gershon Mandelker, "Long-Run Common Stock Performance After Stock Splits: Anomalous Evidence From 1929 to 1988," Unpublished Working Paper, University of Western Ontario (July 1998). These results were pervasive over various subperiods of history as well as for a wide variety of methodologies.

23. Robert Conroy, Robert Harris, and Bruce Benet, "The Effects of Splits on Bid-Ask Spreads," *Journal of Finance* 45:4 (September 1990).

24. Eugene Fama, Lawrence Fisher, Michael Jensen, and Richard Roll, "The Adjustment of Stock Prices to New Information," *International Economic Review* 10 (February 1969).

25. Eugene Pilotte and Timothy Manuel, "The Markets Response to Recurring Events: The Case of Stock Splits," *Journal of Financial Economics* 41 (1996).

26. Justin Pettit, "Is A Share Buyback Right For Your Company?" *Harvard Business Review* (April 2001).

CHAPTER 10

1. Diane Vaza, "Hedging Strategies for Four Oil and Gas Companies," *Standard and Poor's* (August 1, 2005).
2. Antonio S. Mello and John E. Parsons, "Strategic Hedging," *Journal of Applied Corporate Finance* 12:3 (Fall 1999). Rene Stulz, "Rethinking Risk Management," *Journal of Applied Corporate Finance* 9:3 (Fall 1996).
3. Trevor S. Harris, Nahum D. Melumad, and Toshi Shibano, "An Argument Against Hedging by Matching the Currencies of Cost and Revenues," *Journal of Applied Corporate Finance* 9:3 (Fall 1996).
4. We generated 3,000 independent cases of the complete term structure using Monte Carlo simulation to create a probability distribution of EPS and PV of 5-year EPS projections with volatilities for daily short term rates (18 percent) and term spread (31 percent) where the mean EPS is equivalent to the consensus outlook under a bias adjusted forward curve and expected equity returns of 14 percent with a volatility of 17 percent.
5. Diane Vaza, "Hedging Strategies for Four Oil and Gas Companies," *Standard and Poor's* (August 1, 2005).
6. Ibid.
7. "Moody's Findings on Corporate Governance in the United States and Canada," *Moody's Investors Service* (October 2004).

CHAPTER 11

1. Alan C. Shapiro, *Multinational Financial Management, Fourth Edition* (New York: John Wiley & Sons, 1992) pp. 621–655. Justin Pettit, *et al*, "FX Policy Revisited: Strategy & Tactics," (October 2003). Available at SSRN: http://ssrn.com/abstract=463106.
2. Gunter Dufey, "Corporate Finance and Exchange Rate Variations," *Financial Management* 7:2 (Summer 1978) pp. 51–57.
3. S. Waite Rawls, III and Charles Smithson, "Strategic Risk Management," *Journal of Applied Corporate Finance* 2:4 (Winter 1990).
4. M.A. Schrijvers, "M&A Flows and the Foreign Exchange Markets," *Banca Nazionale del Lavoro's Quarterly Review* (March 2002).
5. Robert W. White and Justin Pettit, "Citibank Canada Ltd.—Monetization of Future Oil Production," Richard *Ivey School of Business Case Study* #9A95B032 (1996).

CHAPTER 12

1. Scott Sprinzen, "Standard and Poor's Criteria for Assessing Postretirement Obligations," *Standard & Poor's Ratings Services* (March 2003). Scott Sprinzen, "Pitfalls of U.S. Pension Accounting and Disclosure," *Standard & Poor's Ratings Services* (March 2003).

2. Pension Benefit Guarantee Corporation, "2004 Performance and Accountability Report," (November 2004). As of September 30, 2004, PBGC's best estimate of total underfunding in plans sponsored by companies with credit ratings below investment grade and classified by PBGC as reasonably possible of termination was $96 billion.

3. Based on employers reports to PBGC under section 4010 of ERISA of their December 31, 2003, market value of assets and termination liability.

4. Fischer Black, "The Tax Consequences of Long-Run Pension Policy," *Financial Analyst Journal* Vol. 36: (July/August 1980) pp. 21–28. Justin Pettit, *et al*, "Optimal Capital Structure and the Corporate Pension" (April 2005). Available at SSRN: http://ssrn.com/abstract=707641.

5. Ibid.

6. Jeremy Gold and Nick Hudson, "Creating Value in Pension Plans (or, Gentlemen Prefer Bonds)," *Journal of Applied Corporate Finance* 15:4 (Fall 2003).

7. Li Jin, Robert C. Merton, and Zvi Bodie, "Do a Firm's Equity Returns Reflect the Risk of its Pension Plan?" Working Paper (January 10, 2005).

8. Zvi Bodie, "On the Risk of Stocks in the Long Run," *Financial Analyst Journal* 51:3 (May 1995) pp. 18–22.

9. David Blitzer, Howard Silverblatt, and Dave Guarino, "Pension Status of S&P 500 Member Companies," *Standard and Poor's* (August 2004).

10. Solomon Samson, *et al*, "Standard & Poor's Corporate Ratings Criteria 2005," *Standard & Poor's* (November 2004).

11. Scott Sprinzen, "Adjusting Financials for Postretirement Liabilities," *Standard & Poor's* (March 2003).

12. Fischer Black, "The Tax Consequences of Long-Run Pension Policy," *Financial Analyst Journal* Vol. 36 (July/August 1980) pp. 21–28.

13. Ibid.

14. John Ralfe, Cliff Speed, and Jon Palin, "Pensions and Capital Structure: Why Hold Equities in the Pension Fund?" *North American Actuarial Journal* (July 2004).

15. Andrew Smith and Guy Thomas, "Positive Theory and Actuarial Practice," *The Actuary* (October 1998).

16. Fischer Black, "Tax Consequences of Long-Run Pension Policy," *Financial Analyst Journal* Vol. 36 (July/August 1980) pp. 21–28.

17. Ibid.

18. Irwin Tepper, "Taxation and Corporate Pension Policy," *Journal of Finance* 36:3 (March 1981). Irwin Tepper's arbitrage was published around the same time as Fisher Black's paper.

19. George Oldfield Jr., "Financial Aspects of the Private Pension System," *Journal of Money, Credit, & Banking* (Summer 1977).

20. Thomas Carroll and Greg Niehaus, "Pension Plan Funding and Corporate Debt Ratings," *Journal of Risk and Insurance* 65:2 (June 1998).

21. Li Jin, Robert C. Merton, and Zvi Bodie, "Do a Firm's Equity Returns Reflect the Risk of its Pension Plan?" HBS Finance Working Paper No. 05-011 (January 2005).

22. Ibid.

23. Estimated Credit Score $= 21.50 - 1.52\text{Ln(Revenue)} + 3.48\text{FFO/Debt} +$ 16.55FFO/Sales volatility, based on 10 years of data for 35 comparable companies.

24. John Ralfe, Cliff Speed, and Jon Palin, "Pensions and Capital Structure: Why Hold Equities in the Pension Fund?" *North American Actuarial Journal* (July 2004).

25. Jon Exley, Shyam Mehta, and Andrew Smith, "Pension Funds: A Company Manager's View," *Society of Actuaries* 29:2 (June 2003).

26. Ibid.

27. Ibid.

References

Ahn, Seoungpil and Denis, David J., "Internal Capital Markets and Investment Policy: Evidence from Corporate Spin-Offs," *Journal of Financial Economics*, Vol. 71, No. 3, March 2004.

Amihud, Yakov, and Haim Mendelson, "The Effects of Beta, Bid-Ask Spread, Residual Risk, and Size on Stock Returns," *The Journal of Finance*, Vol. 44, No. 2, June 1989.

Amihud, Yakov, and Haim Mendelson, "The Liquidity Route to a Lower Cost of Capital," *Journal of Applied Corporate Finance*, Vol. 12, No. 4 (Winter 2000).

Angel, James J., "Picking Your Tick: Toward A New Theory of Stock Splits," *Journal of Applied Corporate Finance*, Fall 1997.

Attig *et al*, "Effects of Large Shareholding on Information Asymmetry and Stock Liquidity," SSRN Working Paper Series, August 2004.

Arnold, Tom and Richard L. Shockley, Jr., "Value Creation at Anheuser-Busch: A Real Options Example," in *The Journal of Applied Corporate Finance*, Summer 2001.

Bagwell, Laurie Simon, and John B. Shoven, "Cash Distribution to Shareholders" *Journal of Economic Perspectives*, Vol. 3, No. 3, Summer 1989.

Baker, Kent and Patricia Gallagher, "Management's View of Stock Splits," *Financial Management 9*, Summer 1980.

Bain and Company, "Discipline and the Dilutive Deal," *Harvard Business Review*, 2002.

Berger, Philip and Eli Ofek, "Causes and Effects of Corporate Refocusing Programs," *The Review of Financial Studies*, Summer 1999.

Bharadwaj, Anu and Anil Shivdasani, "Valuation Effects of Bank Financing in Acquisitions," *Journal of Financial Economics*, Vol. 67, No. 1, January 2003.

Biddle, Gary C., and Frederick W. Lindahl, "Stock Price Reactions to LIFO Adoptions: The Association Between Excess Returns and LIFO Tax Savings," *Journal of Accounting Research*, Part II, Autumn 1982, pp. 551–588.

Black, Fischer, "The Tax Consequences of Long-Run Pension Policy," *Financial Analyst Journal*, July/August 1980.

Blitzer, David, Howard Silverblatt, and Dave Guarino, "Pension Status of S&P 500 Member Companies," *Standard and Poor's*, August 2004.

Bodie, Zvi, "On the Risk of Stocks in the Long Run," *Financial Analyst Journal*, May–June 1995.

Botosan, Christine A. "Evidence That Greater Disclosure Lowers the Cost of Equity Capital," *Journal of Applied Corporate Finance*, Vol. 12, No 4, Winter 2000.

Bradley, Michael and Anant Sundaram "Do Acquisitions Drive Performance or Does Performance Drive Acquisitions?" (September 2004.) Available at SSRN: http://ssrn.com/abstract=592761

Brandimarte, Jay P, William C. Fallon, and Robert S. McNish, "Trading the Corporate Portfolio: A Systematic Approach to Buying & Selling Assets Can Deliver Superior Shareholder Returns," *McKinsey on Finance*, No. 2, Autumn 2001.

Breger, Ludovic, Lisa Goldberg, and Oren Cheyette, "Market Implied Ratings," *Barra Research*, July 2003.

Brennan, Michael, and Claudia Tamarowski "Investor Relations, Liquidity, and Stock Prices" *Journal of Applied Corporate Finance*, Vol. 12, No. 4, Winter 2000.

Bruner, Robert F., Kenneth M. Eades, Robert S. Harris, and Robert C. Higgins, "Best Practices in Estimating the Cost of Capital: Survey and Synthesis," *Financial Practice and Education*, Spring/Summer 1998.

Burch, Timothy R., and Vikram Nanda, "Divisional Diversity and the Conglomerate Discount: Evidence from Spin-Offs," *Journal of Financial Economics*, Vol. 70, No. 1, October 2003.

Carroll, Thomas, and Greg Niehaus, "Pension Plan Funding and Corporate Debt Ratings," *The Journal of Risk and Insurance*, June 1998.

Chemmanur, Thomas and Imants Paeglis, "Why Issue Tracking Stock? Insights From a Comparison with Spin-Offs and Carve-Outs," *Journal of Applied Corporate Finance*, Vol. 14, No. 2, 2001.

Christofferson, Scott, Robert McNish, and Diane Sias, "Where Mergers Go Wrong," *McKinsey on Finance*, No. 2, Winter 2004.

Clifton, Gregory *et al*, "Analytical Observations Related to U.S. Pension Obligations," *Moody's Investor Service Global Credit Research*, January 2003.

Comment, Robert, and Gregg A. Jarrell, "The Relative Signaling Power of Dutch Auction and Fixed Price Self-Tender Offers and Open-Market Share Repurchases," *The Journal of Finance* Vol. 46, No. 4, September 1991.

Conroy, Robert, Robert Harris and Bruce Benet, "The Effects of Splits on Bid-Ask Spreads" *The Journal of Finance*, Vol. 45, No. 4 (September 1990).

Cooper, Ian and Evi Kaplanis, "Home Bias in Equity Portfolios and the Cost of Capital for Multinational Firms," *Journal of Applied Corporate Finance*, Vol. 8, No. 3, Fall 1995.

Copeland, Tom, Tim Koller, and Jack Murrin, *Valuation: Measuring and Managing the Value of Companies*, Second Ed. (New York: John Wiley & Sons, 1994).

Copeland, Tom and Fred Weston, *Financial Theory and Corporate Policy, 3rd Edition* (Reading, MA: Addison-Wesley, 1992) pp. 473–478.

Copeland, Thomas E. "Liquidity Changes Following Stock Splits" *The Journal of Finance*, Vol. 34, No. 1, March 1979.

Cusatis, Patrick, James A. Miles, and J. Randall Woolridge, "Some New Evidence that Spin-offs Create Value," *Journal of Applied Corporate Finance*, Vol. 7, No. 2, Summer 1994.

Czarnitzki, Dirk and Kornelius Kraft, "Are Credit Ratings Valuable Information?" *ZEW Discussion Paper*, No. 04–07, May 2004.

Damodaran, Aswath, *Investment Valuation* (New York: John Wiley & Sons, Inc., 1993).

Damodaran, Aswath, *The Dark Side of Valuation* (Upper Saddle River, NJ: Prentice Hall, 2001).

Denis, David J. and Diane K., and Kevin Yost "Global Diversification, Industrial Diversification, and Firm Value," *The Journal of Finance*, Vol. 57, No. 5, October 2002.

Desai, Hemang and Prem Jain, "Long-Run Common Stock Returns Following Stock Split and Reverse Split," *Journal of Business*, July 1997.

Diamond, Douglas, and Robert Verrecchia, disclosure, "Liquidity, and the Cost of Capital," *The Journal of Finance*, Vol. 46, No. 4, September 1991.

Dimson, Elroy, Paul Marsh and Mike Staunton, "Global Evidence on the Equity Risk Premium," *Journal of Applied Corporate Finance*. Vol. 15, No. 4, Fall 2003.

Doukas, John A. and Ozgur B. Kan, "Excess Cash Flows and Diversification Discount," *Financial Management*, Vol. 33, No. 2, Summer 2004.

Dranikoff, Lee, Tim Koller & Antoon Schneider, "Divestiture: Strategy's Missing Link." *Harvard Business Review*, May 2002.

Dufey, Gunter, "Corporate Finance and Exchange Rate Variations," *Financial Management*, No. 2, Summer 1972, pp. 51–57.

Dunbar, Craig, Chuan-Yang Hwang and Gershon Mandelker, "Long-Run Common Stock Performance After Stock Splits: Anomalous Evidence From 1929 to 1988" Unpublished Working Paper, University of Western Ontario (July 1998).

Exley, Jon, Shyam Mehta, and Andrew Smith, "Pension Funds: A Company Manager's View, "Society of Actuaries, June 2003.

Fama, Eugene, Lawrence Fisher, Michael Jensen, and Richard Roll. "The Adjustment of Stock Prices to New Information" *International Economic Review*, February 1969.

Fama, E.F., "Market Efficiency, Long-Term Returns, and Behavioral Finance," Journal of Finance, 1998.

Ferrari, Bernard T., *et al*, "More Restructuring Ahead for Media and Entertainment," *McKinsey on Finance*, Vol. 6, Summer 2003.

Fitch Corporate Ratings Methodology, June 2003.

Fuller, K., J. Netter, and M. Stegemoller, "What do Returns to Acquiring Firms Tell Us? Evidence from Firms that Make Many Acquisitions," *Journal of Finance*, Vol. 57, Issue 4. (August 2002.)

Gagil, Koresh in "The Quality of Corporate Credit Rating: an Empirical Investigation," Berglas School of Economics, Tel-Aviv University Center for Financial Studies, Goethe University of Frankfurt Working paper, June 2003.

Gold, Jeremy and Nick Hudson, "Creating Value in Pension Plans (or, Gentlemen Prefer Bonds)," *Journal of Applied Corporate Finance*, Fall 2003.

Habib, M., D. Johnsen, and N. Naik, "Spin-off and Information," *Journal of Financial Intermediation*, Vol. 6, Issue 2, 1997.

Harris, Trevor S., Nahum D. Melumad, and Toshi Shibano, "An Argument Against Hedging by Matching the Currencies of Cost and Revenues," *Journal of Applied Corporate Finance*, Vol. 9, No. 3, Fall 1996.

Harris, Trevor S., "Overcoming Accounting Differences: A Stockpicker's Guide to the Numbers That Count," *Apples-to-Apples*, February 6, 1998.

Hong, Harrison and Ming Huang. "Talking Up Liquidity: Insider Trading and Investor Relations," *Journal of Financial Intermediation*, Vol. 14, 2005.

Hsi, Paul, Mitchell Jakubovic, Richard Lane, and Brian Oak, "Balancing Growth and Excess Cash in the North American Technology Sector, or Dude, Where's My Cash?" *Moody's Investors Service Credit Research*, October 2004.

Ibbotson, Roger, and Peng Chen, "Long-Run Stock Returns: Participating in the Real Economy," *Financial Analysts Journal* No. 59, pp. 88–98. Mayfield Scott, "Estimating the Market Risk Premium," *Journal of Financial Economics*, Vol. 73, No. 3, September 2004.

Jensen, Marlin R.H., Claire E. Crutchley, and Carl D. Hudson, *Journal of Economics and Finance*, Vol. 18, No.3, Fall 1994 pp. 313–329.

Jensen, Michael, "Agency Costs of Free Cash Flow, Corporate Finance, and Takeovers," *American Economic Review*, May 1986.

Jenson, Michael C., "The Takeover Controversy: Analysis and Evidence" *Midland Corporate Finance Journal* 1991, Vol. 4, No. 2, pp. 6–32.

Jin, Li, Robert C. Merton, and Zvi Bodie, "Do a Firm's Equity Returns Reflect the Risk of its Pension Plan?" Working Paper, January 2005.

Kaplan, Steven and Weisback, Michael, "The Success of Acquisitions: Evidence from Divestitures," Working Paper, October 1990.

Lakonishok, Josef and Theo Vermaelen, "Anomalous Price Behavior Around Repurchase Tender Offers," *The Journal of Finance*, Vol 45, No. 2.

Lakonishok, Josef and Baruch Lev, "Stock Splits and Stock Dividends: Why, Who, and When," *The Journal of Finance*, Vol. 42, No. 4, September 1987.

Lamoureux, Christopher G., and Percy Poon. "The Market Reaction to Stock Splits," *The Journal of Finance*, Vol. 42, 1987.

Lang, L., and R.M. Stulz, "Contagion and Competitive Intra-Industry Effects of Bankruptcy Announcements," *Journal of Financial Economics*, Vol. 32, No. 1. 1992.

Lehmann, Bina "Is it Worth the While?" University of Konstanz, Centre of Finance and Econometrics, Working Paper, April 2003.

Lie, Erik and John J. McConnell, "Earnings Signals in Fixed-Price and Dutch Auction Self-Tender Offers," *Journal of Economics*, Vol. 49, No. 2. December 1998.

Li, Kail and William McNally, "Open Market versus Tender Offer Share Repurchases: A Conditional Event Case Study," University of British Columbia, Working Paper, Spring 1999.

Lindenberg, Eric, and Michael Ross, "To Purchase or To Pool: Does it Matter?" *Journal of Applied Corporate Finance*, Vol. 12, No. 2, Summer 1999.

Loderer, Clauido, and Lukas Roth, "The Pricing Discount for Limited Liquidity: Evidence from SWX Swiss Exchange and the NASDAQ," Vol. 12, No. 2.

Logue, Dennis E., "When Theory Fails: Globalization as a Response to the (Hostile) Market for Foreign Exchange," *Journal of Applied Corporate Finance*, Vol. 8, No. 3, Fall 1995.

Mansi, Sattar A., and David M. Reeb, "Corporate Diversification: What Gets Discounted?" *The Journal of Finance*, Vol. 57, No. 5, October 2002.

Maxwell, William F., and Ramesh P. Rao, "Do Spin-offs Expropriate Wealth from Bondholders?" *Journal of Finance*, Vol. 58, No. 5, Oct 2003.

McConnell, *et al*, "Can Takeover Losses Explain Spin-off Gains?" *Journal of Financial and Quantitative Analysis*, Vol. 30, No. 4, December 1995.

Mello, Antonio S., and John E. Parsons, "Strategic Hedging," *Journal of Applied Corporate Finance*, Vol. 12, No. 3, Fall 1999.

Meulbroek, Lisa, "The Efficiency of Equity-Linked Compensation: Understanding the Full Cost of Awarding Executive Stock Options," *Financial Management*, Vol. 30, No. 2, 2001.

Moeller, Sara B., Schlingermann, F.P. and Stulz, R.M., "Firm Size and the Gains from Acquisitions," *Journal of Financial Economics*, Vol. 73, No. 2, August 2004.

Moody's Rating Methodology Handbook, April 2003.

Moody's Investors Service, "Moody's Findings on Corporate Governance in the United States and Canada," October 2004.

Myers, Stewart and Raghurma Rajan, "The Paradox of Liquidity," *Quarterly Journal of Economics*, August 1998.

Nanda, Vikram and M.P. Narayanan, "Disentangling Value: Financing Needs, Firm Scope and Divestitures," *Journal of Financial Intermediation*, Vol. 8, No. 3. 1999.

Oldfield, George Jr., "Financial Aspects of the Private Pension System," *Journal of Money, Credit, & Banking*, Vol. 9, No. 1. 1977.

Ooghe, Hubert, Tine De Langhe, and Jan Camerlynck, "Profile of Multiple Versus Single Acquirers and Their Targets: A Research Note," Working Paper, 2003.

Opler, Tim, Lee Pinkowitz, Rene Stulz, and Rohan Williamson, "The Determinants and Implications of Corporate Cash Holdings," National Bureau of Economic Research, Working Paper 6234, October 1997.

O'Sullivan, Kate, "Hey! Look at Me" *CFO Magazine*, October 2005.

Pension Benefit Guarantee Corporation, "Performance and Accountability Report," November 2004.

Peterson, David R. and Pamela P., "Dutch Auction Versus Fixed-Price Self-Tender Offers: Do Firms Overpay in Fixed Price Offers?" *The Journal of Financial Research*, Vol. 16, No. 1, 1993.

Pettit, Justin "Corporate Capital Costs: A Practitioner's Guide," *The Journal of Applied Corporate Finance*, Vol. 12, No. 1, Spring 1999.

Pettit, Justin, Mack Ferguson and Robert Gluck, "A Method for Estimating Global Corporate Capital Costs: The Case of Bestfoods," *The Journal of Applied Corporate Finance*. Vol. 12, No. 3, Fall 1999.

Pettit, Justin, "Is A Share Buyback Right For Your Company?" *Harvard Business Review*, April 2001.

Pettit, Justin and Stephen F. O'Byrne, "Stock Splits: What Good Are They?" *Shareholder Value*, May/June 2002.

Pettit, Justin, "The WACC User's Guide" March 2005. Available at SSRN: http://ssrn.com/abstract=683313.

Pettit, Justin, "Optimal Capital Structure and the Corporate Pension" April 2005. Available at SSRN: http://ssrn.com/abstract=707641.

Pettit, Justin, "The New World of Credit Ratings" September 2004. Available at SSRN: http://ssrn.com/abstract=593522.

Pettit, Justin, "Where M&A Pays: Who Wins & How?" December 2004. Available at SSRN: http://ssrn.com/abstract=641621.

Pettit, Justin, "Positioning for Growth: Carve-Outs & Spin-Offs," April 2004. Available at SSRN: http://ssrn.com/abstract=546622.

Pettit, Justin, "How To Find Your Economic Profits," January 2004. Available at SSRN: http://ssrn.com/abstract=505222.

Pettit, Justin, "Renewing Growth: M&A Fact & Fallacy," June 2003. Available at SSRN: http://ssrn.com/abstract=463102.

Pettit, Justin, "The Shareholder Distributions Handbook," May 1, 2003. Available at SSRN: http://ssrn.com/abstract=463104.

Pettit, Justin, "Strategic Decapitalization: Does Excess Cash Matter?" January 2005. Available at SSRN: http://ssrn.com/abstract=644362.

Pettit, Justin, "FX Policy Revisited: Strategy & Tactics," October 2003. Available at SSRN: http://ssrn.com/abstract=463106.

Pettit, Justin, "Rx for Stock Liquidity" November 2005. Available at SSRN: http://ssrn.com/abstract=845544.

Pettit, Justin, "Financial Strategy for a Deflationary Era," March 2003. Available at SSRN: http://ssrn.com/abstract=463004.

Pilotte, Eugene and Timothy Manuel, "The Market's Response to Recurring Events: The Case of Stock Splits" *Journal of Financial Economics*, Vol. 41, No. 1, 1996.

Ralfe, John, Cliff Speed, and Jon Palin, "Pensions and Capital Structure: Why Hold Equities in the Pension Fund?" *North American Actuarial Journal*, July 2004.

Rawls, S. Waite III, and Charles Smithson, "Strategic Risk Management," *Journal of Applied Corporate Finance*, Vol. 2, No. 4, Winter 1990.

Raynor, Michael E. "Tracking Stocks and the Acquisition of Real Options," *Journal of Applied Corporate Finance*, Vol. 13, No. 2, 2000.

Roll, Richard, "A Simple Implicit Measure of the Effective Bid-Ask Spread in an Efficient Market" *The Journal of Finance*, Vol. 39, No. 4, September 1984.

Rowan, Mike and John Lentz, "Speculative Grade Liquidity Ratings," *Moody's Investor Service*, September 2004.

Samson, Solomon, *et al*, *Standard & Poor's Corporate Ratings Criteria 2005*, November 2004.

Schrijvers, M.A., "M&A flows and the foreign exchange markets," *Banca Nazionale del Lavoro's Quarterly Review*, March 2002.

Schwetzler, Bernhard and Carsten Reimund, "Valuation Effects of Corporate Cash Holdings: Evidence from Germany," HHL Leipzig Graduate School of Management, Working Paper, 2004.

Serafin, Marc, Ted Collins, and Thomas Barker, "Property and Casualty Insurance Top Ten Ratios 2001 Update: Relationships Hold as Cycle Bottoms" *Moody's Investors Service, Global Credit Research*, December 2002.

Shapiro, Alan C., *Multinational Financial Management, Fourth Edition* (Boston: Allyn & Bacon, 1992).

Shapiro, Alan C., *Modern Corporate Finance* (New York: MacMillan Publishing, 1990) pp. 239–26.

Siegel, Jeremy, "The Shrinking Equity Premium," *Journal of Portfolio Management,* Vol. 26, No. 1. 1999.

Sirower, Mark and Stephen O'Byrne, "The Measurement of Post-Acquisition Performance: Towards a Value-Based Benchmarking Methodology," *Journal of Applied Corporate Finance,* Summer 1998.

Slovin, M., M. Sushka, and S. Ferraro, "A Comparison of the Information Conveyed by Equity Carve-outs, Spin-offs, and Asset Sell-offs," *Journal of Financial Economics,* Vol. 37, No. 1. 1995.

Smith, Andrew, and Thomas Guy, "Positive Theory and Actuarial Practice," *The Actuary,* October 1998.

Soter, D., E. Brigham, and P. Evanson, "The Dividend Cut Heard Round The World: The Case Of FPL" *Journal of Applied Corporate Finance,* Vol. 9, No. 1. Spring 1996.

Sprinzen, Scott, "Adjusting Financials for Postretirement Liabilities," *Standard & Poor's Ratings Services,* March 2003.

Sprinzen, Scott, "Pitfalls of U.S. Pension Accounting and Disclosure," *Standard & Poor's Ratings Services,* March 2003.

Sprinzen, Scott, "Standard & Poor's Criteria for Assessing Postretirement Obligations," *Standard & Poor's Ratings Services,* March 2003.

Stump, Pamela, "Putting EBITDA In Perspective: Ten Critical Failings of EBITDA as the Principal Determinant of Cash Flow," *Moody's Research,* June 2000.

Standard and Poor's "Hedging Strategies for Four Oil and Gas Companies," August 1, 2005.

S&P's Corporate Ratings Criteria, 2003.

Stein, "Internal Capital Markets and the Competition for Corporate Resources," *Journal of Finance,* Vol. 52, No. 1. 1997.

Stewart, G. Bennett III, *The Quest for Value* (New York: HarperCollins, 1991).

Stulz, Rene M., "Globalization of Capital Markets and the Cost of Capital: The Case of Nestle," *Journal of Applied Corporate Finance,* Vol. 8, No. 3, Fall 1995.

Stulz, Rene, "Rethinking Risk Management," *Journal of Applied Corporate Finance,* Vol. 9, No. 3, Fall 1996.

Stulz, Rene, "Globalization, Corporate Finance, and the Cost of Capital," *Journal of Applied Corporate Finance,* Vol. 12, No. 3, Fall 1999.

Tepper, Irwin, "Taxation and Corporate Pension Policy," *Journal of Finance,* Vol. 36, No. 3, March 1981.

Travlos, N.G., "Corporate Takeover Bids, Method of Payment, and Bidding Firm's Stock Returns," *Journal of Finance,* Vol. 42, No. 4. 1987.

Vermaelen, Theo, "Common Stock Repurchases and Market Signaling: an Empirical Study," *Journal of Financial Economics,* Vol. 9, No. 2. 1981.

Villalonga, Belen, "Does Diversification Cause the "Diversification Discount,"" *Financial Management,* Vol. 33, No. 2, Summer 2004.

Villalonga, Belen, "Diversification Discount or Premium? New Evidence from the Business Information Tracking Series," *The Journal of Finance*, Vol. 59, No. 2, April 2004.

Von Rumohr, Cai, "Strategic Initiatives a Positive Step for 'Show-Me' Stock," SG Cowen Securities equity research, September 28, 1999.

Weber, Steven, "The End of the Business Cycle," *Foreign Affairs*, Vol. 76, No. 4, July/August 1997.

White, Robert W. and Justin Pettit, "Citibank Canada Ltd.—Monetization of Future Oil Production," Ivey Publishing, Richard Ivey Business School, 1995.

Williamson, *Markets and Hierarchies: Analysis and Antitrust Implications* (New York: The Free Press, 1975).

Young, S. David and Stephen F. O'Byrne, *EVA and Value-Based Management* (New York: McGraw-Hill, 2001).

Zimmerman, Jerold L., *Accounting for Decision Making and Control* (New York: McGraw-Hill, 1997).